nge LR

A-Level

Mathematics

for AQA
Mechanics 2

D1335776

CGP

The Complete Course for AQA M2

Contents

Chapter 3

Work, Energy and Power

Chapter 4

Uniform Circular Motion

Reference

About this book

In this book you'll find...

Learning Objectives
Showing which bits of the AQA specification are covered in each section.

Explanations
Clear explanations for every topic, with lots of helpful tips.

Examples
Plenty of step-by-step worked examples.

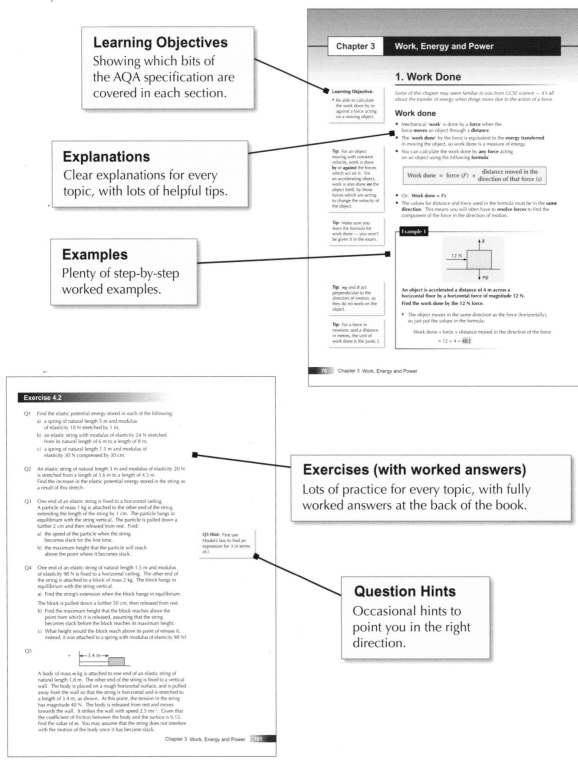

Exercises (with worked answers)
Lots of practice for every topic, with fully worked answers at the back of the book.

Question Hints
Occasional hints to point you in the right direction.

Review Exercise — Chapter 3

Q1　A crate is pushed across a smooth horizontal floor by a force of magnitude 250 N, acting in the direction of motion. Find the work done in pushing the crate a distance of 3 m.

Q2

A roll-along cart is pulled along the ground a distance of 0.4 m by a cord with a tension force, T, acting at 60° to the horizontal. If the work done by the tension is 1.3 J, find T.

Q3　A crane lifts a concrete block 12 m vertically at constant speed. If the crane does 34 kJ of work against gravity, find the mass of the concrete block.

Q4　On the moon, an astronaut lifts a mass of 3 kg through a vertical height of 0.6 m, doing 2.92 J of work against gravity. Find an estimate of the acceleration due to gravity on the moon, g_{moon}. Give your answer correct to 3 significant figures.

Q5

A 25 kg flight case is pushed 10 m up a ramp at an angle of 20° to the horizontal, by a force of magnitude 162 N acting horizontally. The coefficient of friction between the ramp and the case is 0.19. Find the work done on the case as it is pushed up the ramp.

Q6　A horse of mass 450 kg is galloping at a speed of 13 ms⁻¹. Find the horse's kinetic energy.

Q7　An ice skater of mass 65 kg sets off from rest. After travelling 40 m in a straight line across smooth horizontal ice, she has done 800 J of work. Find her speed at this point.

Q8　A supercar of mass 1000 kg moves along a straight horizontal test track. The resistance to motion has a constant magnitude of 590 N. To test the brakes, the driver accelerates to 100 ms⁻¹ and then applies a constant braking force of 8500 N.
　　a) Find the work done by the braking force in bringing the car to a stop.
　　b) Find the work done by the resistance to motion in bringing the car to a stop.
　　c) Show that the work done by the resultant force equals the change in kinetic energy.

Q9　A particle of mass 0.5 kg is projected upwards from ground level and reaches a maximum height of 150 m above the ground. Find the increase in its gravitational potential energy.

Q10　A jubilant cowboy throws his hat vertically upwards with a velocity of 5 ms⁻¹.
　　Use the principle of conservation of mechanical energy to find the maximum height the hat reaches above the point of release.

Review Exercises
Mixed questions covering the whole chapter, with fully worked answers.

Exam-Style Questions — Chapter 3

1

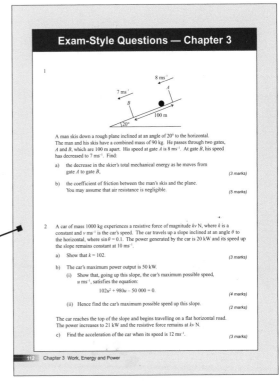

A man skis down a rough plane inclined at an angle of 20° to the horizontal. The man and his skis have a combined mass of 90 kg. He passes through two gates, A and B, which are 100 m apart. His speed at gate A is 8 ms⁻¹. At gate B, his speed has decreased to 7 ms⁻¹. Find:

　a)　the decrease in the skier's total mechanical energy as he moves from gate A to gate B,
　　　　　　　　　　　　　　　　　　　　　　　　　　　　　　(3 marks)

　b)　the coefficient of friction between the man's skis and the plane. You may assume that air resistance is negligible.
　　　　　　　　　　　　　　　　　　　　　　　　　　　　　　(5 marks)

2　A car of mass 1000 kg experiences a resistive force of magnitude kv N, where k is a constant and v ms⁻¹ is the car's speed. The car travels up a slope inclined at an angle θ to the horizontal, where $\sin\theta = 0.1$. The power generated by the car is 20 kW and its speed up the slope remains constant at 10 ms⁻¹.

　a)　Show that $k = 102$.
　　　　　　　　　　　　　　　　　　　　　　　　　　　　　　(3 marks)

　b)　The car's maximum power output is 50 kW.
　　　(i)　Show that, going up this slope, the car's maximum possible speed, u ms⁻¹, satisfies the equation:
　　　　　　$102u^2 + 980u - 50\,000 = 0$.
　　　　　　　　　　　　　　　　　　　　　　　　　　　　　　(4 marks)

　　　(ii)　Hence find the car's maximum possible speed up this slope.
　　　　　　　　　　　　　　　　　　　　　　　　　　　　　　(2 marks)

　　The car reaches the top of the slope and begins travelling on a flat horizontal road. The power increases to 21 kW and the resistive force remains at kv N.

　c)　Find the acceleration of the car when its speed is 12 ms⁻¹.
　　　　　　　　　　　　　　　　　　　　　　　　　　　　　　(3 marks)

Exam-Style Questions
Questions in the same style as the ones you'll get in the exam, with worked solutions and mark schemes.

Glossary
All the definitions you need to know for the exam, plus other useful words.

Practice Exam Papers (on CD-ROM)
Two printable exam papers, with fully worked answers and mark schemes.

A-Level
Mathematics
for AQA
M2
CD-ROM
Exam Practice Papers
& Worked Answers
CGP

Published by CGP

Editors:
Sharon Keeley-Holden, David Ryan, Lyn Setchell, Jonathan Wray, Dawn Wright.

Contributors:
Andrew Ballard, Jean Blencowe, Michael Coe, Barbara Mascetti.

ISBN: 978 1 84762 801 5

With thanks to Janet Dickinson, Simon Little and Glenn Rogers for the proofreading.

Groovy website: www.cgpbooks.co.uk

Printed by Elanders Ltd, Newcastle upon Tyne.
Jolly bits of clipart from CorelDRAW®

1. Moments

In M1 you saw that a force applied to a particle can cause the particle to accelerate in a straight line in the direction of the force.

However, a force acting on a rigid body which is pivoted at a point can cause the body to rotate about the pivot point.

Moments

- A **moment** is the **turning effect** a force has **around a point**.
- The **larger the magnitude** of the force, and the **greater the distance** between the force and the pivot, the **greater the moment**.
- Moments are either **clockwise** or **anticlockwise**.
- You can use the following formula to find the moment of a force about a point:

$$\text{Moment} = \frac{\text{Magnitude of Force}}{} \times \frac{\text{Perpendicular Distance from the line of action of the force to the pivot}}{}$$

- Or, more concisely: **Moment = *Fd*.**
- If the force is measured in newtons and the distance is measured in metres, then the moment is measured in newton-metres, **Nm**.

Tip: The 'line of action' of the force is just the direction that the force acts in.

Example 1

A 2 m long plank is attached to a ship at one end, *O*. The plank is horizontal, and a bird lands on the other end, applying a downward force of magnitude 15 N, as shown. Model the plank as a light rod and find the turning effect about *O* of the bird on the plank.

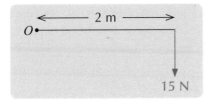

Use the formula:

Moment = *Fd*

    = 15 × 2

    = 30 Nm clockwise

Tip: Modelling the plank as a light rod means that you don't have to worry about its weight.

Tip: The point *O* is the pivot point.

Tip: Make sure you give a direction with your answer — i.e. which way the force will cause the rod to turn.

Example 2

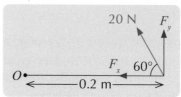

A spanner is attached to a bolt at a point, O. A force of 20 N is applied at an angle of 60° to the other end of the spanner, as shown. Find the turning effect about O of the force upon the bolt.

- This time the force is acting at an angle — resolve the force to find its components, F_x and F_y, acting parallel and perpendicular to the spanner:

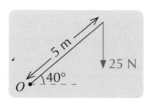

- F_x acts through O, so its moment is zero (it has no turning effect).
- Resolving perpendicular to the spanner, $F_y = 20\sin 60°$.
- F_y is a perpendicular distance of 0.2 m from O, so, using the formula:

    Moment $= 20\sin 60° \times 0.2$

    $= 3.46$ Nm (3 s.f.) anticlockwise

Example 3

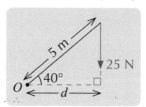

A force of 25 N acts upon a point, O, via a light rod of length 5 m. The 25 N force acts vertically downwards, and the rod makes an angle of 40° with the horizontal, as shown. What is the turning effect of the force about O?

- You need the perpendicular distance, d, between the line of action of the force and the pivot point:

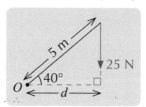

- $d = 5\cos 40°$, so:

    Moment $= 25 \times 5\cos 40° = 95.8$ Nm (3 s.f.) clockwise

Tip: 'Find the turning effect' means the same as 'find the moment'.

Tip: You can either find the component of the force acting perpendicular to the spanner (as done in the example), or you can find the perpendicular distance to the line of action of the force:

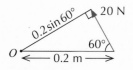

Moment $= 20 \times 0.2\sin 60°$

Tip: You could've resolved the force to find the component acting perpendicular to the rod, as in Example 2:

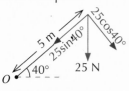

Moment $= 25\cos 40° \times 5$

Finding the sum of moments about a point

- If there are **two or more** forces acting on a rod or beam, then you can find the **sum of the moments** about a particular point.
- If the sum of the moments about a particular point is **zero**, then the rod is in **equilibrium** about **that point** (i.e. it **won't rotate** about that point).
- If the sum of the moments about a particular point is **not zero**, the rod will **turn** clockwise or anticlockwise about **that point**.
- The direction that the rod turns (i.e. clockwise or anticlockwise) is called the **sense** of rotation.

Example 4

The diagram shows the light rod AB. A force of magnitude 5 N acts vertically downwards at point C. A force of magnitude 4 N acts at point B, making an angle of 30° with the rod, as shown:

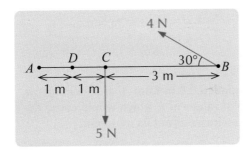

Tip: When you're finding the sum of moments, you have to say which direction is positive — clockwise or anticlockwise.

a) **Show that the rod is in equilibrium about point A.**

- Taking moments about A (with clockwise being the positive direction), and finding their sum:

    Sum of moments $= (5 \times 2) - (4\sin 30° \times 5)$

    $ = 10 - 10$

    $ = \boxed{0 \text{ Nm}}$

    This term is negative because the moment is anticlockwise.

- Total moment equals zero, so the rod is in equilibrium about A.

Tip: Don't forget to resolve so that the line of action of the force and its distance from the pivot are perpendicular to each other.

b) **The rod is now pivoted at point D. Given that the forces acting on the rod are the same as in part a), will the rod rotate clockwise or anticlockwise about this point?**

- Taking moments about D (with clockwise being the positive direction), and finding their sum:

    Sum of moments $= (5 \times 1) - (4\sin 30° \times 4)$

    $ = 5 - 8$

    $ = \boxed{-3 \text{ Nm}}$

- The sum of moments is negative, so the rod will rotate anticlockwise.

Example 5

A light rod, *AB*, of length 4 m, is pivoted at its midpoint.
A 12 N force is applied to *A*, at an angle of 45° above the rod, and a
7 N force is applied to *B*, at an angle of 60° above the rod, as shown:

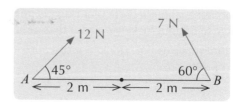

a) **Find the sum of the moments about the midpoint.**

- Taking moments about the midpoint (with clockwise positive), and finding their sum:

Sum of moments $= (12 \sin 45° \times 2) - (7 \sin 60° \times 2)$

$$= (12\sqrt{2} - 7\sqrt{3}) \text{ Nm}$$

$$= \boxed{4.85 \text{ Nm (3 s.f.) clockwise}}$$

Tip: The sense of rotation of the 12 N force is clockwise and the sense of rotation of the 7 N force is anticlockwise.

b) **A force, *F*, is applied 0.5 m from *A*, as shown below. Find the range of values of *F* which would cause the beam to rotate anticlockwise about its midpoint.**

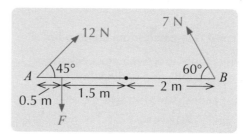

- Taking moments about the midpoint (with clockwise positive), and finding their sum:

Sum of moments $= (12 \sin 45° \times 2) - (7 \sin 60° \times 2) - 1.5F$

$$= 12\sqrt{2} - 7\sqrt{3} - 1.5F$$

- For the beam to rotate anticlockwise, the sum of moments must be negative:

$$12\sqrt{2} - 7\sqrt{3} - 1.5F < 0$$

$$1.5F > 12\sqrt{2} - 7\sqrt{3}$$

$$F > \left(8\sqrt{2} - \frac{14\sqrt{3}}{3}\right) \text{ N}$$

$$\Rightarrow \boxed{F > 3.23 \text{ N (3 s.f.)}}$$

Tip: The sum of moments must be negative for the beam to rotate anticlockwise, as clockwise was taken as the positive direction.

Example 6

PQ is a light rod of length 14 m inclined at an angle of 15° to the horizontal. A vertical force of magnitude 6 N acts at *P* and a horizontal force of magnitude 4 N acts at *Q*, as shown. The rod is pivoted at the point *X*.

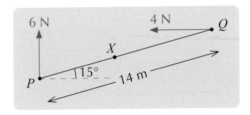

Given that the sum of the moments about *X* is 3 Nm anticlockwise, find the distance between *P* and *X*.

- Let *d* be the distance between *P* and *X*.
- First, find the perpendicular distances from *X* to the line of action of each force:

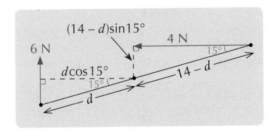

- Now take moments about *X* (with <u>anticlockwise</u> positive), and find their sum:

$$\text{Sum of moments} = [4 \times (14 - d)\sin15°] - (6 \times d\cos15°)$$
$$= 56\sin15° - 4d\sin15° - 6d\cos15°$$
$$= 56\sin15° - d(4\sin15° + 6\cos15°)$$

- Sum of moments is 3 Nm, so:

$$3 = 56\sin15° - d(4\sin15° + 6\cos15°)$$
$$\Rightarrow d = \frac{56\sin15° - 3}{4\sin15° + 6\cos15°}$$
$$= 1.68 \text{ m (3 s.f.)}$$

Tip: Rather than finding perpendicular distances, you could resolve the forces to find their components perpendicular to the rod.

Tip: Here, alternate angles and trigonometry are used to find the perpendicular distances — there are plenty of other ways you can do it.

Tip: You could take clockwise as positive if you wanted — the sum of the moments would then be −3 Nm.

Q1 For each of the following light rods, find
the moment of the force about A.

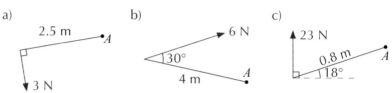

a)   b)   c)

Q2 For each of the following light rods, find
the sum of the moments about X.

a)   b)

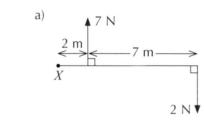   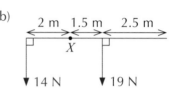

c)   d)

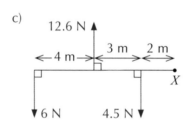   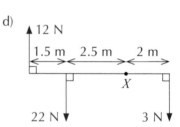

e)   f)

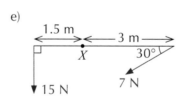   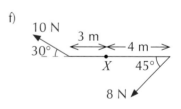

g)   h)

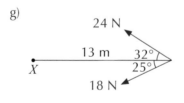   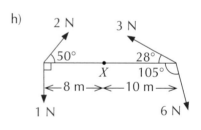

Q3

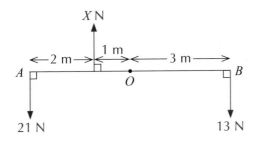

The diagram shows the light rod AB. Find the range of possible values for X, given that AB rotates clockwise about the point O.

Q4

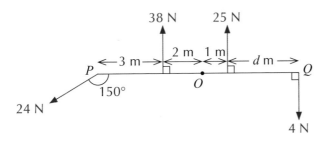

The diagram shows the light rod PQ. Find the range of possible values for d which will cause PQ to rotate anticlockwise about the point O.

Q5

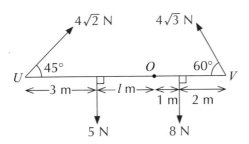

The diagram shows the light rod UV. The sum of the moments about O is 0.5 Nm anticlockwise. Find the value of l.

Q6

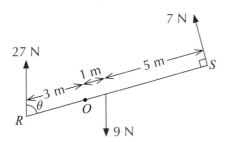

The diagram shows the light rod RS. The 27 N force and the 9 N force both act vertically. The 7 N force acts perpendicular to the rod. Find the value of θ given that the sum of the moments about O is 3 Nm clockwise.

Q6 Hint: You can either resolve forces perpendicular to the rod, or just calculate the perpendicular distances.

Moments in equilibrium

- A rigid body which is in **equilibrium** will **not move**.
- This means that there is **no resultant force** in **any direction** — any forces acting on the body will cancel each other out.
- It also means that the **sum of the moments** on the body **about any point** is **zero**.
- So, for a body in equilibrium:

> Total Clockwise Moment $=$ Total Anticlockwise Moment

- By **resolving forces** and **equating clockwise and anticlockwise moments**, you can solve problems involving bodies in equilibrium.

Example 1

Two weights of 30 N and 45 N are placed on a light 8 m beam. The 30 N weight is at one end of the beam, as shown, whilst the other weight is a distance d from the midpoint, M. The beam is held in equilibrium by a light, inextensible wire with tension T attached at M. Find T and the distance d.

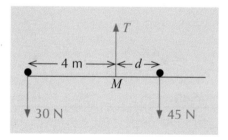

- First resolve forces vertically (forces 'up' = forces 'down'):

$$T = 30 + 45$$
$$= 75 \text{ N}$$

- Then take moments about M (moments clockwise = moments anticlockwise):

$$45d = 30 \times 4$$
$$\Rightarrow d = 120 \div 45$$
$$= 2.67 \text{ m (3 s.f.)}$$

Tip: The line of action of T passes through M, so the moment of T about M is zero.

Example 2

The diagram below shows a light rod AB, of length 10 m.
Particles of mass M_A kg and M_B kg are placed at A and B respectively.
The rod is supported in equilibrium by two vertical reaction forces of
magnitude 145 N and 90 N, as shown below:

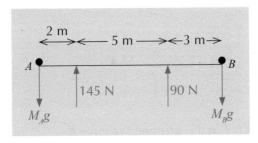

Find the values of M_A and M_B.

- As the rod is in equilibrium, you know that
  clockwise moments = anticlockwise moments.
  So, taking moments about A:

$$M_B g \times 10 = (145 \times 2) + (90 \times 7)$$
$$\Rightarrow M_B = 920 \div 98$$
$$= 9.387... = \boxed{9.39 \text{ kg (3 s.f.)}}$$

Tip: It's a good idea to take moments about a point where an unknown force is acting, as the moment of that force about the point will be zero, and it won't appear in the equation.

- You also know that there is no resultant force acting on the rod.
  So, resolving forces vertically ('forces up' = 'forces down'):

$$145 + 90 = M_A g + M_B g$$
$$\Rightarrow M_A + M_B = 235 \div 9.8 = 23.979...$$
$$\Rightarrow M_A = 23.979... - 9.387...$$
$$= \boxed{14.6 \text{ kg (3 s.f.)}}$$

Centres of mass

- The **centre of mass** (**COM**) of an object is the point where
  the object's **weight** can be considered to act.
- The mass of a **uniform beam** is spread evenly along the length
  of the beam, and so the centre of mass is at its **midpoint**:

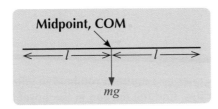

Tip: Up until now, all the beams have been light, so you haven't needed to worry about their weights.

- The centre of mass of a **non-uniform beam**
  could be at **any point** along the beam.
- When you're **taking moments** and **resolving forces** for
  a heavy (i.e. not light) beam, you need to remember to
  include the **weight** of the beam in your calculations.

Example 3

A 6 m long uniform beam *AB* of weight 40 N is supported at *A* by a vertical force *R*. *AB* is held horizontally by a vertical wire attached 1 m from the other end. A particle of weight of 30 N is placed 2 m from the support *R*.

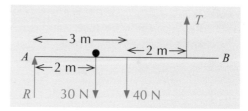

Find the tension *T* in the wire and the force *R*.

■ Taking moments about *A*:

Clockwise moments = Anticlockwise moments

$(30 \times 2) + \boxed{(40 \times 3)} = 5T$ ◁── This is the weight of the beam, acting at its centre.

$\Rightarrow T = 180 \div 5 = \boxed{36 \text{ N}}$

■ Resolving vertically:

$T + R = 30 + 40$

$R = 70 - T = 70 - 36$

$ = \boxed{34 \text{ N}}$

Example 4

A Christmas banner, *AB*, is attached to a ceiling by two pieces of tinsel. One piece of tinsel is attached to *A*, the other to the point *C*, where *BC* = 0.6 m. The banner has mass 8 kg and length 3.6 m and is held in equilibrium in a horizontal position.

a) **Modelling the banner as a uniform rod held in equilibrium and the tinsel as light strings, find the tension in the tinsel at *A* and *C*.**

■ Taking moments about *A*:

$(8g \times 1.8) = 3T_C$

$\Rightarrow T_C = 141.12 \div 3 = \boxed{47.04 \text{ N}}$

- Resolving vertically:

$T_A + T_C = 8g$

$\Rightarrow T_A = 8g - T_C = 78.4 - 47.04$

$= \boxed{31.36 \text{ N}}$

b) **The tinsel at A snaps and a downward force is applied at B to keep the banner horizontal and in equilibrium. Find the magnitude of the force applied at B and the new tension in the tinsel attached at C.**

- Draw a diagram to show the new situation:

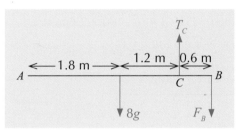

- Taking moments about C:

$8g \times 1.2 = F_B \times 0.6$

$\Rightarrow F_B = 94.08 \div 0.6$

$= \boxed{156.8 \text{ N}}$

- Resolving vertically:

$T_C = 8g + F_B$

$= (8 \times 9.8) + 156.8$

$= \boxed{235.2 \text{ N}}$

Example 5

A non-uniform beam of length 8 m and mass 48 kg is supported by legs attached at P and Q, 1 m from each end of the beam. A gymnast of mass 60 kg balances on the beam, 4 m from P. The reaction in the support at P has magnitude 539 N.

a) **Draw a diagram showing the forces acting on the beam.**

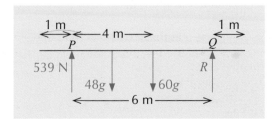

Tip: The beam is non-uniform, so you don't know exactly where its centre of mass is. Just draw the beam's weight acting *somewhere* on the beam.

b) Find the magnitude of the reaction at Q, and d, the distance of the centre of mass of the beam from P.

- Resolving vertically:

  $539 + R = 48g + 60g$

  $\Rightarrow R = 108g - 539$

  $= \boxed{519.4 \text{ N}}$

- Taking moments about P:

  $(60g \times 4) + (48g \times d) = 519.4 \times 6$

  $\Rightarrow 48gd = (519.4 \times 6) - (60 \times 9.8 \times 4)$

  $\Rightarrow d = 764.4 \div (48 \times 9.8)$

  $= \boxed{1.625 \text{ m}}$

The point of tilting

If a rod is '**about to tilt**' about a particular point of support, then any **normal reactions** acting at any other supports along the rod will be **zero**. The **tension** in any strings supporting the rod at any other point will also be **zero**.

Example 6

A non-uniform wooden plank of mass M kg rests horizontally on supports at A and B, as shown. When a bucket of water of mass 18 kg is placed at point C, the plank is in equilibrium, and is on the point of tilting about B.

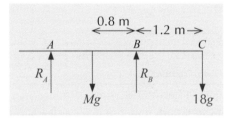

Find the value of M and the magnitude of the reaction at B.

- Taking moments about B:

  $(18g \times 1.2) + 0 = Mg \times 0.8$ ← $R_A = 0$, so the moment of the force is also zero.

  $\Rightarrow M = (18 \times 9.8 \times 1.2) \div (9.8 \times 0.8)$

  $= \boxed{27 \text{ kg}}$

- Resolving vertically:

  $R_A + R_B = Mg + 18g$

  $0 + R_B = 27g + 18g$

  $\Rightarrow R_B = \boxed{441 \text{ N}}$

Tip: The plank is on the point of tilting about B, so the reaction at A, R_A, is zero.

Exercise 1.2

Q1

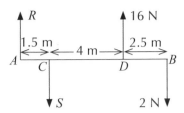

The diagram shows a light rod held horizontally in equilibrium by two vertical strings. Find the magnitudes of the forces R and S.

Q2

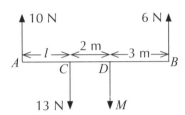

The diagram shows a light rod held horizontally in equilibrium by two vertical strings. Find the magnitude of the force M, and the distance l.

Q3

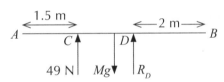

A uniform rod, AB, of length 5 m, rests horizontally in equilibrium on supports at C and D, as shown. If the magnitude of the normal reaction at C is 49 N, find:

a) the magnitude of the normal reaction at D,

b) the mass of the rod.

Q3 Hint: The rod is uniform, so its weight acts halfway along its length.

Q4

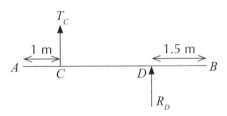

A uniform rod, AB, of mass 9 kg, is held in equilibrium by a vertical wire at C and a support at D, as shown. When an object of mass 3 kg is placed at B, the rod is still horizontal and in equilibrium, but is on the point of tilting about D.
Find the length of the rod.

Q4 Hint: When the rod is on the point of tilting about D, the tension in the wire at C will be zero.

Q5 A uniform beam, AB, has length 5 m and mass 8 kg. It is held horizontally in equilibrium by vertical ropes at B and the point C, 1 m from A.

a) Find the tension in each rope.

b) When a particle of mass 16 kg is placed on the beam, the beam remains horizontal and in equilibrium, but is on the point of tilting about C. Find the distance of the particle from A.

Q6

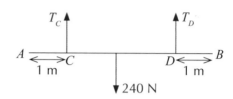

A 9 m long non-uniform beam, AB, of weight 240 N, is suspended between two trees to make a walkway. It is held horizontally and in equilibrium by vertical wires at C and D, as shown. The magnitude of the tension in the wire at C is twice the magnitude of the tension in the wire at D.

a) Find the tension in each wire.

b) Find the distance of the centre of mass of the beam from A.

Q7 A non-uniform plank, AB, of length 6 m, is laid horizontally across a stream to form a bridge. A and B rest on horizontal ground, and the midpoint of the plank rests on a rock protruding from the water. A child of mass 36 kg stands on the bridge 1 m from A and a child of mass 25 kg stands on the bridge 1.5 m from B. The centre of mass of the plank is at point X, 2.5 m from B. The reaction at B is twice the reaction at A, and the reaction of the rock at the midpoint is four times the reaction at A.

a) Draw a diagram to show the forces acting on the plank.

b) Given that the plank is in equilibrium, find its mass.

c) State any modelling assumptions you have made.

Q8 A painter of mass 80 kg stands on a horizontal non-uniform 4 m plank, AB, of mass 20 kg. The plank rests on supports 1 m from each end, at C and D. The painter places paint pots, of mass 2.5 kg, 0.2 m from each end of the plank.

Q8 Hint: The reaction forces at C and D are in the ratio $4:1$, so $R_C = 4R_D$.

a) He stands at the centre of mass of the plank and finds that the reaction forces at C and D are in the ratio $4:1$. Find the distance of the centre of mass of the plank from A.

b) He uses up all the paint in the pot near A, and discards the pot. He then stands on the plank at a point between D and B, and the plank is on the point of tilting about D. How far is he from B?

Friction and limiting equilibrium

Friction

- You should remember from M1 that if a body is in contact with a **rough** surface, then a **frictional force** will act between the body and the surface to oppose motion (or potential motion).

- The frictional force can take a range of values — when the body is **on the point of moving**, the frictional force will reach its **maximum value**. This value is given by the formula:

$$F = \mu R$$

F is the frictional force, μ is the coefficient of friction between the body and the surface, and R is the normal reaction of the surface on the body.

- When the body is on the point of moving, it is said to be in '**limiting equilibrium**'.

- If a **rigid body** rests in contact with a **rough surface**, then a **frictional force** will act between them, **parallel** to the surface, in the opposite direction to any potential motion.

- A **normal reaction** force will also act on the body, **perpendicular** to the surface.

'Ladder' questions

- '**Ladder**' questions, where a rigid body rests at an angle against the ground and a wall, are common in M2.

- In these questions, you'll need to consider the **normal reaction** of the **ground**, the **normal reaction** of the **wall**, and any **frictional forces** which may be acting, as well as the **weight** of the ladder and any other bodies.

- You'll then have to **resolve forces** and **take moments** to find any unknown forces or distances. In these questions, it's often a good idea to resolve forces **parallel** and **perpendicular** to the ladder before taking moments.

- The question will tell you whether the ground and wall are **rough** or **smooth** — this lets you know whether you need to take friction into account in your calculations.

- There are four possible combinations of surfaces for ladder questions:

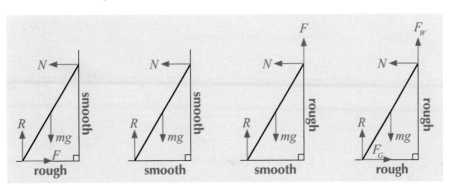

Tip: Friction acts to prevent motion. In each case, think about which way the ladder would slip — the frictional force will act in the opposite direction.

- The most common of these scenarios is **rough ground** and a **smooth wall**, but you should be familiar with all the situations.

Example 1

A ladder rests against a smooth vertical wall at an angle of 65° to rough horizontal ground. The ladder has mass 4.5 kg and length $5x$ m. A cat of mass 1.3 kg sits on the ladder at C, $4x$ m from the base. The ladder is in limiting equilibrium.

Modelling the ladder as a uniform rod and the cat as a particle, find the coefficient of friction between the ground and the ladder.

Tip: N is the normal reaction at the wall, R is the normal reaction at the ground. The wall is smooth, so there is no frictional force. The ground is rough, so there is a frictional force between it and the ladder.

- Draw a diagram to show the weights of the ladder and cat, and also the forces acting between the ladder and the ground, and between the ladder and the wall:

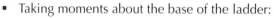

- Taking moments about the base of the ladder:

$$N\sin65° \times 5x = (4.5g\cos65° \times 2.5x) + (1.3g\cos65° \times 4x)$$
$$(4.531...)xN = (46.593..)x + (21.536...)x$$
$$\Rightarrow N = (68.130...)x \div (4.531...)x = 15.034...\text{ N}$$

- Resolving vertically:

$$R = 1.3g + 4.5g = 56.84\text{ N}$$

- Resolving horizontally:

$$F = N$$

- The ladder is in limiting equilibrium, so $F = \mu R$:

$$F = \mu R$$
$$\Rightarrow N = \mu R$$
$$15.034... = \mu \times 56.84$$
$$\Rightarrow \mu = 15.034... \div 56.84 = \boxed{0.26 \text{ (2 d.p.)}}$$

Example 2

A uniform ladder of mass 11 kg and length 3.8 m rests against a smooth vertical wall, at an angle of 58° to rough horizontal ground. The coefficient of friction between the ladder and the ground is 0.45. A painter of mass 83 kg begins to climb the ladder. He stops when the ladder is on the point of slipping.

How far up the ladder is he at this point?

- Draw a diagram to show what's going on:

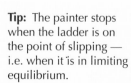

- Resolving vertically:

$$R = 11g + 83g = 921.2\text{ N}$$

- Resolving horizontally:

$$F = N$$

Tip: The painter stops when the ladder is on the point of slipping — i.e. when it is in limiting equilibrium.

- The ladder is in limiting equilibrium, so $F = \mu R$:

$$F = \mu R$$
$$\Rightarrow N = \mu R$$
$$N = 0.45 \times 921.2 = 414.54\text{ N}$$

- Let x be the painter's distance from the base of the ladder.
  Taking moments about the base of the ladder:

$$N\sin 58° \times 3.8 = (11g\cos 58° \times 1.9) + (83g\cos 58° \times x)$$

$$414.54\sin 58° \times 3.8 = 108.538... + (431.036...)x$$

$$\Rightarrow x = 1227.351... \div 431.036... = 2.85 \text{ m (3 s.f.)}$$

Bodies supported along their lengths

Rather than leaning against a wall, a rigid body may be held in equilibrium by resting on **supports** at points along its length. You can solve problems like this just as before, by **resolving forces** and **taking moments**.

You need to know whether the **ground** and **supports** are **rough** or **smooth**, and you should also remember that the **normal reaction** at a **support** will always act **perpendicular** to the body.

Example

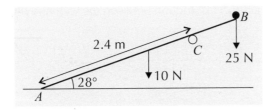

A uniform rod, *AB*, of length 3.3 m and weight 10 N, rests with *A* on rough horizontal ground. The rod is supported by a smooth peg at *C*, where *AC* = 2.4 m, in such a way that the rod makes an angle of 28° with the ground. A particle of weight 25 N is placed at *B*.

Given that the rod is in limiting equilibrium, find the magnitude of the normal reaction, *N*, at the peg and the magnitude of the frictional force, *F*, between the rod and the ground.

- Draw a diagram to show the forces acting on the rod:

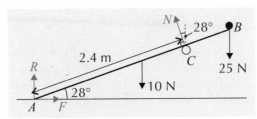

> **Tip:** The peg is smooth, so there is no frictional force at *C*. The normal reaction at *C*, *N*, acts perpendicular to the rod. The rod is on the point of slipping to the left, as viewed in the diagram, so the frictional force at *A* acts to the right.

- Taking moments about *A*:

$$2.4N = (10\cos 28° \times 1.65) + (25\cos 28° \times 3.3)$$

$$\Rightarrow N = 36.421...$$

$$= 36.4 \text{ N (3 s.f.)}$$

The rod's weight acts at its midpoint, 1.65 m from *A*.

- Resolving horizontally:

$$F = N\sin 28° = (36.421...)\sin 28° = 17.1 \text{ N (3 s.f.)}$$

Q1

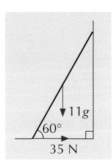

A uniform ladder of mass 11 kg and length 7 m rests against a rough vertical wall, at an angle of 60° to smooth, horizontal ground, as shown. A horizontal force of magnitude 35 N is applied to the base of the ladder, keeping it in limiting equilibrium, with the ladder on the point of sliding up the wall. Find:

a) the magnitude of the normal reaction of the wall on the ladder,

b) the frictional force between the wall and the ladder,

c) the coefficient of friction between the wall and the ladder.

Q2

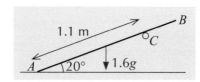

A uniform beam, AB, of mass 1.6 kg and length 1.5 m, rests with A on smooth, horizontal ground. The beam is supported by a rough peg at C, where $AC = 1.1$ m, so that it makes an angle of 20° with the horizontal, as shown. The beam is on the point of slipping. Find:

a) the magnitude of the normal reaction of the peg on the beam,

b) the magnitude of the normal reaction of the ground on the beam,

c) the magnitude of the frictional force between the peg and the beam,

d) the coefficient of friction between the peg and the beam.

Q3   A uniform ladder of mass 10 kg and length 6 m rests with one end on rough, horizontal ground and the other end against a smooth, vertical wall. The coefficient of friction between the ground and the ladder is 0.3, and the ladder makes an angle of 65° with the ground.
A girl of mass 50 kg begins to climb the ladder.
How far up the ladder can she climb before the ladder slips?

Q4   A uniform ladder of mass 9 kg and length 4.8 m rests in limiting equilibrium with one end on rough, horizontal ground and the other end against a rough, vertical wall. The normal reactions at the wall and the ground have magnitude 22 N and 75 N respectively. Find:

a) the angle that the ladder makes with the ground,

b) the coefficient of friction between the wall and the ladder,

c) the coefficient of friction between the ground and the ladder.

2. Centres of Mass — Particles

In the last section, you saw how to use moments to find the location of the centre of mass of a non-uniform rod.

Here, you'll see how to use moments to find the centre of mass of a group of particles.

Particles in a line

- Remember — the **weight** of an object is considered to act at its **centre of mass** (**COM**).

- It's often convenient to model an object as a **particle** (point mass) — the position of the particle will be the centre of mass of the object.

- A **group of objects** also has a centre of mass — this is the point at which the **total weight** of all the objects can be considered to act.

- In this case, the group of objects is modelled as a **group of particles**.

- The centre of mass of a group of particles **isn't** necessarily in the **same position** as any one of the particles.

- If a group of particles all lie in a **line**, then the centre of mass of the group will lie somewhere **on that line**.

- Just as with rigid bodies, you can find the centre of mass of a group of particles using **moments**.

- The **moment** of a particle's **weight** about a **point** is given by the formula:

$$\text{Moment} = \underset{(W = mg)}{\text{Weight}} \times \underset{\text{(from the particle to the point)}}{\text{Horizontal Distance}}$$

Tip: Remember — when you're calculating moments, you need to use the perpendicular distance from the line of action of the force to the point. As weight acts vertically downwards, this distance is horizontal.

Particles in a horizontal line

- The expression for the moment of a particle's weight about a point can be written as mgx, where x is the horizontal distance from the point to the particle.

- The **moment** of a group of particles in a **horizontal line** about a point on the horizontal line can be found by adding together all the individual moments about the point — $\Sigma\, mgx$.

- This has the same effect as the **combined weight** of the particles ($\Sigma\, mg$) acting at the **centre of mass** of the whole group ($\overline{x}$). i.e. $\Sigma\, mgx = \overline{x}\,\Sigma\, mg$, or, cancelling the g's to simplify:

$$\Sigma\, mx = \overline{x}\,\Sigma\, m$$

You need to learn this formula.

Tip: $\overline{x}$ is the horizontal distance from the point you're taking moments about to the centre of mass of the group of particles.

- Use this simplified formula to find the centre of mass, $\overline{x}$, of a group of particles in a horizontal line.

Example

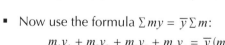

Three particles are placed at positions along the *x*-axis, as shown. Find the coordinates of the centre of mass of the group of particles.

Tip: The *x*-coordinate of each particle gives its distance from the origin (the point about which you're taking moments). Negative coordinates go into the formula as they are (you don't have to change the sign), because weights of particles placed here cause the system to rotate in the opposite direction to those placed at points with positive coordinates.

- Write down the different values you know:

$$m_1 = 3, x_1 = -2 \qquad m_2 = 1.5, x_2 = 3 \qquad m_3 = 0.5, x_3 = 5$$

- Now use the formula $\sum mx = \overline{x}\sum m$:

$$m_1 x_1 + m_2 x_2 + m_3 x_3 = \overline{x}(m_1 + m_2 + m_3)$$
$$(3 \times -2) + (1.5 \times 3) + (0.5 \times 5) = \overline{x}(3 + 1.5 + 0.5)$$
$$1 = 5\overline{x}$$
$$\Rightarrow \overline{x} = 0.2$$

- So the centre of mass of the group has coordinates (0.2, 0).

Particles in a vertical line

Finding the centre of mass of a group of particles arranged in a **vertical line** is pretty much the same — you just need to use the **vertical distance** from the point you're taking moments about to each particle (i.e. just change the *x*'s to *y*'s in the formula):

Tip: $\overline{y}$ is the vertical distance from the point you're taking moments about to the centre of mass of the group of particles.

$$\boxed{\sum my = \overline{y}\sum m}$$ ← Learn this formula too.

Example

A light, vertical rod, *AB*, has particles attached at various positions, as shown. Find the distance of the centre of mass of the loaded rod from *A*.

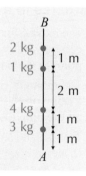

Tip: Remember — 'light' means the rod has negligible mass, so you only need to worry about the masses of the particles when using the formula.

- Write down the values you know — first you'll need to work out the distance of each particle from *A*:

$$m_1 = 3, \ y_1 = 1 \qquad m_2 = 4, \ y_2 = 2$$
$$m_3 = 1, \ y_3 = 4 \qquad m_4 = 2, \ y_4 = 5$$

- Now use the formula $\sum my = \overline{y}\sum m$:

$$m_1 y_1 + m_2 y_2 + m_3 y_3 + m_4 y_4 = \overline{y}(m_1 + m_2 + m_3 + m_4)$$
$$(3 \times 1) + (4 \times 2) + (1 \times 4) + (2 \times 5) = \overline{y}(3 + 4 + 1 + 2)$$
$$25 = 10\overline{y}$$
$$\Rightarrow \overline{y} = 2.5$$

- So the centre of mass of the loaded rod is 2.5 m from *A*.

Q1 Three particles are placed on the x-axis. A particle of mass 4 kg is placed at the point where $x = 3$, a particle of mass 6 kg is placed at the point where $x = 5$, and a particle of mass 10 kg is placed at the point where $x = 7$. Find the centre of mass of the three particles.

Q2 Three particles of mass 8 kg, 4 kg and M kg are placed at the points $(-3, 0)$, $(1, 0)$ and $(13, 0)$ respectively. Given that the centre of mass of the particles is at $(5, 0)$, find the value of M.

Q3 Three objects are attached to a light, horizontal rod, AB. The objects have mass 2 kg, 1 kg and 1.5 kg and are attached at distances of 1 m, 2.5 m and 3 m from A respectively. Find the distance of the centre of mass of the loaded rod from A.

Q4

Three particles are placed in a horizontal line, as shown. Find the distance of the centre of mass of the particles from O.

Q5 Particles of mass 0.8 kg, 1.2 kg, 1.8 kg and 2.1 kg are placed at the points $(0, -2)$, $(0, -2.6)$, $(0, -3.5)$ and $(0, -3.8)$ respectively. Find the coordinates of the centre of mass of the group of particles.

Q6 Particles are placed on the y-axis as follows: 3 kg at $(0, -7)$, 2 kg at $(0, -5)$, 4 kg at $(0, -1)$, 1 kg at $(0, 0)$, 4 kg at $(0, 6)$ and 6 kg at $(0, 8)$. Find the coordinates of the centre of mass of the particles.

Q7 Five particles of mass 1 kg, 2 kg, 3 kg, 4 kg and 5 kg are equally spaced along the x-axis, with the 1 kg particle at the origin and the 5 kg particle at the point $(12, 0)$. Find the coordinates of the centre of mass of the particles.

Q8 Bodies of mass M kg, $2M$ kg and 5 kg are placed at the points $(0, -3)$, $(0, 1)$ and $(0, 2)$ respectively. Given that the centre of mass of the bodies is at the origin, find the value of M.

Q9 Two light, inextensible strings, P and Q, each of length 2 m, are hung vertically from a horizontal ceiling. String P has a particle of mass 5 kg attached at its midpoint and a particle of mass 4 kg attached to its lower end. String Q has a particle of mass 4 kg attached at its midpoint and a particle of mass 5 kg attached to its lower end. Find the vertical distance between the centres of mass of the two strings.

Q10 Four stones are fixed to a light horizontal rod, AB, of length 1 m. A stone of mass 1.5 kg is fixed at A, a stone of mass 0.5 kg is fixed at B, and a stone of mass 2 kg is fixed at the rod's midpoint. A stone of mass 0.2 kg is fixed at the point C. Given that the centre of mass of the loaded rod is at the point C, find the length AC.

Particles in two dimensions

- The same principles from the last few pages apply to finding the centre of mass of a group of particles in a **plane**.
- There are two ways of finding the centre of mass of a group of particles in two dimensions. The first way is to find the values of $\bar{x}$ and $\bar{y}$ **separately** (where $(\bar{x}, \bar{y})$ are the coordinates of the centre of mass of the group).

Tip: A position vector describes the position of a point relative to the origin.

- The second way is to find $\bar{x}$ and $\bar{y}$ at the **same time** using **position vectors**.
- Using position vectors, the formula becomes:

$$\sum m\mathbf{r} = \bar{\mathbf{r}} \sum m$$

where $\bar{\mathbf{r}}$ is the position vector of the centre of mass of the group of particles.

- The quickest way is to use position vectors, but Example 1 below shows both methods, so you can choose which you prefer.

Example 1

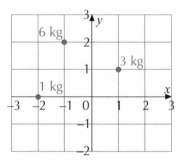

Find the coordinates of the centre of mass of the system of particles shown in the diagram.

THE LONG WAY — finding $\bar{x}$ and $\bar{y}$ separately.

- Write down the values you know:

$$m_1 = 6, x_1 = -1 \qquad m_2 = 3, x_2 = 1 \qquad m_3 = 1, x_3 = -2$$

- Find the x-coordinate of the centre of mass of the group first (pretend the particles are in a horizontal line):

$$\sum mx = \bar{x} \sum m$$
$$m_1x_1 + m_2x_2 + m_3x_3 = \bar{x}(m_1 + m_2 + m_3)$$
$$(6 \times -1) + (3 \times 1) + (1 \times -2) = \bar{x}(6 + 3 + 1)$$
$$-5 = 10\bar{x}$$
$$\Rightarrow \bar{x} = -0.5$$

- Now find the y-coordinate in the same way:

$$y_1 = 2, \qquad y_2 = 1, \qquad y_3 = 0$$
$$\sum my = \bar{y} \sum m$$
$$m_1y_1 + m_2y_2 + m_3y_3 = \bar{y}(m_1 + m_2 + m_3)$$
$$(6 \times 2) + (3 \times 1) + (1 \times 0) = \bar{x}(6 + 3 + 1)$$
$$15 = 10\bar{y}$$
$$\Rightarrow \bar{y} = 1.5$$

- So the centre of mass has coordinates $(\bar{x}, \bar{y}) = (-0.5, 1.5)$.

THE SHORT WAY — using position vectors.

- Write down the mass, m, and position vector, $\mathbf{r}$, for each particle:

$$m_1 = 6, \mathbf{r}_1 = \begin{pmatrix} -1 \\ 2 \end{pmatrix} \qquad m_2 = 3, \mathbf{r}_2 = \begin{pmatrix} 1 \\ 1 \end{pmatrix} \qquad m_3 = 1, \mathbf{r}_3 = \begin{pmatrix} -2 \\ 0 \end{pmatrix}$$

- Use the formula $\sum m\mathbf{r} = \bar{\mathbf{r}} \sum m$:

$$m_1\mathbf{r}_1 + m_2\mathbf{r}_2 + m_3\mathbf{r}_3 = \bar{\mathbf{r}}(m_1 + m_2 + m_3)$$

$$\Rightarrow 6\begin{pmatrix} -1 \\ 2 \end{pmatrix} + 3\begin{pmatrix} 1 \\ 1 \end{pmatrix} + 1\begin{pmatrix} -2 \\ 0 \end{pmatrix} = \bar{\mathbf{r}}(6 + 3 + 1)$$

$$\Rightarrow \begin{pmatrix} -6 \\ 12 \end{pmatrix} + \begin{pmatrix} 3 \\ 3 \end{pmatrix} + \begin{pmatrix} -2 \\ 0 \end{pmatrix} = 10\bar{\mathbf{r}}$$

$$\Rightarrow \begin{pmatrix} -5 \\ 15 \end{pmatrix} = 10\bar{\mathbf{r}}$$

$$\Rightarrow \bar{\mathbf{r}} = \begin{pmatrix} -0.5 \\ 1.5 \end{pmatrix}$$

- So the centre of mass has position vector $\bar{\mathbf{r}} = \begin{pmatrix} -0.5 \\ 1.5 \end{pmatrix}$, and coordinates $(\bar{x}, \bar{y}) = (-0.5, 1.5)$.

Tip: It's easiest to write the particles' positions as column vectors — these are just like coordinates standing upright: $\mathbf{r} = \begin{pmatrix} x \\ y \end{pmatrix}$. When adding column vectors, add the horizontal and vertical components separately.

Example 2

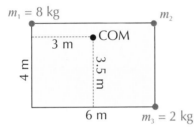

The diagram shows the position of the centre of mass (COM) of a system of three particles attached to the corners of a light, rectangular lamina. Find m_2.

- First of all, pick your origin — the bottom-left corner looks as good as anywhere — and define all your positions from this point:

$$\mathbf{r}_1 = \begin{pmatrix} 0 \\ 4 \end{pmatrix} \qquad \mathbf{r}_2 = \begin{pmatrix} 6 \\ 4 \end{pmatrix} \qquad \mathbf{r}_3 = \begin{pmatrix} 6 \\ 0 \end{pmatrix} \qquad \bar{\mathbf{r}} = \begin{pmatrix} 3 \\ 3.5 \end{pmatrix}$$

- Use the formula $\sum m\mathbf{r} = \bar{\mathbf{r}} \sum m$:

$$m_1\mathbf{r}_1 + m_2\mathbf{r}_2 + m_3\mathbf{r}_3 = \bar{\mathbf{r}}(m_1 + m_2 + m_3)$$

$$\Rightarrow 8\begin{pmatrix} 0 \\ 4 \end{pmatrix} + m_2\begin{pmatrix} 6 \\ 4 \end{pmatrix} + 2\begin{pmatrix} 6 \\ 0 \end{pmatrix} = \begin{pmatrix} 3 \\ 3.5 \end{pmatrix} \times (8 + m_2 + 2)$$

$$\Rightarrow \begin{pmatrix} 0 \\ 32 \end{pmatrix} + \begin{pmatrix} 6m_2 \\ 4m_2 \end{pmatrix} + \begin{pmatrix} 12 \\ 0 \end{pmatrix} = \begin{pmatrix} 3 \\ 3.5 \end{pmatrix} \times (m_2 + 10)$$

$$\Rightarrow \begin{pmatrix} 6m_2 + 12 \\ 4m_2 + 32 \end{pmatrix} = \begin{pmatrix} 3m_2 + 30 \\ 3.5m_2 + 35 \end{pmatrix}$$

- Use the top row to solve for m_2:

$$6m_2 + 12 = 3m_2 + 30$$

$$\Rightarrow m_2 = 6 \text{ kg}$$

Tip: A lamina is a flat body whose thickness can be ignored. This lamina is light, so it also has negligible mass.

Tip: You can check your value of m_2 using the bottom row of the vector equation:
$$4m_2 + 32 = 3.5m_2 + 35$$

Example 3

A particle of mass 0.4 kg is placed at the origin, a particle of mass 0.6 kg is placed at the point (3, –2), and a particle of mass 0.2 kg is placed at the point (1, 5). At what point must a particle of mass 0.8 kg be placed for the centre of mass of the four particles to be at (–0.6, 1.5)?

- Write down the values you know:

$$m_1 = 0.4, \ \mathbf{r}_1 = \begin{pmatrix} 0 \\ 0 \end{pmatrix} \qquad m_2 = 0.6, \ \mathbf{r}_2 = \begin{pmatrix} 3 \\ -2 \end{pmatrix}$$

$$m_3 = 0.2, \ \mathbf{r}_3 = \begin{pmatrix} 1 \\ 5 \end{pmatrix} \qquad m_4 = 0.8, \ \mathbf{r}_4 = \begin{pmatrix} a \\ b \end{pmatrix}$$

$$\bar{\mathbf{r}} = \begin{pmatrix} -0.6 \\ 1.5 \end{pmatrix}$$

a and *b* are constants that you need to find.

- Use the formula $\sum m\mathbf{r} = \bar{\mathbf{r}} \sum m$:

$$m_1\mathbf{r}_1 + m_2\mathbf{r}_2 + m_3\mathbf{r}_3 + m_4\mathbf{r}_4 = \bar{\mathbf{r}}(m_1 + m_2 + m_3 + m_4)$$

$$\Rightarrow \ 0.4\begin{pmatrix} 0 \\ 0 \end{pmatrix} + 0.6\begin{pmatrix} 3 \\ -2 \end{pmatrix} + 0.2\begin{pmatrix} 1 \\ 5 \end{pmatrix} + 0.8\begin{pmatrix} a \\ b \end{pmatrix}$$

$$= \begin{pmatrix} -0.6 \\ 1.5 \end{pmatrix} \times (0.4 + 0.6 + 0.2 + 0.8)$$

$$\Rightarrow \begin{pmatrix} 0 \\ 0 \end{pmatrix} + \begin{pmatrix} 1.8 \\ -1.2 \end{pmatrix} + \begin{pmatrix} 0.2 \\ 1 \end{pmatrix} + 0.8\begin{pmatrix} a \\ b \end{pmatrix} = \begin{pmatrix} -1.2 \\ 3 \end{pmatrix}$$

$$\Rightarrow 0.8\begin{pmatrix} a \\ b \end{pmatrix} = \begin{pmatrix} -3.2 \\ 3.2 \end{pmatrix}$$

$$\Rightarrow \begin{pmatrix} a \\ b \end{pmatrix} = \begin{pmatrix} -4 \\ 4 \end{pmatrix}$$

- So the particle should be placed at the point (–4, 4).

Exercise 2.2

Q1 Find the coordinates of the centre of mass of the following group of particles: a particle of mass 2 kg at the point (3, 1), a particle of mass 3 kg at the point (2, 4), and a particle of mass 5 kg at the point (5, 2).

Q2

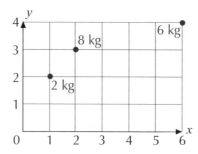

Find the coordinates of the centre of mass of the group of particles shown above.

Q3 A particle of mass 3 kg is placed at (1, 2), a particle of mass 4 kg is placed at (5, 1), a particle of mass 5 kg is placed at (3, 6), and a particle of mass *M* kg is placed at (0, 1). The centre of mass of the group of particles is at (1.9, 2.4). Find the value of *M*.

Q4 Four particles are placed on an x- and y-coordinate grid as follows:
3 kg at (2, 1), 4 kg at (4, 0), M_1 kg at (–4, 0), and M_2 kg at (0, –5).
The centre of mass of the particles is at the origin.

a) Find the value of M_1.

b) Find the value of M_2.

Q5 A light rectangular lamina $ABCD$ has lengths AB = 8 cm and
BC = 10 cm. A stone of mass 200 g is placed at A, a stone of mass
250 g is placed at B, a stone of mass 300 g is placed at C, and a
stone of mass 250 g is placed at D.
Find the distance from the centre of mass of
the loaded lamina to the point A.

Q5 Hint: Don't just find the position of the COM — the question asks for its distance from A.

Q6 Four particles are placed on an x- and y-coordinate grid as follows:
2.5 kg at (–3, 1), 2 kg at (–2, –4), 3 kg at (4, –3), and 1.5 kg at (2, 3).
A fifth particle, of mass 1 kg, is to be placed on the grid so that the
centre of mass of the five particles is at (0.65, –0.8).
Where should this particle be placed?

Q7 A light wire is shaped into a rectangle, $ABCD$, where AB = 30 cm and
BC = 20 cm. A particle of mass 9 kg is fixed to the rectangle at the
midpoint of side AB, a particle of mass 6 kg is fixed to the midpoint
of BC, a particle of mass 12 kg is fixed to the midpoint of CD and a
particle of mass 3 kg is fixed to the midpoint of AD.

a) Taking A to be (0, 0), D to be on the positive x-axis and B to be on
the positive y-axis, find the coordinates of the centre of mass of
the system.

b) A particle of mass M kg is attached to AB in such a way that the
centre of mass of the system lies on the line EF, where E and F
are the midpoints of AD and BC respectively. Find the value of M.

Q8

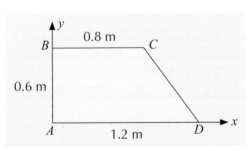

The light trapezium-shaped lamina, $ABCD$, is shown above.
E is the midpoint of AC and F is the midpoint of BD.

a) Taking A as the origin, find the coordinates of E and F.

b) Particles of mass 0.5 kg, 0.75 kg, 0.25 kg and 1 kg
are attached to E, F, C and D respectively.
Find the coordinates of the centre of mass of the loaded lamina.

c) A particle of mass M kg is attached at B in such a way that the
centre of mass of the system lies on AC. Find the value of M.

d) Find the new coordinates of the centre
of mass of the loaded lamina.

Q8 c) Hint: Find the equation of AC to help you form a pair of simultaneous equations. Then solve to find M.

3. Centres of Mass — Laminas

A lamina is a flat body whose thickness can be ignored.
In this section, you'll learn how to find the position of a lamina's centre of mass.

Uniform laminas

- The mass of a **uniform lamina** is **spread out evenly** across the area of the shape.
- The centre of mass of a uniform lamina always lies on the shape's **lines of symmetry** (if it has any).
- For shapes with **more than one** line of symmetry, the centre of mass is where the lines of symmetry **intersect**:

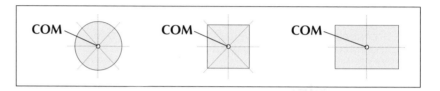

Example

Find the coordinates of the centre of mass of a uniform rectangular lamina with vertices $A(-4, 7)$, $B(2, 7)$, $C(2, -3)$ and $D(-4, -3)$.

- Sketch the lamina:

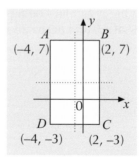

Tip: The dotted lines are the lines of symmetry of the rectangular lamina. The lamina's centre of mass is at the point where the dotted lines intersect.

- Call the coordinates of the centre of mass $(\overline{x}, \overline{y})$.
- $\overline{x}$ is the x-coordinate of the midpoint of AB (or CD):

  $(-4 + 2) \div 2 = -1$

- $\overline{y}$ is the y-coordinate of the midpoint of AD (or BC):

  $(7 + -3) \div 2 = 2$

- So the required coordinates are $(-1, 2)$.

Q1 A uniform square lamina has vertices $A(1, 2)$, $B(1, 5)$, $C(4, 5)$ and $D(4, 2)$. Find the coordinates of the centre of mass of the lamina.

Q2 $A(-5, -5)$ and $B(1, 3)$ are points on a uniform circular lamina such that AB is a diameter of the circle. Find the coordinates of the circle's centre of mass.

Q3 A uniform lamina in the shape of a parallelogram has vertices $E(-2, -1)$, $F(1, 3)$, $G(6, 3)$ and $H(3, -1)$. Find the coordinates of its centre of mass.

Q3 Hint: The COM of a parallelogram is where the diagonals intersect each other.

Q4 The centre of mass of a uniform rectangle is 6.5 cm from each vertex. The length of the shorter side of the rectangle is 5 cm. Find the length of the longer side of the rectangle.

Loaded laminas and composite shapes

Loaded laminas

- You may be asked to find the centre of mass of a **loaded lamina** — i.e. a lamina with **particles attached** to it.
- To do this, first find the centre of mass of the **lamina**.
- Then model the lamina as being replaced by a **particle** of the same mass, in the position of its centre of mass.
- Then you can use one of the methods for finding the centre of mass of a **group of particles** in a **plane** from pages 22 and 23.

Tip: You've seen loaded laminas before — e.g. in Example 2, page 23 — but there the lamina was light. Here, you need to take the lamina's mass into account in your calculations.

Example

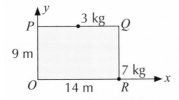

The diagram shows a uniform rectangular lamina, $OPQR$, of height 9 m, width 14 m and mass 10 kg. A particle of mass 3 kg is fixed to the lamina at the midpoint of PQ and a particle of mass 7 kg is fixed to the lamina at R. Find the coordinates of the centre of mass of the loaded lamina relative to O.

- By symmetry, the centre of mass of the unloaded lamina is at its centre, $(7, 4.5)$ m. So imagine the lamina as a particle of mass 10 kg at $(7, 4.5)$ m.

- Combine this with the other two particles — 3 kg at $(7, 9)$ m and 7 kg at $(14, 0)$ m — and use the formula for the centre of mass of particles in a plane.

Tip: This is the formula from page 22.

$$\sum m\mathbf{r} = \bar{\mathbf{r}}\sum m$$

$$\Rightarrow m_1\mathbf{r}_1 + m_2\mathbf{r}_2 + m_3\mathbf{r}_3 = \bar{\mathbf{r}}(m_1 + m_2 + m_3)$$

$$\Rightarrow 10\binom{7}{4.5} + 3\binom{7}{9} + 7\binom{14}{0} = \bar{\mathbf{r}}(10 + 3 + 7)$$

$$\Rightarrow \binom{189}{72} = 20\bar{\mathbf{r}}$$

$$\Rightarrow \bar{\mathbf{r}} = \frac{1}{20}\binom{189}{72} = \binom{9.45}{3.6}$$

- So the centre of mass of the loaded lamina is at (9.45, 3.6) m.

Composite shapes

- A **composite shape** is one that can be **broken up into standard parts**, such as squares, rectangles and circles.
- To find the **centre of mass** of a composite shape, first break it down into its **individual parts**, and find the centre of mass of each part **individually**.
- Once you've found the individual centres of mass, imagine replacing each part with a **particle** of the same mass in the position of its centre of mass.
- You can then find the **centre of mass** of the **group** of 'particles' — this gives you the centre of mass of the **entire composite shape**.
- If the individual parts are made from the **same uniform material**, then the **mass** of each part will be **in proportion** to its area. This means you can use the shapes' **areas** rather than their **masses** in your calculations.

Example 1

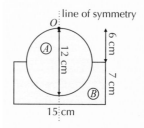

A sign for the 'Rising Sun' restaurant is made from a uniform circular lamina attached to a uniform rectangular lamina made from the same material. The dimensions of the two laminas are shown in the diagram. The line of symmetry of the shape is also shown.
Find the location of the centre of mass of the shape in relation to O.

Tip: In this example, the two laminas overlap — the circle is on top of the rectangle.

- First, split the shape up into a circle (A) and rectangle (B).
- As both bits are made of the same material, the masses of A and B are in proportion to their areas, so you can say:

$$m_A = \pi r^2 = \pi \times 6^2 = 36\pi$$

$$m_B = 15 \times 7 = 105$$

These are just the areas, in cm², of A and B respectively.

- The shape has a line of symmetry, so the centre of mass must be on that line, directly below the point O.

- Find the vertical position of the centres of mass of both A and B individually.

- By symmetry, y_A, the position of the centre of mass of A, is at its centre — i.e. 6 cm down from O.

Tip: Use symmetry where you can — but make sure you explain what you've done.

- Again by symmetry, y_B, the position of the centre of mass of B, is at its centre — i.e. $[6 + (7 \div 2)] = 9.5$ cm down from O.

- Treat the shapes as two particles positioned at the centres of mass of each shape, and use the formula for the centre of mass of particles in a vertical line:

$$\sum my = \overline{y} \sum m$$
$$m_A y_A + m_B y_B = \overline{y}(m_A + m_B)$$
$$(36\pi \times 6) + (105 \times 9.5) = \overline{y}(36\pi + 105)$$
$$1676.08... = (218.09...)\overline{y}$$
$$\Rightarrow \overline{y} = 7.69 \text{ cm (3 s.f.)}$$

Tip: This is the formula from page 20.

- So the centre of mass of the whole shape is 7.69 cm (3 s.f.) vertically below O on the line of symmetry.

Example 2

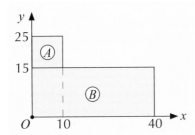

A square and a rectangle are cut from the same uniform lamina. They are fixed together as shown. Find the coordinates of the centre of mass of the composite shape.

- Call the square A and the rectangle B.

- A and B are cut from the same uniform lamina, so the masses of A and B are proportional to their areas:

$$m_A = 10 \times 10 = 100$$

$$m_B = 15 \times 40 = 600$$

- By symmetry, the centre of mass of A is at its centre. So the x-coordinate of the centre of mass of A is $x_A = 5$, and the y-coordinate of the centre of mass of A is $y_A = 15 + 5 = 20$. Therefore, the centre of mass of A is at (5, 20).

- Similarly, the centre of mass of B is at its centre, i.e. at (20, 7.5)

- As in the previous example, treat the shapes as two particles positioned at the centres of mass of each shape.
- This time though, use the formula for the centre of mass of particles in a plane:

$$\sum m\mathbf{r} = \bar{\mathbf{r}}\sum m$$

$$m_A\mathbf{r}_A + m_B\mathbf{r}_B = \bar{\mathbf{r}}(m_A + m_B)$$

$$100\binom{5}{20} + 600\binom{20}{7.5} = \bar{\mathbf{r}}(100 + 600)$$

$$\binom{12\,500}{6500} = 700\bar{\mathbf{r}}$$

$$\Rightarrow \bar{\mathbf{r}} = \frac{1}{700}\binom{12\,500}{6500} = \binom{17.857...}{9.285...}$$

- So the centre of mass of the whole shape is at (17.9, 9.29) (3 s.f.)

Exercise 3.2

Q1 A uniform square lamina of mass 4.5 kg has vertices $A(1, 1)$, $B(1, 7)$, $C(7, 7)$ and $D(7, 1)$. Particles of mass 4 kg and 1.5 kg are fixed to the points (5, 4) and (2, 2) respectively.

Find the coordinates of the centre of mass of the loaded lamina.

Q2 A uniform circular lamina of radius 12 units and mass 8 kg is centred at (10, 8). Particles of mass 7 kg, 10 kg and 6 kg are attached to the lamina at the points (4, 3), (2, 0) and (1, 6) respectively.

Find the coordinates of the centre of mass of the loaded lamina.

Q3 A uniform circular lamina of mass 0.8 kg is centred at (–1, 2). A second uniform circular lamina of mass 1.2 kg, centred at (1, –1), is attached to the first lamina.

Find the coordinates of the centre of mass of the resulting composite shape.

Q4

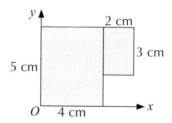

Two rectangles are cut from the same uniform lamina. The rectangles measure 4 cm × 5 cm and 2 cm × 3 cm, and are fixed together as shown in the diagram. Find the coordinates of the centre of mass of the composite shape relative to O.

Q5 A uniform rectangular lamina has vertices $A(1, 2)$, $B(7, 2)$, $C(7, 7)$ and $D(1, 7)$. A uniform circular lamina of radius 1 unit centred at $(4, 5)$ is attached to the lamina.

a) Find the coordinates of the centre of mass of the resulting composite shape, given that the rectangle and circle are made from the same material.

The composite shape has mass 6.5 kg. Objects of mass 2 kg, 2.5 kg and 3 kg are now fixed to the composite shape at points A, C and D respectively.

b) Find the coordinates of the centre of mass of the loaded composite lamina

Q6

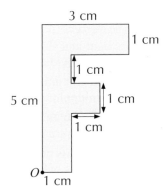

A letter F is cut from a uniform sheet of card, as shown above.
Find the distance of the centre of mass of the letter from the point O.

Q7

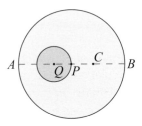

A uniform circular disc of radius 4 cm is attached to a uniform circular disc of radius 12 cm, as shown above. P is the centre of the 12 cm-radius disc, and Q is the centre of the 4 cm-radius disc. P lies on the circumference of the 4 cm-radius disc. C is the centre of mass of the resulting shape. A and B are points on the edge of the shape such that A, Q, P, C and B all lie on the same horizontal line.

Given that the two discs are made from the same material, find the distance AC.

4. Centres of Mass — Frameworks

A framework is made up of rods fixed together or a wire bent into a particular shape. In this section, you'll learn how to find the centre of mass of a framework.

Frameworks

Imagine bending a wire coathanger into something shapely, or fixing a load of rods together. These shapes are called **frameworks**.

In a framework, there's nothing in the middle, so all the mass is within the **wires** or **rods** that make up the shape's edges.

Finding the centre of mass of a framework is similar to finding the centre of mass of a composite shape:

- Imagine each side of the framework as a **separate rod** — even if it's a single wire bent into shape — and find the centre of mass of **each rod individually**.

- If the rods or wires are **straight** and **uniform**, the centre of mass of each one is at the **midpoint** of the rod.

- Next, imagine replacing each rod with a **particle** of the same mass in the position of its centre of mass.

- You can then find the **centre of mass** of the **group** of 'particles' — this gives you the centre of mass of the **framework**.

- If the rods or wires are made from the **same uniform material**, then their **mass** will be in proportion to their **length**. This means you can use the shapes' **lengths** rather than their **masses** in your calculations.

Example

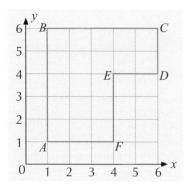

The diagram shows a uniform wire bent into the framework *ABCDEF*.

a) Find the coordinates of the centre of mass of the framework.

- The centre of mass of each side of the framework is at its midpoint.
- Write down the position vector of the centre of mass of each side:

$$\mathbf{r}_{AB} = \begin{pmatrix} 1 \\ 3.5 \end{pmatrix} \qquad \mathbf{r}_{BC} = \begin{pmatrix} 3.5 \\ 6 \end{pmatrix} \qquad \mathbf{r}_{CD} = \begin{pmatrix} 6 \\ 5 \end{pmatrix}$$

$$\mathbf{r}_{DE} = \begin{pmatrix} 5 \\ 4 \end{pmatrix} \qquad \mathbf{r}_{EF} = \begin{pmatrix} 4 \\ 2.5 \end{pmatrix} \qquad \mathbf{r}_{FA} = \begin{pmatrix} 2.5 \\ 1 \end{pmatrix}$$

- The mass of each side is proportional to its length:

$$m_{AB} = 5 \qquad m_{BC} = 5 \qquad m_{CD} = 2$$
$$m_{DE} = 2 \qquad m_{EF} = 3 \qquad m_{FA} = 3$$

Tip: You know that the mass of each side is proportional to its length because each side is made from the same uniform wire.

- You've now got the equivalent of a group of 6 particles, so put it all in the formula from page 22:

$$\sum m\mathbf{r} = \bar{\mathbf{r}}\sum m$$

$$m_{AB}\mathbf{r}_{AB} + m_{BC}\mathbf{r}_{BC} + m_{CD}\mathbf{r}_{CD} + m_{DE}\mathbf{r}_{DE} + m_{EF}\mathbf{r}_{EF} + m_{FA}\mathbf{r}_{FA} =$$
$$\bar{\mathbf{r}}(m_{AB} + m_{BC} + m_{CD} + m_{DE} + m_{EF} + m_{FA})$$

$$5\binom{1}{3.5} + 5\binom{3.5}{6} + 2\binom{6}{5} + 2\binom{5}{4} + 3\binom{4}{2.5} + 3\binom{2.5}{1} =$$
$$(5 + 5 + 2 + 2 + 3 + 3)\bar{\mathbf{r}}$$

$$\binom{5 + 17.5 + 12 + 10 + 12 + 7.5}{17.5 + 30 + 10 + 8 + 7.5 + 3} = 20\bar{\mathbf{r}}$$

$$\Rightarrow \bar{\mathbf{r}} = \frac{1}{20}\binom{64}{76} = \binom{3.2}{3.8}$$

- So the coordinates of the centre of mass are (3.2, 3.8).

b) A particle with the same mass as the whole framework is attached to the frame at A. Find the new centre of mass of the system.

- The system consists of the framework with COM at (3.2, 3.8) (from part a)), plus the particle at (1, 1).

- As they're the same mass, you can call each mass '1'.

- Using the formula $\sum m\mathbf{r} = \bar{\mathbf{r}}\sum m$:

$$1\mathbf{r}_{Frame} + 1\mathbf{r}_{Particle} = 2\bar{\mathbf{r}}$$

$$\Rightarrow \binom{3.2}{3.8} + \binom{1}{1} = 2\bar{\mathbf{r}}$$

$$\Rightarrow \bar{\mathbf{r}} = \frac{1}{2}\binom{4.2}{4.8} = \binom{2.1}{2.4}$$

Tip: You're only really interested in the masses of each part of the system relative to each other. Calling the equal masses '1' is a good way to simplify the calculation.

- So the coordinates of the new centre of mass are (2.1, 2.4).

Q1

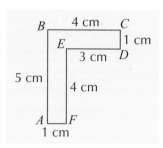

A uniform wire is bent to form the shape *ABCDEF*, as shown. Find:

a) the distance of the centre of mass of the shape from the side *AB*,

b) the distance of the centre of mass of the shape from the side *AF*.

Q2 Hint: Use Pythagoras' theorem to find the distance from *AC* to the COM of each of *AB* and *BC*.

Q2 A framework is made up of three uniform rods forming an isosceles triangle *ABC*. *AC* has length 12 cm and mass 1.5 kg, *AB* has length 10 cm and mass 1 kg and *BC* has length 10 cm and mass 2 kg. Find the distance of the centre of mass of the framework from *AC*.

Q3

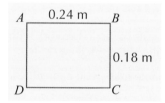

Four uniform rods are fixed together to form the rectangular framework *ABCD*, as shown. Rod *AB* has mass *M* kg, rod *BC* has mass 2*M* kg and rod *CD* has mass 1.5*M* kg.

a) The centre of mass of the framework is 0.15 m from *AD*. Find the mass of rod *AD*, in terms of *M*.

b) Find the distance of the centre of mass of the framework from *AB*.

Q4

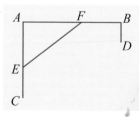

Q4 Hint: A framework doesn't have to be a closed shape — so even though this question looks a bit different, the method for answering it is just the same as for the others.

A bracket for a hanging basket is made from four pieces cut from the same uniform iron rod, as shown. You are given that *AB* = 20 cm, *AC* = 15 cm, *BD* = 4 cm, *AE* = 9 cm and *AF* = 12 cm.

a) Find the distance of the centre of mass of the bracket from *A*.

b) A hanging basket of twice the mass of the bracket is attached at *D*. Modelling the hanging basket as a particle positioned at *D*, find the distance of the centre of mass of the loaded bracket from *A*.

5. Laminas in Equilibrium

Finding the centre of mass of a lamina helps you work out what will happen when the lamina is suspended from a point.

Laminas suspended from a point

When you **suspend** a shape, either from a point on its edge or from a **pivot point** within the shape, it will hang in **equilibrium** so that the **centre of mass** is **vertically below** the **suspension point**.

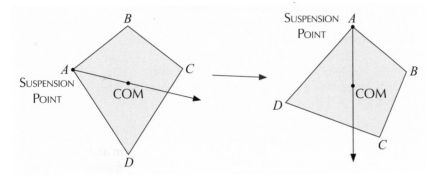

Knowing the position of the centre of mass of the shape will let you work out the **angle** that the shape hangs at.

Example 1

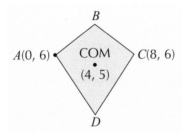

In the shape *ABCD*, shown, *A* is at (0, 6), *C* is at (8, 6), and the centre of mass is at (4, 5). Find the angle *AC* makes with the vertical when the shape is freely suspended from *A*.

- When the shape is suspended from *A*, it will hang with its centre of mass vertically below *A*.

- Draw in the line representing the vertical from *A* to the centre of mass and label the angle you need to find α. You can then use this to form a right-angled triangle:

- You can now find the angle using trigonometry:

$$\alpha = \tan^{-1}\left(\tfrac{1}{4}\right) = \boxed{14.0° \text{ (3 s.f.)}}$$

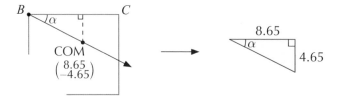

Example 2

B ——14 m—— C
6 m
A | 12 m
E —8 m— D

The diagram shows a uniform wire bent to form the framework _ABCDE_. Find the angle that _BC_ makes with the vertical when the framework is freely suspended from _B_.

Tip: Don't worry that this is asking about a framework rather than a lamina — the principle's the same.

- First find the centre of mass of the framework — it's being suspended from _B_, so you might as well find the position of the centre of mass relative to that point.

- The sides are made of the same uniform material, so the mass of each side is proportional to its length, and, by symmetry, the centre of mass of each side is at its midpoint.

- Write down the individual masses and centres of mass of each side of the framework relative to _B_:

$$m_{AB} = 6, \ \mathbf{r}_{AB} = \begin{pmatrix} 0 \\ -3 \end{pmatrix} \qquad m_{BC} = 14, \ \mathbf{r}_{BC} = \begin{pmatrix} 7 \\ 0 \end{pmatrix}$$

$$m_{CD} = 12, \ \mathbf{r}_{CD} = \begin{pmatrix} 14 \\ -6 \end{pmatrix} \qquad m_{DE} = 8, \ \mathbf{r}_{DE} = \begin{pmatrix} 10 \\ -12 \end{pmatrix}$$

- Now, using the formula $\sum m\mathbf{r} = \bar{\mathbf{r}}\sum m$:

$$m_{AB}\mathbf{r}_{AB} + m_{BC}\mathbf{r}_{BC} + m_{CD}\mathbf{r}_{CD} + m_{DE}\mathbf{r}_{DE} = \bar{\mathbf{r}}(m_{AB} + m_{BC} + m_{CD} + m_{DE})$$

$$6\begin{pmatrix} 0 \\ -3 \end{pmatrix} + 14\begin{pmatrix} 7 \\ 0 \end{pmatrix} + 12\begin{pmatrix} 14 \\ -6 \end{pmatrix} + 8\begin{pmatrix} 10 \\ -12 \end{pmatrix} = \bar{\mathbf{r}}(6 + 14 + 12 + 8)$$

$$\begin{pmatrix} 346 \\ -186 \end{pmatrix} = 40\bar{\mathbf{r}}$$

$$\Rightarrow \bar{\mathbf{r}} = \begin{pmatrix} 8.65 \\ -4.65 \end{pmatrix}$$

- When the framework is suspended from _B_, it will hang with its centre of mass vertically below _B_.

- Draw in the line from _B_ to the centre of mass, and form a right-angled triangle:

B ·—α— C
COM
$\begin{pmatrix} 8.65 \\ -4.65 \end{pmatrix}$

8.65
α
4.65

- You can now find the angle using trigonometry:

$$\alpha = \tan^{-1}\left(\frac{4.65}{8.65}\right) = 28.3° \text{ (3 s.f.)}$$

In some cases, a lamina will be 'free to rotate about a fixed horizontal axis'. This just means that the lamina is **pivoted** about a point somewhere **on the shape**, rather than being suspended from one of its vertices.

Again, the lamina will hang in **equilibrium** with its **centre of mass** directly **below** the pivot.

Tip: The 'horizontal axis' bit just means that the lamina is free to rotate about an axis (line) which passes through the pivot point, perpendicular to the lamina.

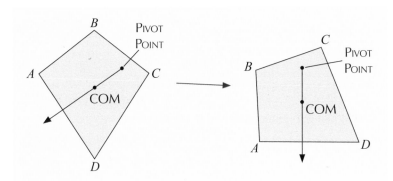

Example

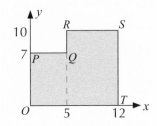

The uniform lamina *OPQRST*, shown, is pivoted at (10, 8) and allowed to freely rotate about this point.

a) Find the angle that *ST* makes with the vertical.

- First you need to find the centre of mass of the shape. Split it into two rectangles, as shown.

- The lamina is uniform, so the masses of *A* and *B* are proportional to their areas:

  $m_A = 5 \times 7 = 35$ $m_B = 7 \times 10 = 70$

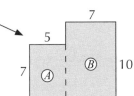

- By symmetry, the centres of mass of each of *A* and *B* are at their centres, so:

  $\mathbf{r}_A = \begin{pmatrix} 2.5 \\ 3.5 \end{pmatrix}$ $\mathbf{r}_B = \begin{pmatrix} 8.5 \\ 5 \end{pmatrix}$

- Using the formula $\sum m\mathbf{r} = \bar{\mathbf{r}} \sum m$:

  $$m_A\mathbf{r}_A + m_B\mathbf{r}_B = \bar{\mathbf{r}}(m_A + m_B)$$

  $$35\begin{pmatrix} 2.5 \\ 3.5 \end{pmatrix} + 70\begin{pmatrix} 8.5 \\ 5 \end{pmatrix} = \bar{\mathbf{r}}(35 + 70)$$

  $$\begin{pmatrix} 682.5 \\ 472.5 \end{pmatrix} = 105\bar{\mathbf{r}}$$

  $$\Rightarrow \bar{\mathbf{r}} = \begin{pmatrix} 6.5 \\ 4.5 \end{pmatrix}$$

- Draw a diagram to show the line from the pivot point to the centre of mass, and draw a right-angled triangle to help you find α, the angle ST makes with the vertical:

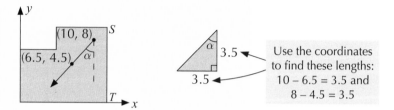

Tip: The dotted line is parallel to ST, so the angle between the vertical and the dotted line is the same as the angle between the vertical and ST.

- Finally, using trigonometry:

$$\alpha = \tan^{-1}\left(\frac{3.5}{3.5}\right)$$

$$= 45°$$

b) **The mass of the shape is 3 kg. A particle of mass M kg is fixed to the shape at the midpoint of ST, such that the shape hangs in equilibrium with ST vertical. Find the value of M.**

- Draw a diagram to show what's going on:

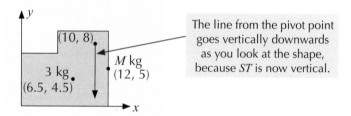

The line from the pivot point goes vertically downwards as you look at the shape, because ST is now vertical.

Tip: Another way to answer this question would be to first find the COM of the loaded lamina in terms of M. Then, for the loaded lamina to hang with ST vertical, the x-coordinate of its COM must be 10. You can use this to find the value of M.

- From page 8, you should remember that, for a rigid body in equilibrium, 'clockwise moments = anticlockwise moments'.
- The pivot point is $(10, 8)$, so you want to take moments about this point.
- When taking moments, you need to use the **perpendicular distance** from the line of action of each force to the pivot.
- The weights of the shape and the particle both act **vertically downwards**, so you need to use the **horizontal** distance from the **position of the particle** to the **pivot**, and the **horizontal** distance from the **centre of mass of the lamina** to the **pivot**:

Tip: Use the x-coordinates of the position of the particle, the COM of the lamina and the pivot point to find the horizontal distances you need for the formula.

Moments clockwise = Moments anticlockwise

$$Mg \times (12 - 10) = 3g \times (10 - 6.5)$$

$$\Rightarrow M = 10.5g \div 2g$$

$$= 5.25 \text{ kg}$$

Q1

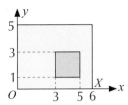

A uniform square lamina is attached to a uniform rectangular lamina made from the same material, as shown.

a) Find the coordinates of the centre of mass of the resulting shape.

b) The shape is freely suspended from O. Find the angle that OX makes with the vertical, where X is the point $(6, 0)$.

Q2

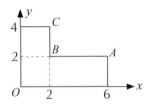

A uniform wire is bent to form the framework shown above.

a) Find the coordinates of the centre of mass of the framework.

b) The framework is freely suspended from $A(6, 2)$. Find the angle that AB makes with the vertical, where B is the point $(2, 2)$.

A particle of mass 2.5 kg is fixed to the framework at $C(2, 4)$, such that, when the framework is suspended from A, AB is vertical.

c) Find the mass of the framework.

Q3 The rectangular lamina $ABCD$ has vertices $A(0, 0)$, $B(12, 0)$, $C(12, 8)$ and $D(0, 8)$. A circular lamina of radius 2 units centred at $(9, 3)$ is fixed to the rectangle. The two laminas are made from the same uniform material. The resulting shape is freely pivoted at the point $(1, 1)$. Find the angle that AB makes with the vertical.

Q4

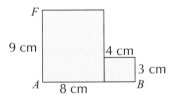

A composite shape consists of two uniform rectangular laminas of the same material, as shown.

a) Find the distance of the centre of mass of the shape from AF.

b) Find the distance of the centre of mass of the shape from AB.

c) The shape is freely suspended from A.
Find the angle that AF makes with the vertical.

d) The shape is now freely suspended from F.
Find the angle that AF now makes with the vertical.

Q5

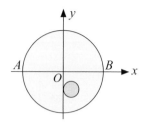

A circular lamina of radius 10 units is centred at O. Another circular lamina of radius 2 units centred at $(2, -4)$ is fixed to the first lamina, as shown. The resulting shape is freely pivoted about an axis perpendicular to the lamina at O. The two laminas are made from the same uniform material.

a) Find the angle that AB makes with the vertical.

A particle of mass 0.9 kg is fixed to the shape at B.

Q5 b) Hint: First find the centre of mass of the loaded shape.

b) Given that the unloaded shape has mass 0.7 kg, find the angle that AB makes with the vertical when the loaded shape is freely pivoted at O.

Q6

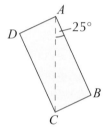

A uniform rectangular lamina, $ABCD$, of mass 0.5 kg, is freely suspended from A. The lamina hangs in equilibrium with AC vertical. The length of AB is 50 cm, and it makes an angle of 25° with the vertical, as shown.

A particle of mass 0.2 kg is fixed to the lamina at D.
Find the angle that AB makes with the vertical
in the new position of equilibrium.

Review Exercise — Chapter 1

Q1

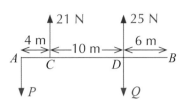

The diagram shows a light rod held horizontally in equilibrium by two vertical strings. Find the magnitudes of the forces P and Q.

Q2

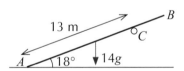

A non-uniform beam of length 13 m is suspended from a vertical wire attached to its midpoint. Downward vertical forces of magnitude 12 N and 17 N are applied to the ends of the beam, as shown. The tension in the wire is 70.16 N, and the beam is horizontal and in equilibrium. Find:

a) the mass of the beam,

b) the distance of the centre of mass of the beam from its midpoint.

Q3

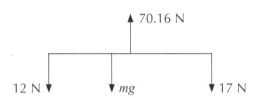

A uniform beam, AB, of mass 14 kg and length 15 m, rests with A on rough, horizontal ground. The beam is supported by a smooth peg at C, where $AC = 13$ m, so that it makes an angle of 18° with the horizontal, as shown. The beam is on the point of slipping.

Find the coefficient of friction between the ground and the beam at A.

Q4 A uniform ladder of mass 20 kg rests with one end on rough, horizontal ground, and the other end against a smooth, vertical wall. The ladder makes an angle of 60° with the horizontal, and is on the point of slipping.

a) Show that the coefficient of friction between the ladder and the ground is $\frac{\sqrt{3}}{6}$.

b) A person of mass 60 kg stands three-quarters of the way up the ladder. Find the magnitude of the minimum horizontal force which must be applied to the base of the ladder to keep it in limiting equilibrium.

Q5 Three particles have mass $m_1 = 1$ kg, $m_2 = 2$ kg and $m_3 = 3$ kg.
Find the centre of mass of the system of particles if their coordinates are, respectively:

a) (1, 0), (2, 0), (3, 0)   b) (0, 3), (0, 2), (0, 1)   c) (3, 4), (3, 1), (1, 0)

Q6 A system of particles located at coordinates $A(0, 0)$, $B(0, 4)$, $C(5, 4)$ and $D(5, 0)$ have masses m kg, $2m$ kg, $3m$ kg and 12 kg respectively. The centre of mass of the system is at $(3.5, 2)$. Find the value of m.

Q7 Find the coordinates of the centre of mass of each of these shapes made from uniform laminas:

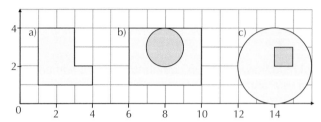

Q7 Hint: The shapes in parts b) and c) consist of one lamina attached to the surface of another.

Q8

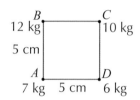

A light square framework has side lengths of 5 cm. Particles are attached to the corners of the square, as shown in the diagram. Find the distance of the centre of mass of the loaded framework from:
a) AD,   b) AB.

Q9 $ABCD$ is a loaded rectangular lamina with dimensions $AB = 60$ cm and $AD = 70$ cm. When $ABCD$ is freely suspended from A, AD makes an angle of $45°$ with the vertical. When $ABCD$ is freely suspended from D, AD makes an angle of $60°$ with the vertical.
a) (i)   Find the distance of the centre of mass of $ABCD$ from AD.
   (ii) Find the distance of the centre of mass of $ABCD$ from AB.
b) Find the angle that BC makes with the vertical when $ABCD$ is freely suspended from B.

Q10

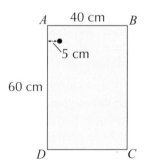

A uniform rectangular lamina, $ABCD$, has dimensions $AB = 40$ cm and $AD = 60$ cm. The lamina is freely pivoted at a point 5 cm from AD, as shown. The lamina hangs in equilibrium with AD at an angle of $35°$ to the vertical. Find the distance of the pivot from AB.

1

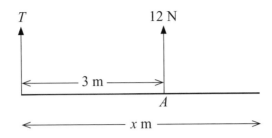

A horizontal uniform beam of length x and weight 18 N is held in equilibrium by two vertical strings. One string is attached to one end of the beam and the other at point A, 3 m from the first string, as shown. The tension in the string at point A is 12 N, and the tension in the other string is T.

a)   Show that $x = 4$ m.

(2 marks)

b)   Find T.

(1 mark)

2   A uniform ladder, AB, is positioned against a smooth vertical wall and rests upon rough horizontal ground at an angle θ to the horizontal, as shown. Clive stands on the ladder at point C, two-thirds of the way along the ladder's length from A. The ladder is 4.2 m long and weighs 180 N. The normal reaction at A is 490 N.

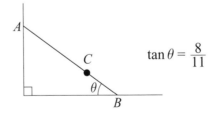

$$\tan \theta = \frac{8}{11}$$

The ladder rests in limiting equilibrium. Modelling Clive as a particle, find:

a)   Clive's mass, m, to the nearest kg,

(3 marks)

b)   the coefficient of friction, μ, between the ground and the ladder.

(5 marks)

3   The diagram below shows three particles, A, B and C, attached to a light rectangular lamina at the points with coordinates $(1, 3)$, $(5, 1)$ and $(4, y)$ respectively.

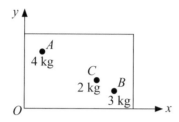

The centre of mass of the system is at $(\overline{x}, 2)$.

a)   Show that $y = 1.5$.

(3 marks)

b)   Show that $\overline{x} = 3$.

(3 marks)

The light lamina is replaced with a uniform rectangular lamina $PQRS$ of mass 6 kg, with vertices at $P(0, 0)$, $Q(0, 5)$, $R(7, 5)$ and $S(7, 0)$. A, B and C remain at their existing positions.

c)   Find the coordinates of the new centre of mass of the whole system.

(6 marks)

d)   The lamina $PQRS$, with the particles still attached, is suspended freely from Q and hangs in equilibrium. Find the angle that PQ makes with the vertical.

(3 marks)

4

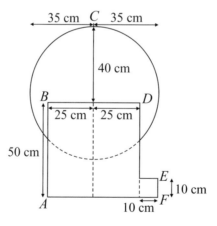

A cardboard advertising sign is modelled as two uniform square laminas with a uniform circular lamina attached, as shown. The masses of the small and large squares are 1 kg and 4 kg respectively. The mass of the circle is 5 kg.

a)   Show that the centre of mass of the sign is 28 cm from AB and 38 cm from AF.

(5 marks)

The sign is suspended from point C, and hangs in equilibrium. A small weight, modelled as a particle, is attached at A, so that the sign hangs with AF horizontal.

b)   Find the mass of the particle needed to make the sign hang in this way.

(3 marks)

1. Variable Acceleration in 1 Dimension

As you know from M1, you can use the uvast equations to describe the motion of a body which is moving with constant acceleration.

However, in M2, you'll also need to be able to describe the motion of a body that is moving with acceleration that varies with time.

To do this, you'll need to use calculus — given an expression for the motion of a body in terms of time, t, you can differentiate or integrate the expression to find out more information.

Differentiating to find velocity and acceleration

Differentiating to find velocity

- You should remember from M1 that a body's **velocity** is the **rate of change** of its **displacement** from a particular point with respect to **time**.

- You should also remember from C1 that to find the **rate of change** of one quantity with respect to another, you can use **differentiation**.

- So if you are given an expression for a body's **displacement** from a particular point **as a function of time**, t, you can find an expression for that body's **velocity** by **differentiating** with respect to time.

Differentiating to find acceleration

- Similarly, a body's **acceleration** is the **rate of change** of its **velocity** with respect to **time**.

- Therefore, if you are given an expression for a body's **velocity** in terms of **time**, t, then you can find an expression for its **acceleration** by **differentiating** with respect to time.

- To find an expression for a body's **acceleration** given an expression for its **displacement**, just **differentiate twice** with respect to time.

Tip: You can also think of this graphically — the gradient of a displacement-time graph gives a body's velocity, and the gradient of a velocity-time graph gives a body's acceleration. To find the gradient of a graph at a particular point, you differentiate.

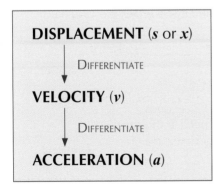

- Remember that displacement, velocity and acceleration are **vector quantities**, so the **direction** of motion is important.

- If the motion is in a straight line, then it's a good idea to choose which direction is **positive**, then any motion in the **opposite direction** will be **negative**.

Tip: You'll often be told that a body is 'moving along the x-axis in the direction of x increasing' — so it makes sense to take this direction as positive.

Example 1

At time $t = 0$, a particle of mass 5 kg leaves the origin and moves along the x-axis in the direction of x increasing. At time t seconds, its displacement from its starting point is given by $x = (7t - 2t^3)$ m.

a) Find the particle's velocity at time $t = 3$ seconds.

- Differentiate the expression for displacement with respect to time:
$$v = \frac{dx}{dt} = (7 - 6t^2) \text{ ms}^{-1}$$

- Substitute $t = 3$ into the expression for velocity:
$$v = 7 - (6 \times 3^2) = -47 \text{ ms}^{-1}$$

Tip: The particle's velocity is negative at time $t = 3$ seconds because it is moving in the negative direction — i.e. in the direction of x decreasing.

b) Find the time after the particle leaves the origin when it is momentarily at rest.

- When the particle is at rest, $v = 0$ ms^{-1}:
$$7 - 6t^2 = 0$$
$$t^2 = 7 \div 6 = 1.166...$$
$$\Rightarrow t = 1.08 \text{ s (3 s.f.)}$$

c) Find the resultant force acting on the particle at time $t = 2$ seconds.

- Differentiate the expression for velocity with respect to time:
$$a = \frac{dv}{dt} = -12t \text{ ms}^{-2}$$

- Substitute $t = 2$ into the expression for acceleration:
$$a = -12 \times 2 = -24 \text{ ms}^{-2}$$

Tip: The examiners will assume you remember everything from M1, like Newton's second law: $F_{net} = ma$, which you need to use here.

- Now use $F_{net} = ma$ to find the resultant force acting on the particle:
$$F_{net} = 5 \times -24 = -120 \text{ N}$$

Example 2

At time t seconds, a particle of mass 5 kg is moving at $(-t^2 + 5t - 2)$ ms^{-1}. Find the particle's speed when its acceleration is momentarily zero.

- Differentiate the expression for velocity with respect to time, then make the resulting expression equal to zero:
$$a = \frac{dv}{dt} = (-2t + 5) \text{ ms}^{-2}$$
$$-2t + 5 = 0$$
$$\Rightarrow t = 2.5 \text{ seconds}$$

Tip: You can also answer this question graphically. The particle's velocity forms an n-shaped quadratic curve, and acceleration will be zero at the curve's turning point. You can find the location of the turning point by completing the square.

- So its acceleration is zero at time $t = 2.5$ seconds. Using the expression for velocity, its speed at this time is:
$$-(2.5)^2 + 5(2.5) - 2 = 4.25 \text{ ms}^{-1}$$

Q1 A particle moves in a straight line along the x-axis in the direction of x increasing. At time t seconds, the particle's displacement from the origin is given by $x = (3t^3 + 5t^2)$ m. Find:

a) an expression for the particle's velocity in terms of t,

b) an expression for the particle's acceleration in terms of t,

c) the particle's mass, given that the resultant force acting on the particle is 480 N when $t = 3$.

Q2 A body moves in a straight line in the direction of the positive x-axis. At time t seconds, the body's displacement from the origin is given by $x = (bt^2 + 6t)$ m, where b is a constant. At time $t = 3$ seconds, its velocity is 18 ms^{-1}.

a) Calculate the value of b.

b) Show that the body is moving with constant acceleration.

Q3 An object moves in a straight line. At time t seconds, its displacement from its starting point is given by $s = (2t^3 - 21t^2 + 60t)$ m. Find:

a) an expression for the object's velocity at time t seconds,

b) the times that the object is momentarily at rest,

c) an expression for the object's acceleration at time t seconds,

d) the object's initial acceleration.

Q4 A particle of mass 1.4 kg moves in a straight line along the x-axis. At time t seconds, the x-coordinate of its position is given by $x = 12t^2 + 60t - t^3$. Find:

a) the particle's initial position,

b) the time that the particle is moving with zero acceleration,

c) the resultant force acting on the particle at time $t = 0.5$ seconds,

d) the particle's maximum positive displacement from the origin.

Q4 d) Hint: The particle will stop momentarily when it reaches its maximum positive displacement from the origin (assuming that it does reach a maximum displacement, and doesn't just carry on in that direction forever).

Q5 A vehicle is travelling along a straight track. At time t hours, its displacement from its initial point is given by $s = (12t - 15t^2 + 4t^3)$ km.

a) Find the times that the vehicle is momentarily at rest.

b) Find the distance travelled by the vehicle between these times.

Q6 A train travels along a straight track between two stations. The train is at rest at both of these stations, and is moving at all times on the journey between the stations. At time t hours, the train's distance from the first station is given by $s = (90t^2 - 45t^3)$ km. Find:

a) the time taken to travel between the two stations,

b) the distance between the two stations,

c) the maximum speed the train reaches in travelling between the two stations.

Integrating to find velocity and displacement

Tip: Again, you can think of this graphically. The area under an acceleration-time graph gives a body's velocity, and the area under a velocity-time graph gives a body's displacement from a particular point. To find the area under a graph, you integrate.

To 'go back the other way', you have to **integrate**:

- Given an expression for a body's **acceleration** in terms of t, you can find its **velocity** at time t by **integrating** with respect to time.
- Similarly, given an expression for a body's **velocity**, you can find its **displacement** from a particular point at time t by **integrating** with respect to time.
- To find a body's **displacement** from a particular point given an expression for its **acceleration**, just **integrate twice** with respect to time.
- When you're integrating, don't forget to add a **constant**. Often, you'll be given enough information in the question to find the value of the constant.

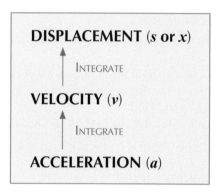

Example 1

A particle is moving in a straight line in the direction of the positive x-axis. At time t seconds, the particle's acceleration is given by $a = (26 - 12t)$ ms^{-2}. At time $t = 4$ seconds, the particle passes through the point where $x = 80$ m with velocity 12 ms^{-1}.

a) Find an expression for the particle's velocity at time t seconds.

Tip: Remember:
$$\int x^n \, dx = \frac{x^{(n+1)}}{n+1} + C$$

- Integrate the expression for acceleration with respect to time to find an expression for the particle's velocity:
$$v = \int a \, dt$$
$$= 26t - 6t^2 + C$$

Tip: Use information given in the question to find the values of the constants.

- When $t = 4$, $v = 12$, so:
$$12 = 26(4) - 6(4)^2 + C$$
$$\Rightarrow C = 4$$

- So the particle's velocity at time t is given by:
$$v = (26t - 6t^2 + 4) \text{ ms}^{-1}.$$

b) Find the particle's displacement from the origin at time $t = 5$ seconds.

- Integrate the expression for velocity with respect to time to find an expression for the particle's displacement:

$$x = \int v \, dt$$
$$= 13t^2 - 2t^3 + 4t + D$$

Tip: You've already used the letter C to represent the constant of integration in part a), so this time use another letter — I've used D.

- When $t = 4$, $x = 80$, so:

$$80 = 13(4)^2 - 2(4)^3 + 4(4) + D$$
$$\Rightarrow D = -16$$

- So the particle's displacement from the origin at time t is given by $x = (13t^2 - 2t^3 + 4t - 16)$ m.

- Therefore, at time $t = 5$ seconds:

$$x = 13(5)^2 - 2(5)^3 + 4(5) - 16$$
$$= 79 \text{ m}$$

Example 2

A particle is moving in a straight line along the x-axis.
At time $t = 0$, the particle passes through the origin, O.
The particle's velocity at time t seconds is given by
$v = (12 - t^2)$ ms^{-1}, measured in the direction of x increasing.
Find the time taken for the particle to return to O.

- Integrate the expression for velocity with respect to time to find the particle's displacement from O:

$$x = \int v \, dt$$
$$= 12t - \frac{t^3}{3} + C$$

- The particle passes through the origin at $t = 0$, so at $t = 0$, $x = 0$:

$$0 = 12(0) - \frac{0^3}{3} + C$$
$$\Rightarrow C = 0$$

- So the particle's displacement from O at time t is given by:

$$x = (12t - \frac{t^3}{3}) \text{ m.}$$

- When the particle is at O, $x = 0$ m:

$$12t - \frac{t^3}{3} = 0$$
$$36t - t^3 = 0$$
$$t(36 - t^2) = 0$$
$$t(6 - t)(6 + t) = 0$$
$$\Rightarrow t = 0, t = 6 \text{ or } t = -6$$

Tip: $t = 0$ is the time that the particle initially passes through O, and $t = -6$ can be ignored because you're looking for a positive time. So the correct solution must be $t = 6$.

- So the particle takes 6 seconds to return to O.

Q1 A particle is travelling in a straight line along the x-axis in the direction of x increasing. At time $t = 0$, the particle passes through the origin, O, with a velocity of 10 ms^{-1}. The particle moves with constant acceleration 5 ms^{-2}. Find:

a) (i) an expression for the particle's velocity in terms of t,

(ii) the particle's velocity 6 seconds after it passes through O,

b) (i) an expression for the particle's displacement from O in terms of t,

(ii) the particle's displacement from O 6 seconds after it passes through O.

Q2 An object is travelling in a straight line. At time t seconds, its velocity is given by $v = (3t^2 - 14t + 8)$ ms^{-1}. When $t = 1$, the object's displacement from its initial position is 8 m. Find:

a) an expression for the object's displacement from its initial position in terms of t,

b) the times that the object is instantaneously at rest,

c) the distance between the two points at which the object is instantaneously at rest.

Q3 A particle is travelling in a straight line in the direction of the positive x-axis. At time $t = 0$, the particle passes through the origin with velocity 6 ms^{-1}. The particle's acceleration at time t seconds is given by $a = (2t - 6)$ ms^{-2}. Find:

a) an expression for the particle's velocity at time t seconds,

b) an expression for the particle's displacement from the origin at time t seconds,

c) the times that the particle passes through the origin for $t > 0$.

Q4 At time $t = 0$, an object sets off from rest at the origin, O, and travels along the x-axis. At time t seconds, the object is accelerating at a rate of $(2t - 4)$ ms^{-2}. Find:

a) the object's velocity 5 seconds after it leaves O,

b) the x-coordinate of the object's position 5 seconds after it leaves O,

c) the value of t at which the object reverses its direction,

d) the value of t at which the object returns to O.

Q5 A particle is travelling in a straight line in the direction of the positive x-axis. At time t seconds, the particle's acceleration is given by $a = (k - 18t^2)$ ms^{-2}, where k is a constant. At time $t = 0$, the particle passes through the origin, O, with velocity 7 ms^{-1}. One second later, the particle passes through the point Q with velocity 9 ms^{-1}. Find:

a) the value of k,

b) the distance of the point Q from O.

Using the chain rule to find velocity and acceleration

The motion of a body can sometimes be defined by an expression which contains **trigonometric** or **exponential functions**.

Just like on the previous pages, you'll need to **differentiate** and **integrate** the expression to find other equations describing the body's motion.

To differentiate expressions like this, you'll need to make a **substitution** $u = f(t)$ and then use the **chain rule**:

To differentiate velocity:
$\dfrac{dv}{dt} = \dfrac{dv}{du} \times \dfrac{du}{dt}$

To differentiate displacement:
$\dfrac{dx}{dt} = \dfrac{dx}{du} \times \dfrac{du}{dt}$

Tip: The chain rule also comes up in C3. It states that:
For $y = f(u)$ and $u = g(x)$,
$\dfrac{dy}{dx} = \dfrac{dy}{du} \times \dfrac{du}{dx}$

Example 1

A particle sets off from the origin at $t = 0$ and moves along the x-axis. At time t seconds, the velocity of the particle is v ms^{-1}, where $v = 5t - 4\cos 4t + 8$.

a) Find an expression for the acceleration of the particle at time t.

- Split the expression for v into two parts:
  $$v_1 = -4\cos 4t \quad \text{and} \quad v_2 = 5t + 8$$

- Use the chain rule to differentiate v_1:
  Let $u = 4t$, then $v_1 = -4\cos u.$ ← *v_1 is now a function of u.*

  So: $\dfrac{du}{dt} = 4$ and $\dfrac{dv_1}{du} = 4\sin u$

  $\dfrac{dv_1}{dt} = \dfrac{dv_1}{du} \times \dfrac{du}{dt} = 4 \times 4\sin u = 16\sin 4t$

Tip: Remember:
$\dfrac{d}{dx}\cos x = -\sin x$

- Then differentiate v_2: $\dfrac{dv_2}{dt} = 5$

- Finally, add the two parts together to find the expression for the particle's acceleration:
  $$a = \dfrac{dv}{dt} = \dfrac{dv_1}{dt} + \dfrac{dv_2}{dt} = (16\sin 4t + 5) \text{ ms}^{-2}$$

Tip: Make sure you keep track of whether you should be differentiating with respect to u or t.

b) Find the particle's displacement from the origin when $t = \pi$.

- Integrate v to find an expression for the particle's displacement from the origin:
  $$x = \int v \, dt = \int_0^\pi (5t - 4\cos 4t + 8) \, dt$$
  The particle is at the origin at $t = 0$, so the lower bound is 0.

  $$= \left[\frac{5}{2}t^2 - \sin 4t + 8t\right]_0^\pi$$

  $$= \left[\frac{5}{2}(\pi)^2 - \sin 4\pi + 8\pi\right] - \left[\frac{5}{2}(0)^2 - \sin 0 + 0\right]$$

  $$= \left(\frac{5}{2}\pi^2 + 8\pi\right) \text{ m}$$
  If you're using a calculator, it should be set to work in radians.

Tip: Remember:
$\int \cos nx \, dx = \dfrac{1}{n}\sin nx$

Tip: Doing a definite integral here means you don't have to find a constant of integration.

Example 2

At time t seconds, a particle moving in a straight line has displacement s m from a particular point, where $s = 3e^{-2t} + 4t$.

a) Find an expression for the particle's velocity at time t seconds.

- Split the expression for s into two parts:

$$s_1 = 3e^{-2t} \quad \text{and} \quad s_2 = 4t$$

- Use the chain rule to differentiate s_1:

  Let $u = -2t$, then $s_1 = 3e^u$.

  So: $\dfrac{du}{dt} = -2$ and $\dfrac{ds_1}{du} = 3e^u$

  $$\frac{ds_1}{dt} = \frac{ds_1}{du} \times \frac{du}{dt} = 3e^u \times -2$$
  $$= -6e^{-2t}$$

- Differentiate s_2 as usual: $\boxed{\dfrac{ds_2}{dt} = 4}$

- Add the two parts together to find the expression for the particle's velocity:

$$v = \frac{ds_1}{dt} + \frac{ds_2}{dt} = (-6e^{-2t} + 4) \text{ ms}^{-1}$$

Tip: You don't have to go through all these steps each time — if you can differentiate $3e^{-2t}$ in one go, then just differentiate the whole expression term-by-term as usual.

b) Find the range of values for the particle's velocity.

- t must be ≥ 0.
- When $t = 0$, $e^{-2t} = 1$, so $v = -6 + 4 = -2$ ms^{-1}.
- As $t \to \infty$, $e^{-2t} \to 0$, so $v \to 4$ ms^{-1}.
- Combining these gives:

$$-2 \text{ ms}^{-1} \leq v < 4 \text{ ms}^{-1}$$

Tip: Remember:
'$\to$' means 'tends to'.

- You can also answer this question by sketching the graph of the velocity function:

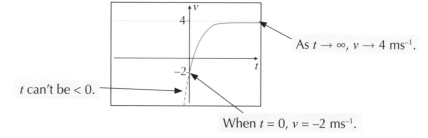

As $t \to \infty$, $v \to 4$ ms^{-1}.

t can't be < 0.

When $t = 0$, $v = -2$ ms^{-1}.

Tip: Take a look at your C3 notes for help with sketching transformations of the graph of e^x.

Exercise 1.3

Q1 A particle is travelling in a straight line along the x-axis. At time t, the particle's velocity is v ms^{-1} and its displacement from the origin is x m. By making the substitution $u = f(t)$, use the chain rule to find an expression for v in terms of t when x is given by:

a) $3\sin 4t$,

b) $4e^{2t}$,

c) $3t^2 - 2\cos 3t + 6t - 7$,

d) $2\sin 3t - 4e^{-t}$.

Q2 A particle travels in a straight line along the x-axis.
At time t seconds, the particle's displacement from the origin is x m, where $x = 3\sin 4t + 24t^2$.

a) Find an expression for the particle's velocity at time t.

b) Calculate the speed of the particle when $t = \frac{\pi}{8}$.

c) Show that the particle's acceleration is zero when $t = \frac{\pi}{8}$.

Q3 A particle moves in a straight line along the x-axis.
At time t seconds, the particle's displacement from the origin is x m, where x is given by $3\cos 4t + e^{-2t}$.

a) Find the particle's initial position.

b) Show that the particle changes direction between the times $t = 0.7$ and $t = 0.8$.

Q4 A body moves in a straight line along the x-axis. Its velocity at time t seconds is given by $v = (6 + 20t - 0.1e^{2t})$ ms^{-1}.

a) Show that the body is at rest at time T, where $3 < T < 4$.

b) Find the time that the body is moving with zero acceleration.

c) Find the body's displacement from the origin when $t = 2$, given that the body is initially at the origin.

> **Q4 a) Hint:** Think about the body's velocity when $t = 3$ and $t = 4$.

Q5 At time t seconds, an object moving in a straight line along the x-axis has displacement x m from the origin, where $x = 3t^2 - 4e^{-t} + 2t$.
Find:

a) an expression for the object's velocity at time t,

b) an expression for the object's acceleration at time t,

c) the range of values for the object's acceleration.

2. Variable Acceleration in 2 and 3 Dimensions

Learning Objectives:

- Be able to find position, velocity and acceleration vectors by differentiating and integrating vectors with respect to time.

- Be able to show that a body's path lies on a circle.

- Be able to use calculus and Newton's second law to find the force acting on a body.

Using calculus to find expressions describing the motion of a body works pretty much the same when the body is moving in two or three dimensions. The only difference is that the expressions will be written in vector form, so you'll have to be able to differentiate and integrate vectors.

Using vectors

Motion in two dimensions

- When you've got a body moving in **two dimensions** (i.e. in a two-dimensional **plane**), you can describe its **position**, **velocity** and **acceleration** using the **unit vectors i** and **j**.

- The **i**-component describes the body's **horizontal** motion, and the **j**-component usually describes the body's **vertical** motion.

- You saw in M1 how to use the *uvast* equations in vector form, but, just like in one dimension, if the body is moving with **variable acceleration**, you'll have to use **calculus** instead.

- The relationships between **displacement** (or **position**), **velocity** and **acceleration** are just the same as on pages 45 and 48:

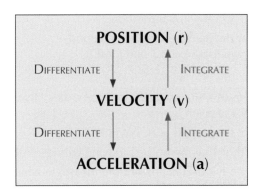

Tip: In two or more dimensions, it's usual to refer to a body's <u>position vector</u>. This is just the vector describing the body's displacement from the origin.

Tip: You could use column vectors instead. The idea's exactly the same — just differentiate or integrate each component separately.

Tip: The shorthand for $\frac{d\mathbf{r}}{dt}$ is $\dot{\mathbf{r}}$ (the single dot means differentiate **r** once with respect to time). The shorthand for $\frac{d^2\mathbf{r}}{dt^2}$ is $\ddot{\mathbf{r}}$ (the double dots mean differentiate **r** twice with respect to time).

- To differentiate or integrate vectors written in **i** and **j** notation, just differentiate or integrate each component **separately**:

Differentiating with i and j vectors

If $\mathbf{r} = x\mathbf{i} + y\mathbf{j}$ is the position vector of a body, then:

the body's velocity, $\mathbf{v} = \dfrac{d\mathbf{r}}{dt} = \dfrac{dx}{dt}\mathbf{i} + \dfrac{dy}{dt}\mathbf{j}$

and the body's acceleration, $\mathbf{a} = \dfrac{d\mathbf{v}}{dt} = \dfrac{d^2\mathbf{r}}{dt^2}$

$$= \dfrac{d^2x}{dt^2}\mathbf{i} + \dfrac{d^2y}{dt^2}\mathbf{j}$$

Integrating with i and j vectors

If $\mathbf{a} = p\mathbf{i} + q\mathbf{j}$ is the acceleration of a body, then:

the body's velocity, $\mathbf{v} = \int \mathbf{a}\,\mathrm{d}t = \int (p\mathbf{i} + q\mathbf{j})\,\mathrm{d}t$

$$= \left(\int p\,\mathrm{d}t\right)\mathbf{i} + \left(\int q\,\mathrm{d}t\right)\mathbf{j}$$

If $\mathbf{v} = w\mathbf{i} + z\mathbf{j}$ is the velocity of a body, then:

the body's position vector, $\mathbf{r} = \int \mathbf{v}\,\mathrm{d}t = \int (w\mathbf{i} + z\mathbf{j})\,\mathrm{d}t$

$$= \left(\int w\,\mathrm{d}t\right)\mathbf{i} + \left(\int z\,\mathrm{d}t\right)\mathbf{j}$$

Tip: When you're integrating, you'll still need to add a constant of integration, **C**, but it will be a vector with **i** and **j** components.

Example 1

A particle is moving in a plane. At time t seconds, its position in the plane is given by r = [(t^2 − 4e$^{-0.5t}$)i + (2 + 5t)j] m relative to a fixed origin O.
Find the particle's speed and direction of motion at time t = 0.5 seconds.

- Differentiate the expression for the particle's position vector to find its velocity. Remember to treat the **i** and **j** components separately:

$$\mathbf{v} = \frac{\mathrm{d}\mathbf{r}}{\mathrm{d}t} = \left[\frac{\mathrm{d}}{\mathrm{d}t}(t^2 - 4e^{-0.5t})\right]\mathbf{i} + \left[\frac{\mathrm{d}}{\mathrm{d}t}(2 + 5t)\right]\mathbf{j}$$

$$= [(2t + 2e^{-0.5t})\mathbf{i} + 5\mathbf{j}]\ \mathrm{ms}^{-1}$$

Tip: Use the chain rule to differentiate the exponential term in the **i**-component.

- Substitute t = 0.5 into this expression:

$$\mathbf{v} = [2(0.5) + 2e^{(-0.5 \times 0.5)}]\mathbf{i} + 5\mathbf{j}$$

$$= [(2.557...)\mathbf{i} + 5\mathbf{j}]\ \mathrm{ms}^{-1}$$

- Use the **i** and **j** components to draw a right-angled triangle:

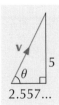

- Now use Pythagoras' theorem to find the particle's speed, and trigonometry to find its direction of motion:

$$\text{speed} = |\mathbf{v}| = \sqrt{(2.557...)^2 + 5^2}$$

$$= \boxed{5.62\ \mathrm{ms}^{-1}\ \text{(3 s.f.)}}$$

$$\theta = \tan^{-1}\left(\frac{5}{2.557...}\right)$$

$$= \boxed{62.9° \text{ (3 s.f.) above } \mathbf{i}}$$

Example 2

A particle is moving in a vertical plane so that at time t seconds it has velocity v ms^{-1}, where $v = (8 + 2t)\mathbf{i} + (t^3 - 6t)\mathbf{j}$. When $t = 2$, the particle has position vector $(10\mathbf{i} + 3\mathbf{j})$ m with respect to a fixed origin O.

a) **Find the acceleration of the particle at time t.**

  ▪ Differentiate the expression for velocity with respect to time:

$$\mathbf{a} = \frac{d\mathbf{v}}{dt} = \left[\frac{d}{dt}(8 + 2t)\right]\mathbf{i} + \left[\frac{d}{dt}(t^3 - 6t)\right]\mathbf{j}$$

$$= [2\mathbf{i} + (3t^2 - 6)\mathbf{j}] \text{ ms}^{-2}$$

b) **Show that the position vector of the particle when $t = 4$ is $\mathbf{r} = (38\mathbf{i} + 27\mathbf{j})$ m.**

  ▪ Integrate the expression for velocity with respect to time:

$$\mathbf{r} = \int \mathbf{v}\, dt = \left(\int (8 + 2t)\, dt\right)\mathbf{i} + \left(\int (t^3 - 6t)\, dt\right)\mathbf{j}$$

$$= (8t + t^2)\mathbf{i} + \left(\frac{t^4}{4} - 3t^2\right)\mathbf{j} + \mathbf{C}$$

  ▪ When $t = 2$, $\mathbf{r} = (10\mathbf{i} + 3\mathbf{j})$. Use these values to find $\mathbf{C}$:

$$10\mathbf{i} + 3\mathbf{j} = (8(2) + 2^2)\mathbf{i} + \left(\frac{2^4}{4} - 3(2)^2\right)\mathbf{j} + \mathbf{C}$$

$$10\mathbf{i} + 3\mathbf{j} = 20\mathbf{i} - 8\mathbf{j} + \mathbf{C}$$

$$\Rightarrow \mathbf{C} = (10 - 20)\mathbf{i} + (3 - -8)\mathbf{j}$$

$$= -10\mathbf{i} + 11\mathbf{j}$$

$$\Rightarrow \mathbf{r} = \left[(8t + t^2 - 10)\mathbf{i} + \left(\frac{t^4}{4} - 3t^2 + 11\right)\mathbf{j}\right] \text{ m}$$

Tip: To find $\mathbf{C}$, collect $\mathbf{i}$ and $\mathbf{j}$ components, and add or subtract to simplify.

  ▪ Substitute $t = 4$ into the equation:

$$\mathbf{r} = (8(4) + (4)^2 - 10)\mathbf{i} + \left(\frac{4^4}{4} - 3(4)^2 + 11\right)\mathbf{j}$$

$$= (32 + 16 - 10)\mathbf{i} + (64 - 48 + 11)\mathbf{j}$$

$$= (38\mathbf{i} + 27\mathbf{j}) \text{ m} \quad\text{— as required.}$$

c) **Find the value of t for which the particle is directly above O.**

  ▪ When the particle is directly above O, the $\mathbf{i}$-component of its position vector will be zero:

$$8t + t^2 - 10 = 0$$

  ▪ Solve for t using the quadratic formula:

$$t = \frac{-8 \pm \sqrt{8^2 - (4 \times 1 \times -10)}}{2}$$

$$\Rightarrow t = 1.099... \quad\text{or}\quad t = -9.099...$$

Tip: You need to check that the $\mathbf{j}$-component of $\mathbf{r}$ is greater than 0 to make sure that the particle is above O (rather than at it or below it).

  ▪ Check that the $\mathbf{j}$-component of $\mathbf{r}$ is greater than zero for $t = 1.099...$

$$\frac{(1.099...)^4}{4} - 3(1.099...)^2 + 11 = 7.741... > 0$$

  ▪ So the particle is directly above O when $t = 1.10$ s (3 s.f.)

Example 3

A body is moving on a plane. At time t seconds, the body's acceleration is given by $\mathbf{a} = [(4 - 18t)\mathbf{i} + 72t\mathbf{j}]$ ms^{-2}, relative to a fixed origin O. When $t = 1$, the body has position vector $\mathbf{r} = 2\mathbf{i}$ m, relative to O. When $t = 2$, the body is moving with velocity $\mathbf{v} = (-20\mathbf{i} + 135\mathbf{j})$ ms^{-1}. Find the body's position vector when it is moving parallel to $\mathbf{i}$.

- First, integrate the expression for acceleration with respect to time to find an expression for velocity:

$$\mathbf{v} = \int \mathbf{a} \, dt = \left(\int (4 - 18t) \, dt \right)\mathbf{i} + \left(\int 72t \, dt \right)\mathbf{j}$$
$$= (4t - 9t^2)\mathbf{i} + 36t^2\mathbf{j} + \mathbf{C}$$

- When $t = 2$, $\mathbf{v} = -20\mathbf{i} + 135\mathbf{j}$. Use these values to find $\mathbf{C}$:

$$-20\mathbf{i} + 135\mathbf{j} = (4(2) - 9(2)^2)\mathbf{i} + 36(2)^2\mathbf{j} + \mathbf{C}$$
$$-20\mathbf{i} + 135\mathbf{j} = -28\mathbf{i} + 144\mathbf{j} + \mathbf{C}$$
$$\Rightarrow \mathbf{C} = 8\mathbf{i} - 9\mathbf{j}$$

- So the particle's velocity at time t is given by:

$$\mathbf{v} = [(4t - 9t^2 + 8)\mathbf{i} + (36t^2 - 9)\mathbf{j}] \text{ ms}^{-1}$$

- When the particle is moving parallel to $\mathbf{i}$, the $\mathbf{j}$-component of its velocity is zero...

$$36t^2 - 9 = 0$$
$$t^2 = 9 \div 36 = 0.25$$
$$\Rightarrow t = 0.5 \text{ seconds}$$

Tip: As always, ignore the negative value of t.

- ...and the $\mathbf{i}$-component of its velocity is non-zero:

$$4(0.5) - 9(0.5)^2 + 8 = 7.75 \neq 0$$

Tip: You need to check that the $\mathbf{i}$ component of velocity is non-zero for the value of t you've found. If it was zero, then the particle wouldn't be moving parallel to $\mathbf{i}$ at this time — it would be stationary.

- So the particle is moving parallel to $\mathbf{i}$ at time $t = 0.5$ seconds. Now integrate the expression for velocity to find an expression for the particle's position vector:

$$\mathbf{r} = \int \mathbf{v} \, dt = \left(\int (4t - 9t^2 + 8) \, dt \right)\mathbf{i} + \left(\int (36t^2 - 9) \, dt \right)\mathbf{j}$$
$$= (2t^2 - 3t^3 + 8t)\mathbf{i} + (12t^3 - 9t)\mathbf{j} + \mathbf{D}$$

- When $t = 1$, $\mathbf{r} = 2\mathbf{i}$. Use these values to find $\mathbf{D}$:

$$2\mathbf{i} = (2(1)^2 - 3(1)^3 + 8(1))\mathbf{i} + (12(1)^3 - 9(1))\mathbf{j} + \mathbf{D}$$
$$2\mathbf{i} = 7\mathbf{i} + 3\mathbf{j} + \mathbf{D}$$
$$\Rightarrow \mathbf{D} = -5\mathbf{i} - 3\mathbf{j}$$

- So the particle's position vector relative to O at time t is given by:

$$\mathbf{r} = [(2t^2 - 3t^3 + 8t - 5)\mathbf{i} + (12t^3 - 9t - 3)\mathbf{j}] \text{ m}$$

- Substitute $t = 0.5$ into this equation to find the particle's position vector when it is travelling parallel to $\mathbf{i}$:

$$\mathbf{r} = (2(0.5)^2 - 3(0.5)^3 + 8(0.5) - 5)\mathbf{i} + (12(0.5)^3 - 9(0.5) - 3)\mathbf{j}$$
$$= (-0.875\mathbf{i} - 6\mathbf{j}) \text{ m}$$

Motion in three dimensions

Tip: Again, you can use column vectors rather than **i**, **j** and **k** notation if you prefer.

When you've got a body moving in **three-dimensional** space, you can describe its **position**, **velocity** and **acceleration** using the **unit vectors i, j** and **k**.

k is just another **unit vector perpendicular** to **i** and **j**.

You can **differentiate** and **integrate three-dimensional vectors** in the same way as two dimensional ones — just deal with each component **separately**, like on pages 54-55.

Example

A body is moving in three-dimensional space. At time t seconds, the body's position is given by r = [(4t^2 + 1)i + t^3j + (1 − t^4)k] m, relative to a fixed origin O.

Find an expression for the body's speed at time t seconds.

- Differentiate the expression for the body's position to get an expression for velocity:

$$\mathbf{v} = \frac{d\mathbf{r}}{dt} = \left[\frac{d}{dt}(4t^2 + 1)\right]\mathbf{i} + \left[\frac{d}{dt}(t^3)\right]\mathbf{j} + \left[\frac{d}{dt}(1 - t^4)\right]\mathbf{k}$$

$$= [8t\mathbf{i} + 3t^2\mathbf{j} - 4t^3\mathbf{k}] \text{ ms}^{-1}$$

- Now use Pythagoras' theorem to find an expression for the body's speed:

$$\text{speed} = \sqrt{(8t)^2 + (3t^2)^2 + (-4t^3)^2}$$

$$= \sqrt{64t^2 + 9t^4 + 16t^6}$$

$$= t\sqrt{64 + 9t^2 + 16t^4} \text{ ms}^{-1}$$

Tip: Using Pythagoras' theorem in 3D is pretty much the same as in 2D, only you can have up to three terms inside the square root.

Exercise 2.1

Q1 Hint: Be careful here — when you're differentiating or integrating trigonometric functions, you need to use radians — so make sure your calculator is set to radians when you're entering t values. You should still give the particle's direction of motion in degrees though.

Q1 A particle is moving in a plane. At time t seconds, the particle's position relative to a fixed origin O is given by
$\mathbf{r} = [(t^3 − 3\sin t)\mathbf{i} + (t^2 + 2e^{-t})\mathbf{j}]$ m.
Find:
a) (i) an expression for the particle's velocity in terms of t,
(ii) the particle's speed and direction of motion at time $t = 3$ s,
b) (i) an expression for the particle's acceleration in terms of t,
(ii) the magnitude of the particle's acceleration at time $t = 4$ s.

Q2 An object is travelling in a plane. Its velocity at time t seconds is given by the expression $\mathbf{v} = [(t^3 − 6t^2 − 36t)\mathbf{i} + 14\mathbf{j}]$ ms^{-1}.
Find the object's velocity when it is moving with zero acceleration.

Q3 A body is moving in a plane. At time t seconds, the body's acceleration is given by $\mathbf{a} = (3t\mathbf{i} + 6\mathbf{j})$ ms^{-2}. At time $t = 2$ seconds, the body has position vector $\mathbf{r} = (2\mathbf{i} - 9\mathbf{j})$ m relative to a fixed origin O, and is travelling at $(4\mathbf{i} + 6\mathbf{j})$ ms^{-1}. $\mathbf{i}$ and $\mathbf{j}$ are the unit vectors directed due east and due north respectively.

Find:

a) an expression for the body's velocity in terms of t,

b) an expression for the body's position vector in terms of t,

c) (i)   the value of t for which the body is due east of O,

   (ii)   the body's distance from O at this time.

Q4 The velocity of a particle at time t seconds ($t \geq 0$) is given by $\mathbf{v} = [(t^2 - 6t)\mathbf{i} + (4t + 5)\mathbf{j}]$ ms^{-1}. The particle is moving in a plane, and at time $t = 0$ the particle passes through the origin, O.

Find:

a) an expression for the particle's acceleration at time t seconds,

b) an expression for the particle's position vector at time t seconds,

c) the values of t for which the particle is travelling parallel to $\mathbf{j}$,

d) the value of b, given that the particle passes through the point with position vector $(b\mathbf{i} + 12\mathbf{j})$ m, where b is a constant.

Q5 A body moves in three-dimensional space. At time t seconds, its velocity, $\mathbf{v}$ ms^{-1}, is given by $\mathbf{v} = 6t\mathbf{i} + 2\mathbf{j} + (3t^2 - 4)\mathbf{k}$. When $t = 0$, the body is at the point $4\mathbf{i}$.

Find:

a) an expression for the body's position at time t seconds,

b) the body's position vector when $t = 3$,

c) an expression for the body's acceleration at time t seconds,

d) the magnitude of the body's acceleration when $t = 4$.

Q6 A particle moves in three-dimensional space. At time t seconds, its position vector, $\mathbf{r}$ m, is given by $\mathbf{r} = (t^2 + 2)\mathbf{i} + (t^3 - 4t)\mathbf{j} + (3t^2 - 3t + 4)\mathbf{k}$.

a) Show that the particle's initial speed is 5 ms^{-1}.

b) Calculate the particle's acceleration at time $t = 3$ seconds.

Q7 At time t seconds, the acceleration of a particle moving in three-dimensional space is $\mathbf{a}$ ms^{-2}, where $\mathbf{a}$ is given by $12t\mathbf{i} + 6\mathbf{j}$. When $t = 0$, the particle passes through the point $2\mathbf{k}$ m with velocity $(-6\mathbf{i} - 6\mathbf{j} + 5\mathbf{k})$ ms^{-1}.

a) Find an expression for the particle's velocity in terms of t.

b) Show that the particle is travelling parallel to $\mathbf{k}$ when $t = 1$.

c) Find an expression for the particle's position vector in terms of t.

d) Show that the particle passes through the point $(4\mathbf{i} + 12\mathbf{k})$ m.

Q8 An object is travelling in a plane. Its velocity, $\mathbf{v}$ ms^{-1}, at time t seconds is given by $\mathbf{v} = 12\cos 4t\mathbf{i} - 12\sin 4t\mathbf{j}$. Initially, the object is at the point $3\mathbf{j}$ m, relative to a fixed origin O.

Show that the object's path lies on a circle, and state the radius of the circle.

Q9 Particle A is moving in a vertical plane. At time t seconds, the particle's position relative to a fixed origin O is given by $\mathbf{r}_A = [(t^3 - t^2 - 4t + 3)\mathbf{i} + (t^3 - 2t^2 + 3t - 7)\mathbf{j}]$ m.

Find:

a) the value of t for which the particle's velocity is $(-3\mathbf{i} + 2\mathbf{j})$ ms^{-1},

b) the value of t for which the direction of motion of the particle is $45°$ above $\mathbf{i}$.

A second particle, B, is moving in the same plane as particle A. At time t seconds, the acceleration of B is given by $\mathbf{a}_B = (6t\mathbf{i} + 6t\mathbf{j})$ ms^{-2}. At time $t = 1$ second, B passes the point $(2\mathbf{i} + 3\mathbf{j})$ m relative to O, with velocity $(4\mathbf{i} - \mathbf{j})$ ms^{-1}.

Find:

c) an expression for the position vector of particle B relative to O in terms of t,

d) an expression for the position vector of particle B relative to particle A in terms of t,

e) the distance between particles A and B at time $t = 4$ seconds.

Forces

Because a **resultant force** causes a body to **accelerate**, you may have to use Newton's second law, $\mathbf{F} = m\mathbf{a}$, as well as calculus, to find expressions describing the motion of a body.

Example 1

A particle P is moving under the action of a single force, F newtons. The position vector, r m, of P after t seconds is given by
$$r = (2t^3 - 3)\mathbf{i} + \frac{t^4}{2}\mathbf{j} + t^2\mathbf{k}.$$

a) Find an expression for the acceleration of P at time t seconds.

- Differentiate the expression for P's position vector to find the expression for velocity:
$$\mathbf{v} = \dot{\mathbf{r}} = (6t^2\mathbf{i} + 2t^3\mathbf{j} + 2t\mathbf{k}) \text{ ms}^{-1}$$

- Differentiate again to find the expression for acceleration:
$$\mathbf{a} = \dot{\mathbf{v}} = \boxed{(12t\mathbf{i} + 6t^2\mathbf{j} + 2\mathbf{k}) \text{ ms}^{-2}}$$

b) P has mass 6 kg. Find the magnitude of F when $t = 3$.

- Substitute $t = 3$ into the expression for acceleration:
$$\mathbf{a} = 12(3)\mathbf{i} + 6(3^2)\mathbf{j} + 2\mathbf{k}$$
$$= (36\mathbf{i} + 54\mathbf{j} + 2\mathbf{k}) \text{ ms}^{-2}$$

- Now use $\mathbf{F} = m\mathbf{a}$, with $m = 6$:
$$\mathbf{F} = (6 \times 36)\mathbf{i} + (6 \times 54)\mathbf{j} + (6 \times 2)\mathbf{k}$$
$$= 216\mathbf{i} + 324\mathbf{j} + 12\mathbf{k}$$

- Finally, use Pythagoras' theorem to find the magnitude:
$$|\mathbf{F}| = \sqrt{216^2 + 324^2 + 12^2} = \boxed{390 \text{ N (3 s.f.)}}$$

Tip: You could find the magnitude of $\mathbf{a}$ first instead if you wanted, then just multiply by m.

Example 2

A particle of mass 4 kg moves in a plane under the action of a single force, F N, where F is given by $\mathbf{F} = 24t\mathbf{i} - 8\mathbf{j}$. At time $t = 0$, the velocity of the particle is $(7\mathbf{i} + 22\mathbf{j})$ ms^{-1}.

a) The velocity of the particle at time t seconds is v ms^{-1}. Show that $\mathbf{v} = (3t^2 + 7)\mathbf{i} + (22 - 2t)\mathbf{j}$.

- Use $\mathbf{F} = m\mathbf{a}$ to find an expression for the acceleration of the particle at time t:
$$24t\mathbf{i} - 8\mathbf{j} = 4\mathbf{a}$$
$$\Rightarrow \mathbf{a} = (6t\mathbf{i} - 2\mathbf{j}) \text{ ms}^{-2}$$

- Integrate the expression for acceleration to find an expression for velocity:
$$\mathbf{v} = \int \mathbf{a}\, dt = \int (6t\mathbf{i} - 2\mathbf{j})\, dt$$
$$= 3t^2\mathbf{i} - 2t\mathbf{j} + \mathbf{C}$$

- When $t = 0$, $\mathbf{v} = (7\mathbf{i} + 22\mathbf{j})$ ms^{-1}. Use this information to find $\mathbf{C}$:
$$7\mathbf{i} + 22\mathbf{j} = 0\mathbf{i} + 0\mathbf{j} + \mathbf{C}$$
$$\Rightarrow \mathbf{C} = 7\mathbf{i} + 22\mathbf{j}.$$

- So $\mathbf{v}$ is given by:
$$\mathbf{v} = 3t^2\mathbf{i} - 2t\mathbf{j} + 7\mathbf{i} + 22\mathbf{j}$$
$$= \boxed{(3t^2 + 7)\mathbf{i} + (22 - 2t)\mathbf{j}} \text{ — as required.}$$

b) Find the value of t when the particle is moving parallel to i.

- When the particle is moving parallel to $\mathbf{i}$, the $\mathbf{j}$ component of $\mathbf{v}$ is 0...
$$22 - 2t = 0$$
$$\Rightarrow t = 11$$

- ...and the $\mathbf{i}$ component is non-zero:
$$3(11)^2 + 7 = 370 \neq 0$$

- So the particle is moving parallel to the vector $\mathbf{i}$ at time $\boxed{t = 11 \text{ s}}$.

Q1 A body moves in a plane under the action of a single force, **F** N. At time $t = 5$ seconds, $\mathbf{F} = 15\mathbf{i} - 8\mathbf{j}$. The velocity of the body at time t seconds is given by $\mathbf{v} = [t^3\mathbf{i} + (1 - 4t^2)\mathbf{j}]$ ms^{-1}. Find the mass of the body.

Q2 An object of mass 1.8 kg moves in three-dimensional space under the action of a single force, **F** N. At time t seconds, the object's position vector relative to a fixed origin, O, is **r** m, where **r** is given by $\mathbf{r} = [(-t^2 + 2)\mathbf{i} + (3t^2 + t)\mathbf{j} + (1 - t^2)\mathbf{k}]$ m. Show that **F** is constant.

Q3 An object of mass 14 kg moves in three-dimensional space under the action of a single force, **F** N. At time t seconds, the object's position vector relative to a fixed origin, O, is given by $\mathbf{r} = [(t^2 - 4t - 5)\mathbf{i} + (t^2 - 4t + 3)\mathbf{j} + 5\mathbf{k}]$ m. Find:
a) the time at which the object is momentarily at rest,
b) the object's distance from O when it is momentarily at rest,
c) an expression for **F**.

Q4 A particle of mass 3 kg moves in a plane under the action of a single force, **F** N. At time t seconds, the force is given by $\mathbf{F} = 3\mathbf{i} + 6t\mathbf{j}$. At time $t = 0$, the particle passes through the origin, O, with velocity $\mathbf{v} = (-2\mathbf{i} + 5\mathbf{j})$ ms^{-1}. Find:
a) the magnitude of the particle's acceleration at time $t = 1$ second,
b) an expression for the particle's velocity in terms of t,
c) the force acting on the particle when it is moving parallel to **j**,
d) an expression for the particle's position vector relative to O in terms of t,
e) the particle's distance from O at time $t = 3$ seconds.

Q5 A particle of mass 0.2 kg moves in a vertical plane under the action of a single force, **F** N. At time t seconds, the particle's velocity is given by $\mathbf{v} = [(5t - 2)\mathbf{i} + 3t^2\mathbf{j}]$ ms^{-1}. At time $t = 1$ second, the particle has position vector $\mathbf{r} = (-16\mathbf{i} - 8\mathbf{j})$ m, relative to a fixed origin, O. Find:
a) an expression for **F** in terms of t,
b) the magnitude of **F** at time $t = 2$ seconds,
c) an expression for the particle's position vector relative to O in terms of t,
d) the value of t for which the particle is directly above O.

Q6 A particle of mass 0.5 kg moves under the action of a single force, **F** N. At time t seconds, **F** is given by $\mathbf{F} = (3t - 4)\mathbf{i} + (t - 3t^2)\mathbf{j}$. At time $t = 0$, the particle passes through the origin, O, with velocity $\mathbf{v} = (-3\mathbf{i} + 45\mathbf{j})$ ms^{-1}. Find:
a) the particle's speed when $t = 3$,
b) the particle's distance from O when $t = 3$.

3. Applying Differential Equations

You can solve problems in kinematics using differential equations. In this section, you'll have to form a differential equation to describe the motion of a body, then solve the equation by separating variables.

You might have seen differential equations before, in C4, so take a look at your C4 notes if you'd like a reminder before you start.

Learning Objectives:

- Be able to form a differential equation to describe the motion of a body experiencing a variable force.

- Be able to solve the differential equation by separating variables and integrating.

Applying differential equations

As you saw on pages 60-61, you can use **calculus** and **Newton's second law** to solve problems where a **resultant force** causes a body to **accelerate**.

If the resultant force is a function of the body's **velocity** (i.e. if it can be written in terms of v), you can use $F = ma$ and $a = \dfrac{dv}{dt}$ to form a **differential equation** describing the body's motion:

$$F = m\frac{dv}{dt}$$

This differential equation will give you an expression for $\dfrac{dv}{dt}$ in terms of v.

Because you can't integrate the variable v with respect to t, you need to **separate the variables** before you integrate to solve the equation.

Example 1

The combined mass of a cyclist and her bike is 75 kg. She is cycling along a horizontal road and stops pedalling when her velocity is 10 ms⁻¹. The only horizontal force acting on the cyclist and her bike is a resistive force of 15v N, where v is the velocity of the bike.

a) **Show that $\dfrac{dv}{dt} = -\dfrac{v}{5}$.**

- Resolving horizontally, taking the direction of motion as positive, and using $F = ma$:

$$F = m\frac{dv}{dt}$$

$$-15v = 75\frac{dv}{dt}$$

$$\frac{dv}{dt} = -\frac{15v}{75}$$

$$\Rightarrow \boxed{\frac{dv}{dt} = -\frac{v}{5}} \text{ — as required.}$$

Tip: The resistive force is the only horizontal force acting on the cyclist, and it acts in the opposite direction to motion. So the resultant force is negative.

b) **How long after she stops pedalling does her speed fall to 3 ms⁻¹?**

- Separate the variables to get all the v's on one side and all the t's on the other:

$$\frac{dv}{dt} = -\frac{v}{5} \quad \Rightarrow \quad \frac{1}{v}\,dv = -\frac{1}{5}\,dt$$

- Now integrate both sides. Take the time that the cyclist stops pedalling (when $v = 10$ ms^{-1}) as $t = 0$ and the time that she has dropped to a speed of $v = 3$ ms^{-1} as $t = T$.
  Use these as the limits for your definite integrals.

$$\int_{10}^{3} \frac{1}{v}\,dv = \int_{0}^{T} -\frac{1}{5}\,dt$$

$$\Rightarrow \left[\ln|v|\right]_{10}^{3} = \left[-\frac{t}{5}\right]_{0}^{T}$$

$$\Rightarrow \ln 3 - \ln 10 = -\frac{T}{5}$$

$$\Rightarrow T = -5\ln 0.3 = \boxed{6.02 \text{ s} \quad (3 \text{ s.f.})}$$

Tip: You could do an indefinite integral if you'd prefer. You'd have to use the initial conditions ($t = 0$, $v = 10$) to find the constant of integration, then plug in $v = 3$ to find the required value of t.

c) **Show that the cyclist's velocity satisfies $v = 10e^{-0.2t}$.**

- As in part b), separate the variables and integrate both sides. This time though, you're dealing with an indefinite integral, so don't forget the constant of integration.

$$\int \frac{1}{v}\,dv = \int -\frac{1}{5}\,dt$$

$$\Rightarrow \ln|v| = -\frac{t}{5} + C$$

Tip: You only need to add one constant for both integrations.

- Take exponentials of both sides to find an expression for v:

$$e^{\ln|v|} = e^{(-0.2t + C)}$$

$$\Rightarrow |v| = e^{-0.2t} \times e^c$$

$$\Rightarrow v = ke^{-0.2t}$$

Tip: To do this step, just rewrite the constant e^c as another constant, k.

(You don't have to do it this way though — you could just find the value of C as usual. Both ways are correct.)

- Now you need to find the value of k.
  When $t = 0$ s, $v = 10$ ms^{-1}, so:
  $$10 = ke^{(-0.2 \times 0)}$$
  $$\Rightarrow k = 10$$

- So $\boxed{v = 10e^{-0.2t}}$ — as required.

Example 2

A particle of mass 0.5 kg moves in a straight horizontal line. At time t seconds, the particle's speed is v ms^{-1}. The only horizontal force the particle experiences as it moves is a resistance to motion of $4v^{0.75}$ N. The particle's initial velocity is 81 ms^{-1}.

a) **Find an expression for v in terms of t, and hence find the value of t when the particle comes to rest.**

- Resolving horizontally, taking the direction of motion as positive, and using $F = ma$:

$$F = m\frac{dv}{dt}$$

$$-4v^{0.75} = 0.5\frac{dv}{dt}$$

$$\Rightarrow -8\,dt = \frac{1}{v^{0.75}}\,dv$$

- Integrate both sides:

$$\int -8 \, dt = \int v^{-0.75} \, dv$$

$$\Rightarrow -8t = 4v^{0.25} + C$$

- When $t = 0$, $v = 81$, so:

$$0 = 4(81)^{0.25} + C$$

$$\Rightarrow C = -12$$

$$\Rightarrow -8t = 4v^{0.25} - 12$$

$$\Rightarrow 3 - 2t = v^{0.25}$$

$$\Rightarrow \boxed{v = (3 - 2t)^4 \text{ ms}^{-1}}$$

- Now find the value of t when the particle comes to rest:

$$0 = (3 - 2t)^4$$

$$\Rightarrow \boxed{t = 1.5 \text{ s}}$$

b) **Find the distance the particle travels as its speed decreases from 81 ms⁻¹ to 1 ms⁻¹.**

- First find the value of t when the particle reaches 1 ms⁻¹:

$$v = (3 - 2t)^4$$

$$1 = (3 - 2t)^4$$

$$\Rightarrow \pm 1 = 3 - 2t$$

$$\Rightarrow t = 1 \text{ or } t = 2$$

- You found in part a) that the particle comes to rest when $t = 1.5$ s, so you can ignore $t = 2$.
  Therefore, the particle reaches 1 ms⁻¹ when $t = 1$ s.

- Remember that $v = \dfrac{ds}{dt}$, so $s = \int v \, dt$.
  So integrate the expression for velocity to find an expression for displacement:

$$s = \int_0^1 v \, dt = \int_0^1 (3 - 2t)^4 \, dt$$

$$= \left[-\frac{1}{10}(3 - 2t)^5 \right]_0^1$$

$$= \left(-\frac{1}{10}(3 - 2(1))^5 \right) - \left(-\frac{1}{10}(3 - 2(0))^5 \right)$$

$$= \left(-\frac{1}{10}(1)^5 \right) - \left(-\frac{1}{10}(3)^5 \right)$$

$$= -\frac{1}{10} - \left(-\frac{243}{10} \right)$$

$$= \frac{242}{10}$$

$$= \boxed{24.2 \text{ m}}$$

Tip: You've just found that the particle reaches 1 ms⁻¹ when $t = 1$, so use this as the upper limit of the definite integral.

Tip: This method uses the C3 formula:

$$\int_p^q (ax + b)^n \, dx = \left[\frac{1}{a(n + 1)}(ax + b)^{n+1} \right]_p^q$$

If you'd prefer, you could expand $(3 - 2t)^4$ and then integrate each term instead.

Q1 A body moves in a straight horizontal line, decelerating at a rate of $4\sqrt{v}$ ms^{-2}, where v ms^{-1} is its speed at time t seconds. The body's initial speed is 9 ms^{-1}.

Find an expression for v in terms of t.

Q2 A car of mass m kg is travelling along a smooth horizontal road. At time t seconds, the car's speed is v ms^{-1}. When $t = 0$, $v = 30$, and the driver takes her foot off the accelerator. The only horizontal force then experienced by the car is a resistance to motion of magnitude kmv N, where k is a positive constant.

a) Show that $\dfrac{dv}{dt} = -kv$.

b) Hence find an expression for v in terms of k and t.

c) It takes 11 seconds for the car's speed to reduce from 30 ms^{-1} to 10 ms^{-1}. Find the value of k, to 1 decimal place.

Q3 An object of mass 2 kg travels in a straight horizontal line. The only horizontal force acting on the object is a resistance to motion of magnitude $(4 + 2v)$ N, where v ms^{-1} is the object's speed at time t seconds. When $t = 0$, $v = 20$. Find:

a) the value of t for which $v = 12$,

b) the value of v when $t = 1.5$.

Q4 A vehicle of mass 400 kg freewheels along a smooth horizontal road. The only horizontal force it experiences is a resistive force of magnitude $20v^{1.5}$ N, where v ms^{-1} is the vehicle's speed at time t seconds.

a) Show that $\dfrac{dv}{dt} = -0.05v^{1.5}$.

b) Find the time it takes for the vehicle's speed to decrease from 25 ms^{-1} to 15 ms^{-1}.

Q5 A particle of mass 0.2 kg moves in a straight horizontal line against a resistive force of magnitude $\dfrac{v^2}{6}$ N, where v ms^{-1} is its speed at time t seconds. This is the only horizontal force experienced by the particle. Given that the initial speed of the particle is U ms^{-1}, find:

a) an expression for v in terms of U and t,

b) the time it takes the particle's speed to reach half its initial speed, in terms of U.

Q6 Hint: You'll need to use:

$\displaystyle\int \frac{1}{ax + b}\, dx =$

$\dfrac{1}{a}\ln|ax + b| + C$

Q6 At time $t = 0$ seconds, a ball of mass 5 kg is dropped from a window and falls vertically downwards. It experiences a resistance to motion of magnitude $4v$ N, where v ms^{-1} is the ball's speed at time t seconds. Find:

a) an expression for the ball's speed in terms of g and t,

b) the distance the ball travels between the times $t = 0.5$ and $t = 1.5$.

Review Exercise — Chapter 2

Q1   A particle sets off from the origin at $t = 0$ and moves along the x-axis with velocity $v = (3t^2 - 4\cos 2t + 8)$ ms^{-1}. Find an expression for:

a) the acceleration of the particle at time t seconds,

b) the displacement of the particle at time t seconds.

Q2   An object of mass 0.1 kg moves in a straight line along the x-axis. At time t seconds, the object's velocity is given by $v = (3t^2 - 9t + 4)$ ms^{-1}. Find:

a) an expression for the object's acceleration in terms of t,

b) the resultant force acting on the object when $t = 3$,

c) the value of t for which the resultant force acting on the object is momentarily zero.

Q3   At time $t = 0$, a particle sets off from rest at the origin, O, and moves in a plane with velocity $\mathbf{v} = (4t\mathbf{i} + t^2\mathbf{j})$ ms^{-1}, where t is the time in seconds. Find:

a) the particle's acceleration at time t,

b) the particle's position vector at time t.

Q4   A particle moves in a vertical plane. At time t seconds, the particle's position vector relative to a fixed origin, O, is given by $\mathbf{r} = [(t^2 - 3t + 2)\mathbf{i} + (t^2 - 5)\mathbf{j}]$ m. Find:

a) the particle's initial position,

b) the values of t for which the particle is directly below O,

c) the velocity of the particle when $t = 4$.

Q5   A body is moving in a plane with acceleration $\mathbf{a} = -10\mathbf{j}$ ms^{-2} relative to a fixed origin, O. The body's initial velocity is $(15\mathbf{i} + 12\mathbf{j})$ ms^{-1}. At time $t = 1$ second, the body passes through the point with position vector $(15\mathbf{i} + 16\mathbf{j})$ m. Given that $\mathbf{i}$ and $\mathbf{j}$ are unit vectors directed due east and due north respectively, find:

a) an expression for the body's velocity at time t seconds,

b) an expression for the body's position vector at time t seconds,

c) the body's velocity when it is due east of O.

Q6   A particle of mass 7.5 kg moves under the action of a single force, $\mathbf{F}$ N. At time t seconds, the particle has velocity $\mathbf{v}$ ms^{-1}, where $\mathbf{v}$ is given by $\mathbf{v} = (3t^2 - 8t)\mathbf{i} + (6 + 4t)\mathbf{j} - t^3\mathbf{k}$. When $t = 3$, the particle has position vector $(-4\mathbf{i} + 32\mathbf{j} - 0.25\mathbf{k})$ m, relative to a fixed origin O. Find:

a) an expression for $\mathbf{F}$ in terms of t,

b) an expression for the particle's position vector in terms of t.

Q7   A car's engine is switched off when the car is travelling along a smooth horizontal road at 15 ms^{-1}. The only horizontal force acting on the car from this point is a resistive force of $0.025mv$ newtons, where m kg is the mass of the car and v ms^{-1} is its speed at time t s.

a) Show that $\dfrac{dv}{dt} = -0.025v$.

b) Hence find the car's speed when $t = 60$.

1   A particle moves in a straight line along the x-axis.
At time t, the particle has velocity v ms^{-1} and acceleration a ms^{-2}, where:

$$a = 8t^2 + 6\sin 2t$$

When $t = 0$, $v = 0$.

     a)   Find an expression for v in terms of t.

(4 marks)

     b)   Show that when $t = \frac{\pi}{2}$, $v = \frac{\pi^3}{3} + 6$.

(2 marks)

2   A particle of mass m kg moves in a straight line from the origin, O.
Its velocity, v ms^{-1}, at time t seconds is:

$$v = 2t - 3e^{-2t} + 4$$

     a)   Find an expression for the particle's acceleration at time t.

(2 marks)

     b)   Find the range of values for the particle's acceleration.

(3 marks)

     c)   The resultant force acting on the particle when $t = 2$ is 6 N.
Find the value of m.

(2 marks)

     d)   Find an expression for the particle's displacement from O at time t.

(4 marks)

3   A particle is moving in a curved path. Its velocity, $\mathbf{v}$ ms^{-1}, at time t seconds is given by:

$$\mathbf{v} = (2\cos 3t + 5t)\mathbf{i} + (2t - 7)\mathbf{j}$$

where the unit vectors $\mathbf{i}$ and $\mathbf{j}$ are directed due east and due north respectively.
Find:

     a)   an expression for the particle's acceleration after t seconds.

(2 marks)

     b)   the magnitude of the particle's maximum acceleration. Give an exact value.

(4 marks)

4   A particle P is moving in a horizontal plane under the action of a single force, $\mathbf{F}$ N.
    After t seconds, P has position vector:

$$\mathbf{r} = [(2t^3 - 7t^2 + 12)\mathbf{i} + (3t^2 - 4t^3 - 7)\mathbf{j}] \text{ m}$$

where the unit vectors $\mathbf{i}$ and $\mathbf{j}$ are directed due east and due north respectively.

Find:

a)   an expression for the velocity of P after t seconds,

(2 marks)

b)   the speed of P when $t = \frac{1}{2}$, and the direction of motion of P at this time.

(3 marks)

At $t = 2$, the magnitude of $\mathbf{F}$ is 170 N. Find:

c)   the acceleration of P at $t = 2$,

(3 marks)

d)   the mass of the particle,

(3 marks)

e)   the value of t when $\mathbf{F}$ is acting parallel to $\mathbf{j}$.

(3 marks)

5   A plane of mass m kg is taxiing along a runway. Its engines exert a horizontal driving force
    of $10\,000v^{-1}$ N, and it experiences a horizontal resistive force of $0.1mv^2$, where v is the
    velocity of the plane in ms^{-1}.
    Assume that these are the only two forces acting horizontally on the plane.

a)   Show that the equation of motion of the plane is:

$$\frac{\mathrm{d}v}{\mathrm{d}t} = \frac{10\,000}{mv} - 0.1v^2$$

(2 marks)

b)   The pilot switches the engines off. Write down the new equation of motion
     for the plane.

(1 mark)

c)   If the pilot switched off the engines when the plane was travelling at 20 ms^{-1},
     find the time it would take for the plane to slow down to 10 ms^{-1}.

(5 marks)

6   A 2 kg bowling ball moves along a smooth horizontal surface with initial velocity 12 ms^{-1}.
    The ball experiences a horizontal resistive force of kv N, where v is the velocity of the ball
    in ms^{-1} and k is a constant.

Assuming that this is the only horizontal force experienced by the ball, show that:

a) $\dfrac{\mathrm{d}v}{\mathrm{d}t} = -\dfrac{kv}{2}$,

(2 marks)

b) $v = 12\sqrt{e^{-kt}}$.

(4 marks)

1. Work Done

Some of this chapter may seem familiar to you from GCSE science — it's all about the transfer of energy when things move due to the action of a force.

Work done

- Mechanical '**work**' is done by a **force** when the force **moves** an object through a **distance**.
- The '**work done**' by the force is equivalent to the **energy transferred** in moving the object, so work done is a measure of energy.
- You can calculate the work done by **any force** acting on an object using the following **formula**:

> **Work done = force (F) × distance moved in the direction of that force (s)**

- Or: **Work done = Fs**.
- The values for distance and force used in the formula must be in the **same direction**. This means you will often have to **resolve forces** to find the component of the force in the direction of motion.

Learning Objective:

- Be able to calculate the work done by or against a force acting on a moving object.

Tip: For an object moving with constant velocity, work is done **by** or **against** the forces which act on it. For an accelerating object, work is also done **on** the object itself, by those forces which are acting to change the velocity of the object.

Tip: Make sure you learn the formula for work done — you won't be given it in the exam.

Tip: mg and R act perpendicular to the direction of motion, so they do no work on the object.

Tip: For a force in newtons, and a distance in metres, the unit of work done is the joule, J.

Example 1

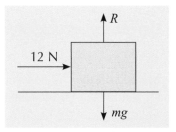

An object is accelerated a distance of 4 m across a horizontal floor by a horizontal force of magnitude 12 N. Find the work done by the 12 N force.

- The object moves in the same direction as the force (horizontally), so just put the values in the formula:

  Work done = force × distance moved in the direction of the force

  = 12 × 4 = 48 J

Example 2

A rock is pulled across a smooth horizontal surface by a rope
attached at an angle of 25° above the horizontal.
Given that the work done by the tension in the rope is 470 J and the
tension in the rope is 120 N, find the distance the rock is moved.

- Resolving horizontally and using
  the formula 'Work done = Fs':

  $470 = 120\cos 25° \times s$

  $\Rightarrow s = 470 \div 120\cos 25°$

  $= \boxed{4.32 \text{ m (3 s.f.)}}$

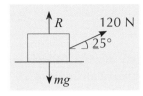

Tip: The block moves
horizontally, so you
need the horizontal
component of the
tension.

- If a **resistive force** acts on a body to oppose motion,
  then work is done **against** the resistive force.

- You may also see this referred to as the work done **by** the resistive force.
  In this case, if the direction of motion is taken as positive, then
  the work done by the resistive force will be **negative** — because
  the resistive force acts in the **opposite** direction to motion.

Tip: It may seem
odd for work done
to be negative — but
remember that work
done is a transfer of
energy. So, if the work
done on the body is
negative, then the body
experiences a loss of
energy.

Example 3

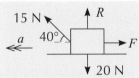

A block of weight 20 N is pulled 1.4 m across a rough horizontal floor by
a rope. The tension in the rope is 15 N, acting at 40° above the horizontal.
The coefficient of friction between the floor and the block is 0.3.

a) **Find the work done against friction.**

- There is no vertical motion, so, resolving vertically:

  $R + 15\sin 40° = 20$

  $\Rightarrow R = 20 - 15\sin 40° = 10.358... \text{ N}$

- Friction is limiting, so, using $F = \mu R$:

  $F = 0.3 \times 10.358... = 3.107... \text{ N}$

- Now, using 'Work done = Fs':

  Work done against friction = $3.107... \times 1.4$

  $= \boxed{4.35 \text{ J (3 s.f.)}}$

Tip: Remember — for
a body moving across
a rough surface, the
frictional force, F,
between the two is given
by $F = \mu R$.

Tip: You're asked for
the work done against
friction, so don't worry
about the tension in the
rope just yet.

b) **Find the work done on the block as it moves this distance.**

- In part a), you were only interested in the work done against friction.
  Now, you're looking for the work done **on the block**.

- This is equal to the product of the **resultant force** acting on the block
  and the **distance** through which the block is moved.

- Resolving horizontally, taking the direction of motion (left) as
  positive, and using the formula for work done:

  Work done = $(15\cos 40° - 3.107...) \times 1.4$

  $= \boxed{11.7 \text{ J (3 s.f.)}}$

Tip: You can think of the
work done on the block
as being the work done
by the resultant force.

Example 4

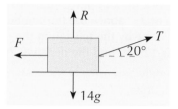

A body of mass 14 kg is pulled across a rough, horizontal plane by a rope inclined at an angle of 20° above the horizontal. The body moves 4 m at a constant speed. The work done against friction is 96 J.

a) Find the magnitude of the tension in the rope.

- Work done against friction is 96 J, so:

$$\text{Work done} = Fs$$
$$96 = F \times 4$$
$$\Rightarrow F = 24 \text{ N}$$

- The body is moving at a constant speed (i.e. acceleration is zero), so resolving horizontally and using $F_{net} = ma$:

$$T\cos 20° - 24 = 14 \times 0$$
$$\Rightarrow T = 24 \div \cos 20° = 25.540...$$
$$= 25.5 \text{ N (3 s.f.)}$$

b) Find the coefficient of friction between the plane and the block.

- Resolving vertically:

$$R + (25.540...)\sin 20° = 14g$$
$$\Rightarrow R = 128.464... \text{ N}$$

- Now, using $F = \mu R$:

$$24 = \mu \times 128.464...$$
$$\Rightarrow \mu = 0.19 \text{ (2 d.p.)}$$

Exercise 1.1

Q1 A train travels 0.3 km along a horizontal stretch of track. The resistance to motion is modelled as a constant horizontal force of magnitude 500 N. Find the work done against this resistive force.

Q2 A toy car travels 1.6 m along a smooth horizontal floor. It is powered by a horizontal driving force, P. If the work done is 8 J, find P.

Q3 A dart is thrown at a board, strikes it horizontally, and penetrates to a distance of d metres. The resistance to motion caused by the board is 84 N. If the work done against this resistive force is 0.428 J, find d.

Q4

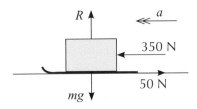

A package is placed on a sledge at rest on rough horizontal ground. A horizontal force of magnitude 350 N is applied to the sledge, which then moves a distance of 0.7 m. A frictional force of magnitude 50 N acts between the ground and the sledge. Find:

a) the work done against friction,

b) the work done on the sledge as it moves along the ground.

Q5 An object is pulled 1150 m along smooth horizontal ground by a rope. The rope is attached at an angle of 18° above the horizontal, and the tension in the rope is 2000 N.
Find the work done by the tension in the rope.

Q6 A particle is pushed 25 m across a rough, horizontal plane by a force, P, applied to the particle at an angle of 30° above the horizontal. The particle moves at constant speed. Given that the work done against friction is 55 J, find the magnitude of P.

Q7 A body of mass 0.15 kg is accelerated 6 m along rough, horizontal ground by a wire. The wire is attached to the body at an angle of 24° above the horizontal, and the tension in the wire is 2.2 N.
The coefficient of friction between the ground and the body is 0.14.

a) Find the work done against friction.

b) Find the work done on the body as it moves along the ground.

Q8 A box of mass 12 kg is pulled with increasing speed along rough, horizontal ground by a light, inextensible string. The string is attached to the box at an angle of 15° above the horizontal, and the magnitude of the tension in the string is 32 N. The coefficient of friction between the ground and the box is 0.18.

a) Given that the work done against friction is 45 J, find the distance the box moves.

b) Hence find the work done on the box as it moves this distance.

Q9

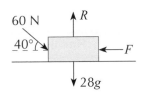

A parcel of mass 28 kg is pushed 3.5 m across a rough, horizontal floor by a pushing force of magnitude 60 N, applied to the parcel at an angle of 40° to the horizontal, as shown above.
The work done on the parcel as it moves this distance is 28 J.
Find the coefficient of friction between the parcel and the floor.

Gravity

- When a body **falls freely under gravity**, **work is done** by **gravity**.
- The force that causes the body to fall is the body's **weight**: $W = mg$.
- So for a body which falls through a height h:

$$\text{Work done by gravity} = \text{Weight} \times \text{Height}$$
$$= mgh \longleftarrow \qquad \text{Learn this formula.}$$

- A force **lifting** a body vertically does work **against gravity**.
- The work done by a force **against** gravity is also given by mgh:

A body of mass m kg is attached to a vertical rope and raised h m at a **constant speed**. The tension in the rope is T.

Tip: $a = 0$ because the body is moving at a constant speed.

Resolving vertically, taking up as positive, and using $F_{net} = ma$:

$$F_{net} = ma$$
$$T - mg = m \times 0$$
$$\Rightarrow T = mg$$

Using the formula for **work done**:

$$\text{Work done} = Fs$$
$$= T \times h$$
$$= mgh$$

So the **work done against gravity** for an object moving **vertically upwards** is given by:

$$\textbf{Work done} = \textit{mgh}$$

Tip: For a body moving at a constant speed, the work done **on the body** is zero.

- For a body being lifted vertically, mgh only gives you the work done **against gravity**. If the body is moving at **constant speed**, there will be **no resultant force** on the body, and the tension in the rope (or whatever force is doing the lifting) will be **equal** to the body's weight. So the **work done by the tension** in the rope will be equal to the **work done against gravity**.

- However, if the body is **accelerating**, then there **will** be a **resultant force**, and the work done by the tension in the rope and the work done against gravity **won't** be equal. Some of the work done overcomes the **resistance** of gravity, and the rest of the work is done **on the body** and causes it to **accelerate**.

Example 1

A 20 kg sack of flour is raised vertically by a light rope at a constant speed. The work done is 1400 J. Find the distance, d, the sack is raised.

Tip: The sack is moving at constant speed, so the work done in lifting it is just the work done against gravity.

- The sack is being lifted vertically at a constant speed, so:

$$\text{Work done} = mgh$$
$$1400 = 20 \times 9.8 \times d$$
$$\Rightarrow d = 1400 \div 196$$
$$= 7.14 \text{ m (3 s.f.)}$$

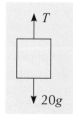

Example 2

A particle of mass 1.8 kg is lifted vertically upwards by a light, inextensible string. The particle accelerates uniformly from rest to a speed of 6 ms^{-1} in 4 seconds.

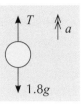

a) **Find the work done against gravity.**

- First, find the distance the particle travels.
  Taking up as positive:

  $u = 0, \; v = 6, \; s = s, \; t = 4$

  $s = \left(\dfrac{u + v}{2}\right)t$

  $s = \left(\dfrac{0 + 6}{2}\right) \times 4 = 12$ m

- Now, using the formula for work done against gravity:

  Work done = mgh

  $= 1.8 \times 9.8 \times 12$

  $= 211.68$ J

b) **Find the work done on the particle.**

- First, find the particle's acceleration.
  Taking up as positive:

  $u = 0, \; v = 6, \; a = a, \; t = 4$

  $v = u + at$

  $6 = 0 + 4a$

  $\Rightarrow \; a = 1.5$ ms^{-2}

Tip: In this example, the particle is accelerating, so the work done by the tension in the string is not equal to the work done against gravity.

- Now, resolving vertically, taking up as positive, and using $F_{net} = ma$:

  $F_{net} = 1.8 \times 1.5$

  $= 2.7$ N

- Finally, using the formula for work done:

  Work done = $F_{net} \times s$

  $= 2.7 \times 12$

  $= 32.4$ J

Exercise 1.2

Q1 A pebble of mass 1.3 g is dropped a distance of 37 m.
Find the work done by gravity in the pebble's fall.

Q2 A person of mass 57 kg is lifted by a rescue helicopter.
If 16 367 J of work is done against gravity, calculate the vertical height through which the person is raised.

Q3 A car is lifted through a vertical distance of 2.7 m at constant speed. The work done in lifting the car is 22 491 J. Find the car's mass.

Q4

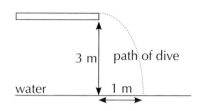

Q4 Hint: The path of the dive doesn't matter — it's only the vertical height that you're interested in.

A diver of mass 48 kg dives from a height of 3 m. The path of the dive is shown below. How much work is done by gravity on the diver before she hits the water?

Q5 A light, inextensible wire raises a bucket of water, with a total mass of 3 kg, from the bottom to the top of a well. The depth of the well is 9.5 m.

a) Assuming that the bucket is raised at a constant speed, find:

    (i)   the tension in the wire,

    (ii)   the work done by the tension in the wire.

b) Now assume that the bucket is raised with a constant acceleration of 1.5 ms^{-2}. Find:

    (i)   the tension in the wire,

    (ii)   the work done on the bucket as it is raised to the top of the well.

Q6 A stone of mass 2 kg is dropped from the top of a cliff. It falls freely under gravity and lands in the sea below after 3 s.

a) Calculate the height of the cliff.

b) Find the work done by gravity on the stone.

c) List any assumptions you have made.

Q7 A particle is lifted 9 m vertically upwards by a light, inextensible string. The tension in the string has magnitude 44 N. Given that the particle accelerates at a rate of 0.16 ms^{-2}, find:

a) the mass of the particle,

b) the work done on the particle.

Q8 An object of mass 25 kg is lifted vertically upwards by a light, inextensible wire. The object accelerates uniformly from rest to a speed of 4.2 ms^{-1} in 10 seconds. Find:

a) the work done against gravity,

b) the magnitude of the tension in the wire,

c) the work done by the tension in the wire.

Friction and gravity

- If a body slides **down a rough slope**, work will be done **by gravity**. Some of this work will be done **against friction** between the body and the slope.
- If a force moves a body **up a rough slope** then work will be done **by that force**, **against friction** and **against gravity**.
- To find the work done by or against each force, you need to **resolve forces** to find the **component** of each force in the **direction of motion**.
- Then the formula '**Work done = Fs**' can be used as normal.

Example 1

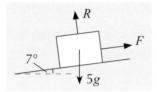

A block of mass 5 kg slides 0.5 m down a rough plane inclined at an angle of 7° to the horizontal. The coefficient of friction between the block and the plane is 0.12.

a) Find the work done by gravity in moving the block.

- The block moves 0.5 m down the plane.
- Resolving vertically, taking down as positive, the block moves through a vertical distance of $0.5\sin 7°$ m.
- Using the formula for work done by gravity:

$$\text{Work done by gravity} = mgh$$
$$= 5 \times 9.8 \times 0.5\sin 7°$$
$$= 2.99 \text{ J (3 s.f.)}$$

Tip: Instead of finding the vertical distance, you could resolve the block's weight to find its component parallel to the plane, then use Work done = Fs = $5g\sin 7° \times 0.5$

b) Find the work done against friction as the block slides.

- Resolving perpendicular to the plane:

$$R = 5g\cos 7°$$

- Now, using $F = \mu R$:

$$F = 0.12 \times 5g\cos 7°$$
$$= 5.836... \text{ N}$$

- Now, using the formula for work done:

$$\text{Work done against friction} = \text{Force} \times \text{distance}$$
$$= F \times 0.5$$
$$= 5.836... \times 0.5$$
$$= 2.92 \text{ J (3 s.f.)}$$

Example 2

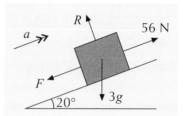

A block of mass 3 kg accelerates 9 m up a rough plane inclined at an angle of 20° to the horizontal. The block is pulled by a rope which is parallel to the plane. The tension in the rope has magnitude 56 N. The coefficient of friction between the block and the plane is 0.36.

Find the work done on the block as it is pulled up the plane.

- First find the frictional force, F, between the plane and the block.
- Resolving perpendicular to the plane:

$$R = 3g\cos 20° \text{ N}$$

- Now, using $F = \mu R$:

$$F = 0.36 \times 3g\cos 20° = 9.945... \text{ N}$$

- Now, resolving parallel to the plane, taking up the plane as positive, and using the formula for work done:

$$\text{Work done} = (56 - 9.945... - 3g\sin 20°) \times 9$$
$$= 324 \text{ N (3 s.f.)}$$

Tip: The block is accelerating, so there is a resultant force acting on it. It's this resultant force that you want to use to find the overall work done on the block.

Exercise 1.3

Q1 A body of mass 90 kg slides 1.4 m down a smooth plane inclined at an angle of 70° to the horizontal. Find the work done by gravity.

Q2

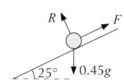

A particle of mass 0.45 kg slides 2 m down a rough plane inclined at an angle of 25° to the horizontal. The coefficient of friction between the plane and the particle is 0.37. Find:

a) the work done by gravity,

b) the work done against friction.

Q3 A package of mass 8 kg is pulled 1.5 m up a rough plane by a light, inextensible rope which is parallel to the plane. The plane is inclined at an angle of 22° to the horizontal, and the coefficient of friction between the package and the plane is 0.55.

a) Find the work done against gravity.

b) Find the work done against friction.

Q4

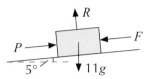

A rock of mass 11 kg is pushed up a rough plane by a force P, applied to the rock in a direction parallel to the plane. The plane is inclined at an angle of 5° to the horizontal, and the rock moves at a constant speed. Given that the coefficient of friction between the plane and the rock is 0.08, find the work done by P in pushing the rock 16 m up the plane.

Q5

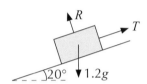

A light, inextensible string pulls a particle of mass 1.2 kg a distance of 4.5 m up a smooth ramp inclined at an angle of 20° to the horizontal. The particle is initially at rest, and it accelerates uniformly to a final speed of 5 ms⁻¹. The string is parallel to the ramp. Find the work done on the particle as it is pulled up the ramp.

Q6

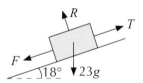

A light, inextensible rope pulls a block of mass 23 kg a distance of 0.75 m up a rough plane inclined at an angle of 18° to the horizontal. The rope is parallel to the plane and the block accelerates up the plane at a rate of 0.95 ms⁻². The coefficient of friction between the block and the plane is 0.36. Find:

a) the magnitude of the tension in the rope,

b) the work done on the block as it is pulled up the plane.

2. Kinetic and Gravitational Potential Energy

In mechanics, two types of energy you'll be dealing with a lot are kinetic energy and gravitational potential energy. A body could experience a change in either of these if the body moves and work is done.

The big thing to remember about energy is that it's always conserved — you can't lose or gain energy, it just gets converted to another form.

Kinetic energy

- Any body that is **moving** has **kinetic energy** (K.E.).
- You can find the kinetic energy of a body using the formula:

$$\text{Kinetic Energy} = \frac{1}{2} \times \text{mass} \times \text{speed}^2$$

$$\text{or } \textbf{K.E.} = \frac{1}{2}mv^2$$

You need to learn this formula.

- If mass, m, is measured in kg, and speed, v, in ms^{-1}, then kinetic energy will be measured in joules, J.

Example

An ice skater of mass 60 kg is moving at a constant velocity of 8 ms^{-1}. Find the ice skater's kinetic energy.

Just put the values for mass and velocity straight in the formula:

Kinetic energy $= \frac{1}{2}mv^2 = \frac{1}{2} \times 60 \times 8^2 = \boxed{1920 \text{ J}}$

Exercise 2.1

Q1 A golf ball has a mass of 45 g. In flight it has a velocity of 20 ms^{-1}. Find the kinetic energy of the golf ball.

Q2 At a point on her fall, a skydiver of mass 60 kg has kinetic energy 94 080 J. Find her speed at this point.

Q3 A plane has mass 11 249 kg and is flying at 1462 kmh^{-1}. Find the kinetic energy of the plane.

Q4 An alpha particle has a mass of 6.64×10^{-27} kg and is moving at 1.5×10^6 ms^{-1}. What is its kinetic energy?

Q5 A particle travels 14 m in 3.5 seconds at a constant speed. Its kinetic energy is 22 J. Find the particle's mass.

Q6 Two cars, A and B, have the same mass, but A is travelling at twice the speed of B. Find the ratio of the kinetic energy of A to the kinetic energy of B.

Kinetic energy and work done

- Remember, **work done** is a **transfer of energy**.
- The **work done** by a **resultant force** on a body moving **horizontally** is equal to the change in that body's **kinetic energy**:

Tip: You need to remember to find the work done by the **resultant** force, rather than any individual force. If there's no resultant force, there'll be no change in speed, and hence no change in kinetic energy.

Consider a **resultant force**, F_{net}, acting horizontally on a body of mass m kg, causing it to **accelerate** horizontally from u ms^{-1} to v ms^{-1}.

The force is given by Newton's second law: $F_{net} = ma$

The body's acceleration can be found using a **constant acceleration equation**:

$v^2 = u^2 + 2as$

$\Rightarrow a = \dfrac{v^2 - u^2}{2s}$

So, $F_{net} = m\left(\dfrac{v^2 - u^2}{2s}\right)$

The work done by this force can then be found using the formula 'Work done = Force × Distance':

$$\text{Work done} = Fs$$
$$= m\left(\frac{v^2 - u^2}{2s}\right) \times s$$
$$= \frac{1}{2}mv^2 - \frac{1}{2}mu^2$$

Therefore, **Work done = change in kinetic energy**

Example 1

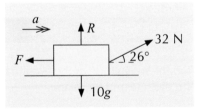

A body of mass 10 kg is pulled along a rough horizontal plane by a rope inclined at an angle of 26° above the horizontal. The magnitude of the tension in the rope is 32 N. The body starts from rest, and accelerates to a speed of 8 ms^{-1} over a distance of 14 m.

a) Find the work done on the body as it is pulled along the plane.

- The work done on the body is equal to the body's change in kinetic energy:

$$\text{Work done} = \frac{1}{2}mv^2 - \frac{1}{2}mu^2$$
$$= \frac{1}{2} \times 10 \times 8^2 - \frac{1}{2} \times 10 \times 0^2$$
$$= 320 \text{ J}$$

b) Find the coefficient of friction between the plane and the body.

- Resolving horizontally, the resultant force, F_{net}, acting on the body is:
$$F_{net} = 32\cos 26° - F$$

- Using the formula 'Work done = Force × distance':
$$320 = (32\cos 26° - F) \times 14$$
$$22.857... = 32\cos 26° - F$$
$$\Rightarrow F = 5.904... \text{ N}$$

- Now, resolving vertically:
$$R + 32\sin 26° = 10g$$
$$\Rightarrow R = 83.972... \text{ N}$$

- So, using $F = \mu R$:
$$5.904... = \mu \times 83.972...$$
$$\Rightarrow \boxed{\mu = 0.07 \text{ (2 d.p.)}}$$

Example 2

A particle of mass 6 kg is pulled along a rough horizontal plane by a horizontal force of magnitude 40 N. The particle travels 4 m in a straight line between two points on the plane, *A* and *B*. The particle passes *B* with speed 8 ms⁻¹. Given that the coefficient of friction between the particle and the plane is 0.35, find the particle's speed as it passes *A*.

- Draw a diagram to show what's going on:

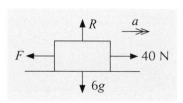

- First, you need to find the magnitude of the frictional force, *F*, between the particle and the plane.

- Resolving vertically:
$$R = 6g$$

- Now, using $F = \mu R$:
$$F = 0.35 \times 6g = 20.58 \text{ N}$$

- So, the resultant force, F_{net}, acting on the particle is:
$$F_{net} = 40 - 20.58 = 19.42 \text{ N}$$

- Now, using Work done = Force × distance:
$$\text{Work done by resultant force} = 19.42 \times 4$$
$$= 77.68 \text{ J}$$

- The work done by this force is equal to the change in the particle's kinetic energy, so:

$$77.68 = \frac{1}{2}mv^2 - \frac{1}{2}mu^2$$

$$77.68 = \frac{1}{2} \times 6 \times 8^2 - \frac{1}{2} \times 6 \times u^2$$

$$\Rightarrow u^2 = 38.106...$$

$$\Rightarrow u = 6.17 \text{ ms}^{-1} \text{ (3 s.f.)}$$

Exercise 2.2

Q1 A particle is pulled across a rough, horizontal surface by a horizontal wire. The tension in the wire has magnitude 0.6 N, and resistance to motion is modelled as a constant horizontal force of magnitude 0.0147 N.

a) If the particle's kinetic energy increases by 3.62×10^{-3} J, calculate the distance, s, it has travelled.

b) Calculate the particle's mass, given that its initial speed was 0.210 ms⁻¹ and its final speed is 1.222 ms⁻¹.

Exam Hint: Drawing a diagram can help you picture what's going on in these questions.

Q2 A lorry of mass 1800 kg is driven along a straight horizontal road. It undergoes a constant horizontal resistance to motion of magnitude R. At the point where the speed of the lorry is 11 ms⁻¹, the engine is switched off and the lorry coasts to a stop over a distance of 96 m. Find R.

Q2 Hint: Don't confuse the resistance to motion, R, with the normal reaction force, which is also often denoted R.

Q3 A body of mass 3 kg is pulled along a rough, horizontal surface by a horizontal rope. The tension in the rope has magnitude 15.88 N and the coefficient of friction between the body and the surface is 0.2. Given that the body is accelerated from an initial speed of 3 ms⁻¹ to a final speed of 7 ms⁻¹, find:

a) the change in the body's kinetic energy,

b) the magnitude of the frictional force between the body and the surface,

c) the distance travelled by the body.

Q4 A dart of mass 22 g is thrown towards a vertical dartboard. It hits the board horizontally at a speed of 8 ms⁻¹ and its point enters to a depth of 0.5 cm. Find:

a) the kinetic energy of the dart as it strikes the board,

b) the work done on the dart,

c) the magnitude of the constant resultant force experienced by the dart.

Q5 A body of mass 11 kg is pulled along a rough, horizontal plane by a rope inclined at an angle of 15° above the horizontal. The tension in the rope has magnitude 65 N. The coefficient of friction between the body and the plane is 0.19. Find the distance the body travels as it accelerates from a speed of 2 ms⁻¹ to a speed of 14 ms⁻¹.

Gravitational potential energy

- The **gravitational potential energy** (G.P.E.) of a body is the energy it has due to its **height**. The greater the height of a body above some 'base level', the greater that body's gravitational potential energy.

- G.P.E. can be calculated using the following formula:

> Gravitational Potential Energy = mass × g × vertical height above base level
> or **G.P.E. = mgh**

Tip: This formula should be familiar to you — it's the same as the formula for the work done by or against gravity when a body moves vertically.

- If mass, m, is in kg, acceleration due to gravity, g, is in ms⁻², and the vertical height above the base level, h, is in m, then G.P.E. is measured in joules, J.

Example 1

A lift has a total mass of 750 kg. The lift moves vertically from the 1st floor of a building, 6.1 m above the ground, to the 17th floor, 64.9 m above the ground.

Find the gravitational potential energy gained by the lift in travelling between the two floors.

Tip: Here, the 'base level' is the 1st floor, not the ground. So h is the difference in height between the two floors, not the height of the 17th floor.

- You want the gravitational potential energy gained by the lift in moving between the two floors, so use the formula G.P.E. = mgh, where h is the vertical distance between the two floors:

$$\text{G.P.E. gained} = 750 \times 9.8 \times (64.9 - 6.1)$$
$$= \boxed{432\,000 \text{ J (3 s.f.)}} \text{ or } \boxed{432 \text{ kJ (3 s.f.)}}$$

- When you're working out the G.P.E. of a body, the value of h you use should always be the **vertical** height above the 'base level'.

- So, for a particle moving on a **slope**, you'll have to use **trigonometry** to find the vertical distance travelled.

Example 2

A skateboarder and her board have a combined mass of 65 kg. She starts from rest and freewheels down a slope inclined at 15° to the horizontal. She travels 40 m down the line of greatest slope.

a) Find the gravitational potential energy lost by the skateboarder.

- You need to find h, the vertical distance she travels:

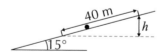

- Using trigonometry:
$$h = 40\sin 15°$$

- So, using G.P.E. = mgh:
$$\text{G.P.E. lost} = 65 \times 9.8 \times 40\sin 15°$$
$$= \boxed{6590 \text{ J (3 s.f.)}} \text{ or } \boxed{6.59 \text{ kJ (3 s.f.)}}$$

b) She reaches the bottom of the incline and starts to freewheel up a different slope, inclined at an angle θ to the horizontal. After travelling 5 m up the slope she has gained 2 kJ of G.P.E. Find θ.

- Using G.P.E. = mgh:

  $2000 = 65 \times 9.8 \times 5\sin\theta$

  $\sin\theta = 0.627...$

  $\Rightarrow \theta = \boxed{38.9° \text{ (3 s.f.)}}$

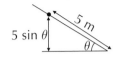

5 sin θ

Tip: Don't forget to change the energy in kJ to J first.

Exercise 2.3

Q1 A cat of mass 3.7 kg jumps onto a chair of height 41 cm and from there onto a table of height 73 cm. Find the gravitational potential energy gained by the cat in jumping from the chair to the table.

Q2 A fly loses 7.2×10^{-5} J of gravitational potential energy dropping from a height of 1.63 m to a height of 1.02 m. Find the fly's mass.

Q3 A rocket of mass 3039 tonnes leaves the ground and travels vertically upwards. At its highest point, it has 5×10^{12} J of gravitational potential energy. Find, to the nearest km, the maximum height reached by the rocket. You may assume that the rocket's mass remains constant, and that g remains constant at 9.8 ms^{-2}.

Q4 A postman pushes a trolley of mass 20 kg a distance of 3.7 m up a slope inclined at an angle θ to the horizontal, where $\theta = \sin^{-1}\left(\frac{1}{8}\right)$. Find the gravitational potential energy gained by the trolley.

Q5

13°

240 m

A cable car travels 240 m, at an angle of 13° below the horizontal. It loses 1 MJ of gravitational potential energy. Find its mass.

Q6 A lump of snow of mass 0.6 kg slides 3 m down a roof inclined at θ to the horizontal. It loses 6.032 J of gravitational potential energy. Find θ.

Q7

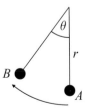

θ

r

B

A

A particle of mass m kg is fixed to the end of a light, inextensible string of length r, the other end of which is fixed in position. As part of its movement, it swings from its lowest point, A, through an angle θ, to the point B. Find an expression for the particle's gain in gravitational potential energy in moving from A to B.

Q7 Hint: Use trigonometry to find the change in height of the particle.

3. The Work-Energy Principle

Learning Objectives:

- Be able to find a body's mechanical energy.
- Be able to solve problems using the principle of conservation of mechanical energy.
- Be able to solve problems using the work-energy principle.

In the last section you saw how the kinetic and gravitational potential energies of a body can change as it moves. The mechanical energy of a body is the sum of its kinetic and gravitational potential energies.

As work done is a transfer of energy, you'll see in this section the effect that doing work on a body can have on its mechanical energy.

The principle of conservation of mechanical energy

Mechanical energy

The **mechanical energy** of a body is the sum of its **kinetic** and **gravitational potential** energies:

> Total Mechanical Energy =
> Kinetic Energy + Gravitational Potential Energy

Tip: Strictly speaking, mechanical energy also includes elastic potential energy — you'll find out plenty more about this on pages 95-102, but you can ignore it in the calculations on the next few pages.

Example

A paper plane weighs 20 g. At the highest point in its flight it has a mechanical energy of 0.6 J and is 2.8 m above the ground. Find its speed at this point in the flight.

- Mechanical energy = Kinetic energy + Gravitational potential energy

$$= \tfrac{1}{2}mv^2 + mgh$$

- Substituting in the values from the question:

$$0.6 = (\tfrac{1}{2} \times 0.02 \times v^2) + (0.02 \times 9.8 \times 2.8)$$
$$0.6 = 0.01v^2 + 0.5488$$
$$v^2 = 5.12$$
$$\Rightarrow v = 2.26 \text{ ms}^{-1} \text{ (3 s.f.)}$$

The principle of conservation of mechanical energy

- The principle of conservation of mechanical energy says that:

> If there is **no resultant external force** acting on a body, the **total** mechanical energy of the body will remain **constant**.

An **external force** is any force other than the body's **weight**. So this includes things like friction, air resistance, tension in a rope, etc.

- This means that the **sum** of a body's gravitational potential and kinetic energies **remains the same** throughout the body's motion.

- So a **decrease** in **gravitational potential energy** will mean an **increase** in **kinetic energy** of the **same amount**.

Example 1

A BASE jumper of mass 88 kg jumps from a ledge on a building and falls vertically downwards. When he is 150 m above the ground, his velocity is 6 ms⁻¹. When he is 60 m above the ground, he releases his parachute.

a) Find the kinetic energy of the jumper when he is 150 m above the ground.

Initial K.E. $= \frac{1}{2}mu^2$

$\qquad = \frac{1}{2} \times 88 \times 6^2 = \boxed{1584 \text{ J}}$

b) Use the principle of conservation of mechanical energy to find the jumper's kinetic energy and speed at the point where he releases his parachute.

- Applying the principle of conservation of mechanical energy:
  Increase in K.E. = Decrease in G.P.E.

  Decrease in G.P.E. $= mgh$

  $\qquad = 88 \times 9.8 \times (150 - 60)$

  $\qquad = 77\ 616 \text{ J}$

Tip: The principle states that the total mechanical energy is conserved, so any loss in gravitational potential energy must result in an equal gain in kinetic energy.

- So, at the point where he opens his parachute, he has 77 616 J more K.E. than he had at a height of 150 m. So:

  K.E. when parachute released = K.E. at 150 m + Decrease in G.P.E.

  $\qquad = 1584 + 77\ 616 = 79\ 200 \text{ J} = \boxed{79.2 \text{ kJ}}$

- Using K.E. $= \frac{1}{2}mv^2$ to find the speed at this point:

  $79\ 200 = \frac{1}{2} \times 88 \times v^2$

  $v = \sqrt{\dfrac{79\ 200}{\frac{1}{2} \times 88}} = \boxed{42.4 \text{ ms}^{-1} \text{ (3 s.f.)}}$

c) State one assumption you have made in modelling this situation.

The only force acting on the jumper is his weight
(i.e. there's no air resistance or any other external forces).

Tip: if you don't make this assumption, then you can't use the principle of conservation of mechanical energy.

Example 2

A package is projected up a smooth plane inclined at an angle of 4° to the horizontal. At the bottom of the incline it has a speed of 5 ms⁻¹. How far up the plane will it travel before instantaneously coming to rest?

- When the package comes to rest, it will have no kinetic energy.
- By the principle of conservation of mechanical energy, assuming that there are no external forces acting on the package, all of the package's kinetic energy at the bottom of the incline will have been converted to gravitational potential energy at the point where it comes to rest.

  i.e. Initial K.E. = Final G.P.E.

  $\Rightarrow \frac{1}{2}mu^2 = mgh$

- Cancelling m from both sides and substituting in the values from the question:

$$\frac{1}{2} \times 5^2 = 9.8 \times h$$
$$12.5 = 9.8h$$
$$\Rightarrow h = 1.275... \text{ m}$$

- h is the vertical height travelled, but you need to find the distance travelled **up the slope**. Call this x.

- Using trigonometry:

$$\sin 4° = \frac{h}{x}$$
$$\Rightarrow x = 1.275... \div \sin 4° = 18.3 \text{ m (3 s.f.)}$$

Exercise 3.1

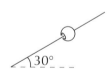

Hint: Throughout this exercise, you may assume that there are no external forces acting.

Q1 At its highest point, a carriage of a roller coaster has 70 560 J of mechanical energy. At its lowest point, it has 52 920 J of kinetic energy. Find the carriage's gravitational potential energy at its lowest point.

Q2 A tennis ball of mass 57 g is dropped from a height of 1.13 m. Find:
  a) the total mechanical energy of the ball immediately before it is dropped,
  b) the ball's speed at the instant it hits the ground.

Q3 An object is dropped and falls freely under gravity. It hits the ground with speed 11 ms⁻¹.
Find the height from which the object was dropped.

Q4

Q4 Hint: Watch out for units here:
1 J = 1000 mJ.

A bead is threaded on a smooth, straight wire. The wire is held at an angle of 30° above the horizontal, as shown. The bead is flicked upwards. It travels a distance of 6 cm along the wire and loses 1.47 mJ of kinetic energy. Find the mass of the bead.

Q5 A projectile of mass 50 g is launched vertically upwards from ground level and moves freely under gravity. When it is 52 m above the ground, the projectile is moving upwards at a speed of 10.1 ms⁻¹. Find:
  a) the total mechanical energy of the projectile at this point,
  b) the maximum height the projectile reaches,
  c) the speed of projection of the projectile.

Q6

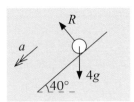

A particle of mass 4 kg slides 7 m down a smooth plane inclined at an angle of 40° to the horizontal. Its initial velocity is 3 ms⁻¹. Find:

a) the change in the particle's gravitational potential energy,

b) the particle's final velocity.

Q7 A body is released from rest at the top of a smooth ramp inclined at an angle of 19° to the horizontal. It slides down the ramp and reaches the bottom with speed 4.5 ms⁻¹.

Find the length of the sloped surface of the ramp.

Q8 A particle of mass 13 kg is fired up a smooth plane inclined at 25° to the horizontal. Its initial speed is 16 ms⁻¹. Find:

a) the distance the particle travels up the plane before it first comes to rest,

b) the distance the particle has travelled up the plane when it is travelling with speed 10 ms⁻¹.

The work-energy principle

- As you saw on pages 86-88, if there is **no resultant external force acting** on a body, then the **total mechanical energy** of the body remains **constant**.

- However, if there **is a resultant external force acting** on a body, then work is done and the total mechanical energy of the body will **change**.

- This is the **work-energy principle**:

> The **work done** on a body by external forces is equal to the **change** in the **total mechanical energy** of that body.

- In M2, the 'external force' will usually be a **resistive force**, such as **friction**. Remember — talking about a resistive force doing work **on** a body is really just another way of saying that work is being done **against** the resistive force.

- If the **only** external forces acting on the body are **resistive forces**, then **doing work against** these resistive forces will cause the overall mechanical energy of the body to **decrease**.

- In this case, the best way to think of the work-energy principle is:

Initial Mechanical Energy of a body		Final Mechanical Energy of the body		Work Done against resistive forces
	−		=	

Tip: Doing work on a body will always cause a change in the body's K.E. — no matter the direction of movement. If some (or all) of the work is done in moving the body vertically (i.e. if work is done by or against gravity), then there will also be a change in the body's G.P.E.

Example 1

A particle of mass 1.5 kg slides down a rough plane inclined at an angle of 40° to the horizontal. The particle passes through point A with speed 7.5 ms⁻¹ and point B with speed 6.5 ms⁻¹. The distance AB is 6.8 m.

Find the coefficient of friction between the plane and the particle.

Tip: The 'base level' is the point where the particle has no G.P.E.

- Take B as the 'base level' — i.e. the point where the particle's height is measured from.

- First, you need to find the particle's initial mechanical energy — i.e. its mechanical energy at A:

    Initial Mechanical Energy = Initial K.E. + Initial G.P.E.

    $= \frac{1}{2}mu^2 + mgh_{initial}$

    $= (\frac{1}{2} \times 1.5 \times 7.5^2) + (1.5 \times 9.8 \times 6.8\sin 40°)$

    $= 106.440... \text{ J}$

- Next, find the particle's final mechanical energy — i.e. its mechanical energy at B:

    Final Mechanical Energy = Final K.E. + Final G.P.E.

    $= \frac{1}{2}mv^2 + mgh_{final}$

    $= (\frac{1}{2} \times 1.5 \times 6.5^2) + (1.5 \times 9.8 \times 0)$

    $= 31.6875 \text{ J}$

- Now, using the work-energy principle:

Tip: The only external force doing work on the particle is the frictional force.

$$\begin{matrix} \text{Initial Mechanical} \\ \text{Energy} \end{matrix} - \begin{matrix} \text{Final Mechanical} \\ \text{Energy} \end{matrix} = \begin{matrix} \text{Work done} \\ \text{against friction} \end{matrix}$$

$\Rightarrow 106.440... - 31.6875 = 74.753... \text{ J}$

- So the work done against friction is 74.753... J.

- Now, using 'Work done = Fs' to find the magnitude of F, the frictional force acting on the particle:

    $74.753... = F \times 6.8$

    $\Rightarrow F = 10.993... \text{ N}$

- Finally, resolving perpendicular to the plane and using $F = \mu R$:

    $10.993... = \mu \times 1.5g\cos 40°$

    $\Rightarrow \mu = 0.98 \text{ (2 d.p.)}$

Example 2

A particle of mass 3 kg is projected up a rough plane inclined at an angle θ to the horizontal, where $\tan\theta = \frac{5}{12}$. The particle moves through point A with speed 11 ms⁻¹. The particle continues to move up the line of greatest slope and comes to rest at point B before sliding back down the plane. The coefficient of friction between the particle and the slope is $\frac{1}{3}$.

a) Use the work-energy principle to find the distance AB.

- Take A as the base level. Let the distance AB be x.

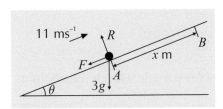

Tip: You're told that $\tan\theta = \frac{5}{12}$, so using Pythagoras' theorem and trigonometry you can work out that $\sin\theta = \frac{5}{13}$ and $\cos\theta = \frac{12}{13}$.

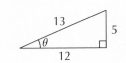

- First find the particle's initial mechanical energy — i.e. its mechanical energy at A:

  Initial Mechanical Energy = Initial K.E. + Initial G.P.E.

  $= \frac{1}{2}mu^2 + mgh_{initial}$

  $= (\frac{1}{2} \times 3 \times 11^2) + (3 \times g \times 0) = \boxed{181.5 \text{ J}}$

- Next, find the particle's final mechanical energy — i.e. its mechanical energy at B:

  Final Mechanical Energy = Final K.E. + Final G.P.E.

  $= \frac{1}{2}mv^2 + mgh_{final}$

  $= (\frac{1}{2} \times 3 \times 0^2) + (3 \times g \times x\sin\theta)$

  $= 3gx \times \frac{5}{13} = \boxed{\frac{15gx}{13}} \text{ J}$

Tip: $v = 0$ as the particle is at rest at B.

- Now, using the work-energy principle:

  $$\begin{array}{ccc} \text{Initial Mechanical} & \text{Final Mechanical} & \text{Work done} \\ \text{Energy} & - \quad \text{Energy} & = \quad \text{against friction} \end{array}$$

  $\Rightarrow \boxed{181.5 - \frac{15gx}{13}} = \boxed{\begin{array}{c}\text{Work done} \\ \text{against friction}\end{array}}$ — call this **equation 1**

- To find x, you need to find the work done against friction.

- Resolving perpendicular to the plane:

  $R = 3g\cos\theta = 3g \times \frac{12}{13} = \boxed{\frac{36g}{13}} \text{ N}$

- So, using $F = \mu R$:

  $F = \frac{1}{3} \times \frac{36g}{13} = \boxed{\frac{12g}{13}} \text{ N}$

- Now, using 'Work done = Fs':

$$\text{Work done against friction} = \frac{12g}{13} \times x = \frac{12gx}{13} \text{ J} \quad \text{— call this \textbf{equation 2}}$$

- So, using the work-energy principle, substitute **equation 2** into **equation 1**:

$$181.5 - \frac{15gx}{13} = \frac{12gx}{13}$$

$$181.5 = \frac{27gx}{13}$$

$$\Rightarrow x = \frac{181.5 \times 13}{27g} = 8.917...$$

$$= 8.92 \text{ m (3 s.f.)}$$

b) **Find the speed of the particle when it returns to A.**

- From part a), the particle's initial mechanical energy (i.e. its mechanical energy the first time it's at A) is 181.5 J.

- The particle's final mechanical energy (i.e. its mechanical energy the second time it's at A) is given by:

$$\text{Final Mechanical Energy} = \text{Final K.E.} + \text{Final G.P.E.}$$

$$= \frac{1}{2}mv^2 + mgh_{\text{final}}$$

$$= \left(\frac{1}{2} \times 3 \times v^2\right) + (3 \times g \times 0)$$

$$= \frac{3v^2}{2} \text{ J}$$

- The work done against friction as the particle moves from A to B and back to A again is given by:

$$\text{Work done} = Fs$$

$$= \frac{12g}{13} \times 2x$$

$$= \frac{12g}{13} \times 2(8.917...)$$

$$= 161.333... \text{ J}$$

Tip: s, the distance travelled by the particle, is $2x$ m, because it moves x m from A to B, then x m back to A again, and friction always acts in the same direction relative to motion (i.e. to oppose motion or likely motion).

- So, using the work-energy principle:

$$\text{Initial Mechanical Energy} - \text{Final Mechanical Energy} = \text{Work done against friction}$$

$$\Rightarrow 181.5 - \frac{3v^2}{2} = 161.333...$$

$$\frac{3v^2}{2} = 20.166...$$

$$v^2 = 13.444...$$

$$\Rightarrow v = 3.67 \text{ ms}^{-1} \text{ (3 s.f.)}$$

Exercise 3.2

Q1

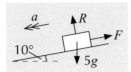

A block of mass 5 kg is released from rest and slides down a
rough ramp inclined at an angle of 10° to the horizontal.
After sliding 12 m down the ramp, the block has speed 3.5 ms^{-1}.
Find the work done against friction as the block slides down the ramp.

Q2

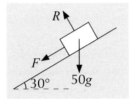

A body of mass 50 kg is projected up a rough slope inclined at an
angle of 30° to the horizontal. The body's initial speed is 8 ms^{-1}.
After travelling 3.4 m up the slope, the body's speed is 1.5 ms^{-1}.

a) Find the work done against friction during this time.

b) Find the magnitude of the frictional force
   between the body and the slope.

Q3 A body of mass 7.9 kg is released from rest at the top of a slide
inclined at an angle of 45° to the horizontal. The body accelerates
down the rough surface of the slide, reaching a speed of 6 ms^{-1} after
it has travelled a distance of 5 m. Find:

a) the work done against friction during this time,

b) the coefficient of friction between the body and the slide's surface.

Q4

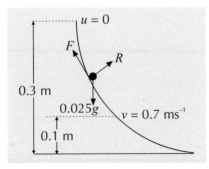

An object of mass 25 g is placed on a curved surface. It starts from
rest a height of 0.3 m above the ground and slides down a rough
track which follows an arc of a circle. When the object is a height of
0.1 m above the ground, its speed is 0.7 ms^{-1}.

Find the work done against friction during this time.

Q5   A particle of mass 9 kg is projected vertically upwards from ground level with speed 14 ms⁻¹. The particle reaches a maximum height of 9 m above the ground, then begins to fall back down again. Throughout its motion, the particle experiences a constant resistive force, F, acting in the opposite direction to the particle's motion.

a) Find the work done by the resistive force from the time that the particle is projected to the time that it reaches its maximum height.

b) Find the particle's speed as it lands back on the ground.

Q6   An object of mass 5.5 kg is projected with speed 6.25 ms⁻¹ up a rough plane inclined at an angle of 17° to the horizontal. The coefficient of friction between the object and the plane is 0.22.

a) Find the distance that the object travels up the plane before it comes to rest.

b) The object then slides down the plane. Find the object's speed as it passes back through its initial point of projection.

Q7

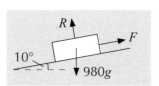

A vehicle of mass 980 kg is travelling down a rough road inclined at an angle of 10° to the horizontal. The driver stops accelerating, so that the only external force acting on the vehicle is the frictional force between the vehicle and the road. The vehicle passes through point A with speed U ms⁻¹, and then through point B with speed 10 ms⁻¹. The coefficient of friction between the vehicle and the road is 0.32, and the distance between the points A and B is 65 m.

Find the value of U.

4. Elastic Potential Energy

This section is all about elasticity. When an elastic body is stretched or compressed, elastic potential energy (E.P.E.) is stored in the body, and the body exerts a force to try to return to its original length.

Hooke's law

- An **elastic string** is a string which, when **stretched** and released, will return to its **initial length**. If you apply a **force** to **stretch** an elastic string, then **tension** in the string will act to try and return the string to its initial length.

  Hooke's law is a formula for finding the magnitude of this **tension**:

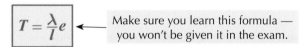

  $$T = \frac{\lambda}{l}e \qquad \longleftarrow \begin{array}{l}\text{Make sure you learn this formula —}\\ \text{you won't be given it in the exam.}\end{array}$$

  - T is the magnitude of the **tension** in the string (or equivalently, the magnitude of the **force** required to keep the string **stretched**).

  - l is the **length** of the string when it is **not being stretched** — it is called the **natural length** of the string.

  - e is the distance the string has been stretched — it is usually referred to as the **extension** of the string.

  - λ is the **modulus of elasticity** of the string. This is a measure of how easily the string can be stretched, assuming that it will return to its **original shape** afterwards. The greater the value of λ, the greater the force needed to stretch the string. If T is measured in newtons, N, then λ will also be measured in newtons.

- Hooke's law can also be used to find the force required to **stretch** or **compress** a **spring** by a distance e. For a **compressed spring**, T is equal to the **thrust** the spring exerts to try to return to its natural length.

Learning Objectives:

- Know and be able to use Hooke's law.
- Be able to find the work done by a variable force.
- Be able to derive and use the formula for finding the elastic potential energy stored in a stretched or compressed elastic body.
- Be able to solve energy problems involving stretched or compressed elastic bodies.

Tip: Because $\frac{\lambda}{l}$ is a constant, Hooke's law says that the force required to stretch the string is proportional to the length it is being extended. So, to double the length of extension, you need to double the force applied.

Examples

a) **A wooden block is suspended in equilibrium from an elastic string, as shown. The string is extended from its natural length of 5 m to a length of 8 m. Given that the modulus of elasticity of the string is 30 N, find the mass of the block.**

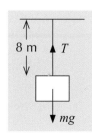

- Use Hooke's law to find the tension in the string:

$$T = \frac{\lambda}{l}e = \frac{30}{5} \times (8 - 5)$$
$$= 6 \times 3 = 18\ \text{N}$$

- Now, resolving vertically, taking up as positive and using $F_{net} = ma$:

$$T - mg = m \times 0$$
$$\Rightarrow m = 18 \div 9.8$$
$$= \boxed{1.84\ \text{kg (3 s.f.)}}$$

Tip: Remember that e is the length that the string has been extended (i.e. the difference between its natural length and its new length).

**b) A force of magnitude 11 N compresses a spring to a length of 0.8 m.
Given that the modulus of elasticity of the spring is 16 N, find the
natural length of the spring.**

- Using Hooke's law, $T = \frac{\lambda}{l}e$:

$$11 = \frac{16}{l} \times (l - 0.8)$$

$$11 = 16 - \frac{12.8}{l}$$

$$\frac{12.8}{l} = 5$$

$$\Rightarrow l = 12.8 \div 5 = \boxed{2.56 \text{ m}}$$

Tip: The formula works just the same when a spring is being compressed. The only difference is that e is now the distance the spring has been compressed, rather than the length it has been extended.

Exercise 4.1

Q1 Find the magnitude of the tension in each of the following springs:
   a) a spring with modulus of elasticity 6 N and natural length 2 m is stretched by 50 cm,
   b) a spring with modulus of elasticity 10 N is stretched from its natural length of 4 m to a length of 5 m,
   c) a spring with modulus of elasticity 25 N is stretched to double its natural length.

Q2 Find the magnitude of the force required to compress a spring of natural length 5 m and modulus of elasticity 30 N to a length of 3 m.

Q3 An elastic string is stretched from its natural length of 80 cm to a length of 1 m. The tension in the string has magnitude 12 N. Find the modulus of elasticity of the string.

Q4 A spring has modulus of elasticity 40 N. Find the magnitude of the force needed to compress the spring to half its natural length.

Q5 An elastic string of natural length 2 m and modulus of elasticity 49 N is attached at one end to a horizontal ceiling. An object of mass 3 kg is attached to the other end of the string and hangs in equilibrium with the string vertical. Find:
   a) the magnitude of the tension in the string,
   b) the distance the string is extended by the object.

Q6 A particle of mass 3.2 kg is attached to one end of an elastic string, the other end of which is fixed in place. The particle hangs in equilibrium with the string vertical. The string's modulus of elasticity is 38 N. The particle extends the string's length to 6 m. Find the natural length of the string.

Q7 A spring of natural length 1.2 m and modulus of elasticity 35 N is placed inside a smooth vertical tube. A particle of mass m kg is placed on top of the spring, compressing it to a length of 0.9 m. Find the value of m.

Elastic potential energy

When an elastic string is **stretched**, the **work done** in stretching it is converted into **elastic potential energy** (**E.P.E.**). This is another form of **mechanical energy**, which is stored in the string.

If you want to find the work done, you can't use the standard 'work done = force × distance' formula, as this only works for **constant forces**.

The force required to stretch an elastic string isn't constant — it's a **variable force** which is proportional to the **distance** the string is stretched. This means that the **further** you try to stretch the string, the **more difficult** it becomes to do so.

For a force which **varies** with **distance**, **integrating** the **force**, F, with respect to **distance**, x, gives you the work done by the force.

$$W = \int F \, dx$$

You can use this to derive a **formula** for **elastic potential energy**:

Tip: You can see this from Hooke's law — the greater the value of e, the greater the value of T.

Tip: You could be asked to derive the formula for E.P.E. in your exam — so make sure you learn how to do it.

The formula for elastic potential energy

From **Hooke's law**, the **tension** in an **elastic string** extended a distance x **m** is: $T = \frac{\lambda}{l}x$

So the **work done against tension** is given by:

$$W = \int_0^e T \, dx = \int_0^e \frac{\lambda}{l}x \, dx$$

$$= \left[\frac{\lambda}{2l}x^2\right]_0^e$$

$$= \frac{\lambda}{2l}e^2$$

The work done against tension is converted into **elastic potential energy**, so:

$$\text{E.P.E.} = \frac{\lambda}{2l}e^2 \quad \longleftarrow \quad \text{You need to learn this formula.}$$

Tip: The limits of the integral are chosen to be [0, e] rather than [0, x] to avoid using x, the variable you're integrating with respect to, as a limit. Another variable, e, is picked to represent the length of extension.

Tip: This formula also works for the E.P.E. stored in a compressed spring.

Elastic potential energy and mechanical energy

The total **mechanical energy** of a system also includes elastic potential energy, so the equation from page 86 becomes:

$$\text{Mechanical Energy} = \text{Kinetic Energy} + \text{Gravitational Potential Energy} + \text{Elastic Potential Energy}$$

You can still use the **principle of conservation of mechanical energy** and the **work-energy principle** for systems involving elastic bodies.

Like the **weight** of a body, the **tension** in a stretched string is **not** considered to be an **external force**. So, as work done **against gravity** is equivalent to a change in **gravitational potential energy**, the work done **against tension** in a string is equivalent to the change in **elastic potential energy** in that string.

This means that if the only forces acting in a system are **weight** and **elastic tension**, you can use the **principle of conservation of mechanical energy**.

However, if there are any **external forces**, such as **friction**, acting on a system, you'll have to use the **work-energy principle**.

Tip: Take a look back at pages 86-92 for a reminder about the principle of conservation of mechanical energy and the work-energy principle.

Example 1

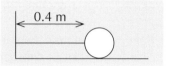

0.4 m

A particle of mass 1.5 kg is attached to one end of a horizontal spring, the other end of which is fixed to a vertical wall. The particle is pushed towards the wall and then held in place so that the spring is compressed from its natural length of 0.85 m to a length of 0.4 m, as shown. The modulus of elasticity of the spring is 24 N.

a) **Find the elastic potential energy stored in the spring.**

- Use the formula for elastic potential energy:

$$\text{E.P.E.} = \frac{\lambda}{2l}e^2 = \frac{24}{2 \times 0.85} \times (0.85 - 0.4)^2$$

$$= 2.858... = \boxed{2.86 \text{ J (3 s.f.)}}$$

b) **The particle is released from rest. Given that the coefficient of friction between the particle and the horizontal ground is 0.25, find the particle's speed when the spring first returns to its natural length.**

- Use the work-energy principle:

$$\begin{matrix} \text{Initial Mechanical} \\ \text{Energy} \end{matrix} - \begin{matrix} \text{Final Mechanical} \\ \text{Energy} \end{matrix} = \begin{matrix} \text{Work done} \\ \text{against friction} \end{matrix}$$

Tip: Friction is the only external force acting on the particle.

- The particle is initially at rest, so the initial mechanical energy of the system is equal to the elastic potential energy stored in the spring — i.e. Initial mechanical energy = 2.858... J

- When the spring has returned to its natural length, it has no elastic potential energy, so the total mechanical energy of the system is equal to the particle's kinetic energy:

Tip: There is no vertical motion, so there is no change in G.P.E. So you only need to worry about K.E. and E.P.E.

$$\text{Final mechanical energy} = \frac{1}{2}mv^2 = \frac{1}{2} \times 1.5 \times v^2$$

$$= 0.75v^2 \text{ J}$$

- The work done against friction as the particle moves is given by:

$$\text{Work done} = \text{Force} \times \text{Distance}$$
$$= \mu R \times (0.85 - 0.4)$$
$$= 0.25 \times 1.5g \times 0.45 = 1.65375 \text{ J}$$

- So, using the work-energy principle:

$$2.858... - 0.75v^2 = 1.65375$$
$$v^2 = 1.606...$$
$$\Rightarrow \boxed{v = 1.27 \text{ ms}^{-1} \text{ (3 s.f.)}}$$

Example 2

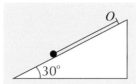

One end of a light elastic string is attached at point O to a smooth plane inclined at an angle of 30° to the horizontal, as shown.
The other end of the string is attached to a particle of mass 8 kg.
The string has a natural length of 1 m and modulus of elasticity 40 N.
The particle is released from rest at O and slides down the slope.

a) **Find the length of the string when the particle's acceleration is zero.**

- Resolving parallel to the slope, taking up the slope as positive and using $F_{net} = ma$:

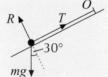

$$T - mg\sin 30° = 8 \times 0$$
$$\Rightarrow T = 8 \times 9.8 \times \sin 30°$$
$$= 39.2 \text{ N}$$

- Now using Hooke's law to find the length of extension at this point:

$$T = \frac{\lambda}{l}e$$
$$\Rightarrow e = \frac{Tl}{\lambda} = \frac{39.2 \times 1}{40}$$
$$= 0.98 \text{ m}$$

- So the length of the string at this point is $l + e = 1 + 0.98 = \boxed{1.98 \text{ m}}$

b) **The string extends to a total length of x m before the particle first comes to rest. Show that $x^2 - 3.96x + 1 = 0$.**

- The particle starts and ends at rest, so the change in the particle's kinetic energy is zero.

- So, by the principle of conservation of mechanical energy:

Loss in G.P.E. = Gain in E.P.E.

Loss in G.P.E. $= mgh = 8 \times 9.8 \times x\sin 30°$
$$= 39.2x$$

Gain in E.P.E. $= \frac{\lambda}{2l}e^2 = \frac{40}{2 \times 1} \times (x - 1)^2$
$$= 20(x - 1)^2$$

So: $20(x - 1)^2 = 39.2x$
$$\Rightarrow x^2 - 2x + 1 = 1.96x$$
$$\Rightarrow \boxed{x^2 - 3.96x + 1 = 0} \text{ — as required.}$$

Tip: In this example, there are no external forces acting, so you can use the principle of conservation of mechanical energy.

Tip: The total length of the extended string is x m, and its natural length is 1 m, so the length of extension is $(x - 1)$ m.

c) Hence find the distance from O at which the particle first comes to rest.

- Solving $x^2 - 3.96x + 1 = 0$ using the quadratic formula:

$$x = \frac{3.96 \pm \sqrt{(-3.96)^2 - (4 \times 1 \times 1)}}{2 \times 1}$$

$$\Rightarrow x = 3.688... \text{ or } x = 0.271...$$

- 0.271 can be ignored as you know that the string is extended, so x must be greater than 1 (the natural length of the string).

- So the particle is first stationary when it is $\boxed{3.69 \text{ m (3 s.f.)}}$ from O.

The particle is held at point A, 3 m down the slope from O, where it is released from rest and moves up the slope with speed v ms^{-1}.

d) Show that, while the string is taut, the particle's motion satisfies the equation $v^2 = -5y^2 + 19.8y - 14.4$, where y is the particle's distance from O down the slope.

Tip: 'Taut' means that the string is stretched to some length greater than its natural length, so there is tension in the string.

- Take A as the base level. At this point, the particle has no K.E. and no G.P.E. So the total mechanical energy of the system at A is equal to the elastic potential energy stored in the string:

$$\text{E.P.E.} = \frac{\lambda}{2l}e^2 = \frac{40}{2 \times 1} \times (3 - 1)^2$$

$$= 80 \text{ J}$$

- By the principle of conservation of mechanical energy, during the motion of the particle after release from A:

The value of e is now $(y - 1)$ m, not 2 m as it was in the previous step.

$$\frac{\lambda}{2l}e^2 + mgh + \frac{1}{2}mv^2 = 80$$

$$\frac{40}{2 \times 1}(y - 1)^2 + (8 \times 9.8 \times (3 - y)\sin 30°) + (\frac{1}{2} \times 8 \times v^2) = 80$$

$$20(y - 1)^2 + 39.2(3 - y) + 4v^2 = 80$$

$$20y^2 - 40y + 20 + 117.6 - 39.2y + 4v^2 = 80$$

$$4v^2 = -20y^2 + 79.2y - 57.6$$

$$\Rightarrow \boxed{v^2 = -5y^2 + 19.8y - 14.4} \text{ — as required.}$$

Tip: $(3 - y)\sin 30°$ is the vertical distance between A (3 m from O) and the particle's position (y m from O).

e) Find the speed of the particle at the point where the string becomes slack.

Tip: 'Slack' means that the string is not being stretched to a length greater than its natural length, so there is no tension in the string.

- The string becomes slack when it is no longer stretched, i.e. when it is at its natural length.
- So, substituting $y = 1$ into the equation from part d) and solving for v:

$$v^2 = -5 + 19.8 - 14.4 = 0.4$$

$$\Rightarrow \boxed{v = 0.632 \text{ ms}^{-1} \text{ (3 s.f.)}}$$

Q1 Find the elastic potential energy stored in each of the following:
   a) a spring of natural length 5 m and modulus
      of elasticity 10 N stretched by 1 m,
   b) an elastic string with modulus of elasticity 24 N stretched
      from its natural length of 6 m to a length of 8 m,
   c) a spring of natural length 1.5 m and modulus of
      elasticity 30 N compressed by 30 cm.

Q2 An elastic string of natural length 3 m and modulus of elasticity 20 N
   is stretched from a length of 3.6 m to a length of 4.5 m.
   Find the increase in the elastic potential energy stored in the string as
   a result of this stretch.

Q3 One end of an elastic string is fixed to a horizontal ceiling.
   A particle of mass 1 kg is attached to the other end of the string,
   extending the length of the string by 1 cm. The particle hangs in
   equilibrium with the string vertical. The particle is pulled down a
   further 2 cm and then released from rest. Find:
   a) the speed of the particle when the string
      becomes slack for the first time,

   b) the maximum height that the particle will reach
      above the point where it becomes slack.

Q3 Hint: First use
Hooke's law to find an
expression for λ in terms
of l.

Q4 One end of an elastic string of natural length 1.5 m and modulus
   of elasticity 98 N is fixed to a horizontal ceiling. The other end of
   the string is attached to a block of mass 2 kg. The block hangs in
   equilibrium with the string vertical.
   a) Find the string's extension when the block hangs in equilibrium.

   The block is pulled down a further 50 cm, then released from rest.
   b) Find the maximum height that the block reaches above the
      point from which it is released, assuming that the string
      becomes slack before the block reaches its maximum height.
   c) What height would the block reach above its point of release if,
      instead, it was attached to a spring with modulus of elasticity 98 N?

Q5

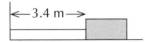

A body of mass m kg is attached to one end of an elastic string of
natural length 1.8 m. The other end of the string is fixed to a vertical
wall. The body is placed on a rough horizontal surface, and is pulled
away from the wall so that the string is horizontal and is stretched to
a length of 3.4 m, as shown. At this point, the tension in the string
has magnitude 40 N. The body is released from rest and moves
towards the wall. It strikes the wall with speed 2.5 ms⁻¹. Given that
the coefficient of friction between the body and the surface is 0.12,
find the value of m. You may assume that the string does not interfere
with the motion of the body once it has become slack.

Q6 An elastic rope of natural length 15 m and modulus of elasticity 60 N is attached at one end to a fixed point Q. The other end of the rope is attached to an object of mass 20 kg. The object is released from rest at Q and falls freely under gravity until the rope becomes taut, and then begins to stretch the rope vertically.

When the object is y m below Q, it is moving with speed v ms⁻¹.

a) Show that the object's motion when the rope is taut satisfies the equation $v^2 = -0.2y^2 + 25.6y - 45$.

b) Find the object's speed when the rope has been extended to double its natural length.

c) Find the extension of the rope when the object's speed is 4 ms⁻¹. You may assume that the rope does not snap or become deformed before this point.

Q6 c) Hint: The rope not becoming 'deformed' just means that it will still return to its natural length when the object is removed — i.e. the rope remains elastic.

Q7

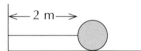

A spring of natural length 1.25 m and modulus of elasticity 32 N is fixed at one end to a vertical wall and at the other end to a particle of mass 0.2 kg. The particle is placed on rough horizontal ground, so that the spring is horizontal and stretched to a length of 2 m, as shown. The coefficient of friction between the particle and the ground is 0.3. The particle is released from rest. Find the speed of the particle when it first passes through the point A, 0.6 m from the wall.

Q8

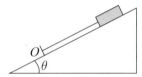

One end of a spring of natural length 8 m and modulus of elasticity 44 N is attached to a fixed point O, on a plane inclined at an angle θ to the horizontal, where $\sin\theta = \frac{3}{5}$.

The other end of the spring is attached to a block of mass 1.6 kg, which is placed up the plane from O, as shown. The block is pushed down the plane, so that the spring is compressed to a length of 1 m. The block is then released from rest and begins to move up the plane.

a) Assuming that the plane is smooth, find the speed of the block when the spring returns to its natural length.

b) Now assume that the plane is rough, and that the coefficient of friction between the block and the plane is 0.55. Find the speed of the block when the spring first returns to its natural length.

5. Power

So far in this chapter, you've learnt all about work done and how it relates to the transfer of energy from one form to another. This section is about the rate at which all this happens.

Learning Objectives:

- Be able to use the formula for power to find the rate at which a force does work on a body.
- Be able to solve problems involving variable resistive forces.

Power

- **Power** is a measure of the **rate** at which a force does **work** on a body:

$$\text{Power} = \frac{\text{Work Done}}{\text{Time}}$$

The unit for power is the watt (W), where 1 watt = 1 joule per second.

Using the formula 'Work Done = Force × Distance', this becomes

$\text{Power} = \frac{\text{Force} \times \text{Distance}}{\text{Time}}$, but as $\frac{\text{Distance}}{\text{Time}}$ is speed, you can then derive:

$$\text{Power} = \text{Force} \times \text{Speed}$$

- So for an engine generating a **driving force** of magnitude F N, moving a vehicle at a **speed** v ms^{-1}, the power of the engine in watts is given by $P = Fv$.

This is the version of the formula you'll end up using most of the time. But don't forget what power **means** — it's the **rate of doing work**.

Tip: You won't be given the power formula in the exam — so make sure you know it.

Examples

a) **A motor boat moves horizontally through water with speed 12 ms^{-1}. The driving force of the engine is 4250 N. Find the engine's power.**

$\text{Power} = Fv = 4250 \times 12$
$\qquad = 51\,000 \text{ W} = \boxed{51 \text{ kW}}$

b) **A car with a 95 kW engine is driven at its maximum speed on a straight horizontal race track. The car experiences a constant resistance to motion of 2375 N. Find the car's maximum speed.**

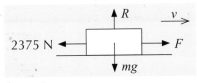

- The car is driven at its maximum speed, so there is no acceleration. So, resolving horizontally in the direction of motion gives:

$F_{net} = ma$
$F - 2375 = m \times 0$
$\Rightarrow F = 2375 \text{ N}$

- Now, using the formula for power:

$\text{Power} = Fv$
$95\,000 = 2375 \times v_{max}$
$\Rightarrow v_{max} = 40 \text{ ms}^{-1}$

Tip: Remember to change the units from kW to W in your calculations.

You can apply the same principles to situations where an object is moving on an **inclined plane**.

Example

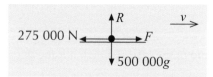

A train of mass 500 tonnes is travelling along a straight horizontal track with a constant speed of 20 ms⁻¹. The train experiences a constant resistance to motion of magnitude 275 000 N.

a) **Find the rate at which the train's engine is working. Give your answer in kW.**

- Resolving horizontally:

  $F - 275\ 000 = m \times 0$

  $\Rightarrow F = 275\ 000$ N

- Power = Fv

  $= 275\ 000 \times 20$

  $= 5\ 500\ 000$ W = 5500 kW

b) **The train now moves up a hill inclined at 2° to the horizontal. If the engine continues to work at the same rate and the magnitude of the non-gravitational resistance to motion remains the same, find the new constant speed of the train.**

- Draw a diagram to show what's going on:

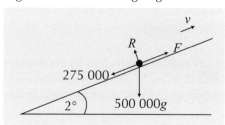

- Resolving parallel to the slope (taking up the slope as positive):

  $F - 275\ 000 - (500\ 000 \times 9.8 \times \sin 2°) = m \times 0$

  $\Rightarrow F = 275\ 000 + (500\ 000 \times 9.8 \times \sin 2°)$

  $= 446\ 007.5...$ N

- Now using Power = Fv:

  $5\ 500\ 000 = 446\ 007.5... \times v$

  $\Rightarrow v = 5\ 500\ 000 \div 446\ 007.5...$

  $= 12.3$ ms⁻¹ (3 s.f.)

Tip: The speed is constant, so $a = 0$ ms⁻².

Tip: The driving force and non-gravitational resistance to motion stay the same as in part a), but now you have to think about the effect of the train's weight.

If an object is moving with **constant acceleration**, you'll have to resolve in the direction of motion to find the **resultant force** acting on it, then use $F_{net} = ma$.

Because the velocity of the object will be **constantly changing**, you can only use the formula $P = Fv$ if you consider the object's motion at a particular **instant**, rather than considering its entire motion.

Example

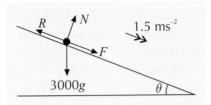

A tractor of mass 3000 kg is moving down a hill inclined at an angle of θ to the horizontal, where $\sin\theta = \frac{1}{24}$.

When the tractor is travelling at a speed of 8 ms^{-1}, its acceleration is 1.5 ms^{-2}, and its engine is working at a constant rate of 130 kW.

Find the magnitude of the resistance to motion, R, at the instant when the tractor is travelling at a speed of 8 ms^{-1}.

- First, use $P = Fv$ to find the driving force, F:

  $130\,000 = F \times 8$

  $\Rightarrow F = 16\,250$ N

- Now, resolving parallel to the slope, taking down the slope as positive, and using $F_{net} = ma$:

  $F + 3000g\sin\theta - R = 3000 \times 1.5$

  $16\,250 + (3000 \times 9.8 \times \frac{1}{24}) - R = 4500$

  $\Rightarrow R = 16\,250 + 1225 - 4500$

  $= 12\,975$ N

Tip: N has been used to denote the normal reaction force of the slope on the tractor, as R has been used to denote the resistance to motion.

Exercise 5.1

Q1 A model boat has a maximum speed of 1.8 ms^{-1} when moving horizontally through the water against a resistance to motion of magnitude 85 N. Find the power of its engine.

Q2 A car of mass 900 kg is driven along a straight horizontal road. It undergoes a constant acceleration and experiences a constant horizontal resistance to motion of magnitude 1140 N. The power generated by the engine when the car is moving at a speed of 11 ms^{-1} is 23.1 kW. Find the car's acceleration.

Q3 A van is towing a trailer along a straight horizontal road. The van and trailer experience horizontal resistances to motion of magnitude 1360 N and 1070 N respectively. The maximum power output of the van's engine is 95 kW. Find the maximum speed of the van and trailer on this road.

Q4 a) A motorbike and its rider have a combined mass of 250 kg. It travels along a straight, flat road at a constant speed of 32 ms^{-1}, with its engine working at a rate of 96 kW. Find R, the constant resistance to motion experienced by the motorbike.

   b) The motorbike moves onto a section of road that slopes upwards at an angle θ to the horizontal. The engine's power and the constant resistance to motion remain unchanged. The motorbike climbs the hill at a constant speed of 28 ms^{-1}. Find θ.

Q5 A man uses a rope to lift an object of weight 52 N through a vertical distance of 2.4 m in 11 s. The object moves at constant speed and experiences a constant resistance to motion of 4.2 N. Find the rate at which the man does work as he lifts the object.

Q6 A vehicle of mass 660 kg travels up a ramp inclined at an angle of 17° to the horizontal. Its engine is working at 16 kW. The vehicle experiences a constant non-gravitational resistance to motion of magnitude 140 N.

   a) Find the vehicle's maximum speed up the ramp.

   b) When the vehicle is travelling at its maximum speed, its engine cuts out. Assuming that the resistance to motion is unchanged, find the distance the vehicle will travel before first coming to rest.

Q7 A vehicle of mass 1230 kg travels up a slope inclined at an angle of 25° to the horizontal. It experiences a non-gravitational resistance to motion of magnitude 305 N. The vehicle decelerates at a rate of 0.28 ms^{-2}. Find the power output of the vehicle's engine when the vehicle is travelling at 8 ms^{-1}.

Q8

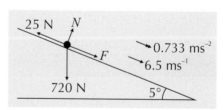

A cyclist and her cycle have a combined weight of 720 N. As she rides down a hill with a slope of 5° to the horizontal, her acceleration is 0.733 ms^{-2}. She experiences a constant resistance to motion of 25 N. Find her power when her speed is 6.5 ms^{-1}.

Variable resistive forces

There's a good chance you'll get a power question where a vehicle (or some other powered body) experiences a resistive force which **isn't constant**. Instead, the resistance will be dependent on the vehicle's **speed**. This is a more **realistic** model of resistive force — **resistance to motion** tends to **increase** as a vehicle's **speed increases**.

Like the examples on the previous pages, these questions require **resolving of forces** and the careful use of *F = ma*.

Tip: You've seen resistive forces that depend on velocity before — in the differential equations section in Chapter 2. Take a look back at pages 63-65 for a reminder.

Example 1

A van of mass 1500 kg moves up a road inclined at an angle of 5° to the horizontal. The van's engine works at a constant rate of 25 kW and the van experiences a resistive force of magnitude *kv* N, where *k* is a constant and *v* ms⁻¹ is the van's velocity.
At the point where the van has speed 8 ms⁻¹, its acceleration is 0.5 ms⁻².

a) **Show that *k* = 137 to 3 significant figures.**

- A diagram is always useful:

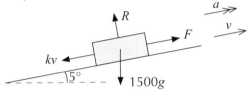

- Using $P = Fv$ to find F, the driving force of the van's engine:

$$F = \frac{P}{v} = \frac{25\,000}{8}$$

$$= 3125 \text{ N}$$

- Now resolving forces parallel to the slope, taking up the slope as positive, and substituting in the values you know:

$$F_{net} = ma$$

$$F - kv - 1500g\sin 5° = 1500a$$

$$3125 - 8k - (1500 \times 9.8 \times \sin 5°) = 1500 \times 0.5$$

$$\Rightarrow k = \tfrac{1}{8}(3125 - (1500 \times 9.8 \times \sin 5°) - (1500 \times 0.5))$$

$$= 137 \text{ (3 s.f.)} \quad \text{— as required.}$$

b) **Using *k* = 137, show that *U* ms⁻¹, the maximum speed of the van working at this power going up this road, satisfies the equation:**

$$U^2 + 9.35U - 182 = 0,$$

where the coefficients are given to 3 significant figures.

- Using $P = Tv$, the driving force, T, of the van's engine at speed U is:

$$T = \frac{P}{v} = \frac{25\,000}{U} \text{ N}$$

Tip: You've already used F to represent the driving force in part a), so it's a good idea to use a different variable (like T) here.

- Resolving forces parallel to the slope, taking up the slope as positive, and substituting in the values you know:

$$F_{net} = ma$$

$$\frac{25\,000}{U} - 137U - (1500 \times 9.8 \times \sin 5°) = 0$$

- Multiplying throughout by U:

$$25\,000 - 137U^2 - (1281.18...)U = 0$$

$$\Rightarrow 137U^2 + (1281.18...)U - 25\,000 = 0$$

$$\Rightarrow U^2 + (9.351...)U - 182.481... = 0$$

- So, to 3 significant figures:

$$U^2 + 9.35U - 182 = 0 \quad \text{— as required.}$$

Tip: The van is travelling at its maximum speed, so $a = 0$.

Example 2

A car of mass 1200 kg travels on a straight horizontal road. It experiences a resistive force of magnitude 30v N, where v ms^{-1} is the car's velocity. The maximum speed of the car on this road is 70 ms^{-1}.

a) Find the car's maximum power.

- When the car is travelling at its maximum speed, $a = 0$.
- Resolving horizontally, taking the direction of motion as positive:

$$F_{net} = ma$$

$$F - 30v = 1200 \times 0$$

$$\Rightarrow F = 30v$$

- Now using $P = Fv$:

$$P = 30v^2 = 30 \times 70^2$$

$$= 147 \text{ kW}$$

b) Find the car's maximum possible acceleration when its speed on this road is 40 ms^{-1}.

- Call the new driving force of the car T. Using $P = Tv$:

$$T = \frac{P}{v} = \frac{147\,000}{40}$$

$$= 3675 \text{ N}$$

Tip: Maximum acceleration will only be possible when the car's engine is working at maximum power.

- Resolving horizontally, taking the direction of motion as positive:

$$F_{net} = ma$$

$$3675 - 30v = 1200a$$

$$3675 - (30 \times 40) = 1200a$$

$$\Rightarrow a = 2.06 \text{ ms}^{-2} \text{ (3 s.f.)}$$

Q1   A car of mass 800 kg travels along a straight horizontal road. It experiences a resistance to motion of magnitude $22v$ N, where v ms^{-1} is the car's velocity. The maximum power output of the car's engine is 62 kW. Find the car's maximum speed on this road.

Q2   The maximum speed of a vehicle travelling along a straight horizontal road is 52 ms^{-1}. The resistance to motion experienced by the vehicle has magnitude $0.9v^2$ N, where v ms^{-1} is the vehicle's velocity. Find the maximum power output of the vehicle's engine.

Q3   A bus accelerates along a straight horizontal street against a resistive force of magnitude $89v$ N, where v ms^{-1} is the velocity of the bus. At the point where the bus is moving with speed 17 ms^{-1}, its acceleration is 1.05 ms^{-2} and the power generated by its engine is 200 kW. Find the mass of the bus.

Q4   A car of mass 600 kg accelerates at a rate of 2 ms^{-2} along a straight horizontal road. Its engine is generating a power output of 40 kW and the car experiences a resistance force of magnitude $25v$, where v ms^{-1} is the car's velocity.
   a) Show that the car's velocity satisfies the equation
       $v^2 + 48v - 1600 = 0$.
   b) Hence find the car's velocity.

Q5   A body of mass 1.2 tonnes is powered along a straight horizontal track against a resistance to motion of magnitude $1.3v^2$ N, where v ms^{-1} is the body's velocity. The maximum speed of the body along this track is 216 kmh^{-1}. Find:
   a) the maximum power of the body's engine,
   b) the maximum possible acceleration of the body when its velocity is 70 kmh^{-1}.

Q6   A vehicle of mass 1800 kg travels up a straight slope inclined at an angle of 10° to the horizontal. The vehicle experiences a resistive force of $80v$ N, where v ms^{-1} is its velocity. When the vehicle's acceleration is 0.8 ms^{-2}, its engine is working at a rate of 30 kW.
   a) Show that its speed, u ms^{-1}, satisfies the equation:
       $u^2 + 56.3u - 375 = 0$,
       with coefficients given to 3 significant figures.
   b) Hence find the value of u.

Review Exercise — Chapter 3

Q1 A crate is pushed across a smooth horizontal floor by a force of magnitude 250 N, acting in the direction of motion. Find the work done in pushing the crate a distance of 3 m.

Q2

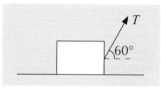

A roll-along cart is pulled along the ground a distance of 0.4 m by a cord with a tension force, T, acting at 60° to the horizontal. If the work done by the tension is 1.3 J, find T.

Q3 A crane lifts a concrete block 12 m vertically at constant speed. If the crane does 34 kJ of work against gravity, find the mass of the concrete block.

Q4 On the moon, an astronaut lifts a mass of 3 kg through a vertical height of 0.6 m, doing 2.92 J of work against gravity. Find an estimate of the acceleration due to gravity on the moon, g_{moon}. Give your answer correct to 3 significant figures.

Q5

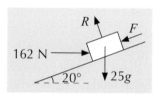

A 25 kg flight case is pushed 10 m up a ramp at an angle of 20° to the horizontal, by a force of magnitude 162 N acting horizontally. The coefficient of friction between the ramp and the case is 0.19. Find the work done on the case as it is pushed up the ramp.

Q6 A horse of mass 450 kg is galloping at a speed of 13 ms⁻¹. Find the horse's kinetic energy.

Q7 An ice skater of mass 65 kg sets off from rest. After travelling 40 m in a straight line across smooth horizontal ice, she has done 800 J of work. Find her speed at this point.

Q8 A supercar of mass 1000 kg moves along a straight horizontal test track. The resistance to motion has a constant magnitude of 590 N. To test the brakes, the driver accelerates to 100 ms⁻¹ and then applies a constant braking force of 8500 N.
a) Find the work done by the braking force in bringing the car to a stop.
b) Find the work done by the resistance to motion in bringing the car to a stop.
c) Show that the work done by the resultant force equals the change in kinetic energy.

Q9 A particle of mass 0.5 kg is projected upwards from ground level and reaches a maximum height of 150 m above the ground. Find the increase in its gravitational potential energy.

Q10 A jubilant cowboy throws his hat vertically upwards with a velocity of 5 ms⁻¹. Use the principle of conservation of mechanical energy to find the maximum height the hat reaches above the point of release.

Q11 A boy tries to score a goal in football. Unfortunately, when he shoots, the ball just passes over the top of the goal. The height of the goal is 1.94 m and the ball's mass is 0.4 kg. The boy's kick gives the ball an initial kinetic energy of 39.2 J. By modelling the ball as a particle, find its kinetic energy at the instant it passes over the top of the goal.

Q12 A particle of mass 15 kg is released from rest and slides down from the top of a rough ramp of length 9 m, inclined at an angle of 11° to the horizontal. It reaches the bottom of the ramp with speed 4.2 ms⁻¹. Find the work done against friction as the particle slides down the ramp.

Q13

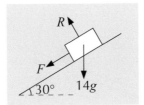

A body of mass 14 kg is projected up a rough slope inclined at an angle of 30° to the horizontal. The body's initial speed is 5.5 ms⁻¹.
After travelling 2.5 m up the slope, the body's speed is 0.4 ms⁻¹.

a) Find the work done against friction during this time.

b) Find the coefficient of friction between the body and the slope.

Q14 A spring of natural length 3 m is compressed so that its new length is 1.5 m. Given that the modulus of elasticity of the spring is 25 N, find:

a) the compression force in the spring,

b) the elastic potential energy stored in the spring.

Q15 One end of an elastic string is attached to a vertical wall. The other end of the string is attached to a particle of mass 3 kg, which is on a smooth horizontal floor. The natural length of the string is 2 m and its modulus of elasticity is 10 N. The string is stretched so that the particle is 8.4 m from the wall, with the string horizontal. The particle is released from rest. Assuming that the string doesn't interfere with the motion of the particle when it is slack, find:

a) the particle's speed when it is 4.2 m from the wall,

b) the particle's speed when it hits the wall.

Q16 A car's engine is working at a rate of 350 kW. The car moves with speed 44 ms⁻¹. Find the driving force of the engine.

Q17 A vehicle of mass 820 kg drives down a slope inclined at an angle of 5° to the horizontal. It accelerates at a rate of 0.75 ms⁻² and experiences a constant resistance to motion of magnitude 188 N. Find the power output of the vehicle's engine when its speed is 10 ms⁻¹.

Q18 A motorbike and its rider, of combined mass 295 kg, travel up a ramp inclined at an angle of 8° to the horizontal. The motorbike's engine works at a rate of 22 kW. The motorbike and rider experience a constant non-gravitational resistance to motion of magnitude 128 N. Find the motorbike's maximum speed up the ramp.

Q19 A cyclist and her bicycle travel along a straight, horizontal track with velocity v ms⁻¹. They experience a resistance of magnitude kv N, where k is a constant. The cyclist works at a rate of 240 W, and the bicycle can reach a maximum speed of 16 ms⁻¹ on this track. Find the value of k.

1

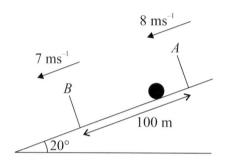

A man skis down a rough plane inclined at an angle of 20° to the horizontal.
The man and his skis have a combined mass of 90 kg. He passes through two gates,
A and B, which are 100 m apart. His speed at gate A is 8 ms⁻¹. At gate B, his speed
has decreased to 7 ms⁻¹. Find:

a) the decrease in the skier's total mechanical energy as he moves from
   gate A to gate B,

   (3 marks)

b) the coefficient of friction between the man's skis and the plane.
   You may assume that air resistance is negligible.

   (5 marks)

2   A car of mass 1000 kg experiences a resistive force of magnitude kv N, where k is a
    constant and v ms⁻¹ is the car's speed. The car travels up a slope inclined at an angle θ to
    the horizontal, where $\sin\theta = 0.1$. The power generated by the car is 20 kW and its speed up
    the slope remains constant at 10 ms⁻¹.

a)   Show that $k = 102$.

     (3 marks)

b)   The car's maximum power output is 50 kW.

     (i)   Show that, going up this slope, the car's maximum possible speed,
           u ms⁻¹, satisfies the equation:

           $$102u^2 + 980u - 50\,000 = 0.$$

           (4 marks)

     (ii) Hence find the car's maximum possible speed up this slope.

           (2 marks)

     The car reaches the top of the slope and begins travelling on a flat horizontal road.
     The power increases to 21 kW and the resistive force remains at kv N.

c)   Find the acceleration of the car when its speed is 12 ms⁻¹.

     (3 marks)

3

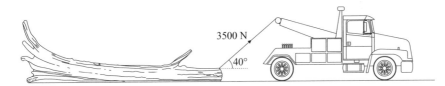

3500 N

40°

A log of mass 1100 kg is towed 820 m along straight, horizontal rough ground by a rope attached to a truck. The rope is attached to the log at an angle of 40° to the horizontal, as shown, and the tension in the rope has magnitude 3500 N.

The log experiences a constant resistance to motion from friction.

a) Find the work done by the towing force.

(3 marks)

b) Over the 820 m, the truck's speed increases from 5 ms^{-1} to 6 ms^{-1}.
Assuming that the magnitude of the towing force remains constant at 3500 N,
find the coefficient of friction between the log and the ground.

(4 marks)

4   A cyclist is riding up a road at a constant speed of 4 ms^{-1}. The road is inclined at an angle α to the horizontal. The cyclist is working at a rate of 250 W and experiences a constant non-gravitational resistance to motion of magnitude 35 N. The cyclist and his bike have a combined mass of 88 kg.

a) Find the angle of the slope, α.

(4 marks)

b) The cyclist now increases his work rate to 370 W. If all resistances to motion remain unchanged, find the cyclist's acceleration when his speed is 4 ms^{-1}.

(4 marks)

5   A block of mass 3 kg is attached to one end of a light elastic string of natural length 2 m.
The other end of the string is attached to a fixed point A, above the block.
The weight of the block extends the length of the string to 5 m.
The system is in equilibrium, with the block hanging directly below A. Find:

a) the modulus of elasticity of the string,

(3 marks)

b) the elastic potential energy in the string.

(2 marks)

The block is pulled down to a distance of 8 m directly below A,
where it is released from rest and begins to move upwards.

c) Find the speed of the block when it is a distance of 3 m below A.

(4 marks)

6   A van of mass 2700 kg is travelling at a constant speed of 16 ms⁻¹ up a road inclined at an angle of 12° to the horizontal. The non-gravitational resistance to motion is modelled as a single force of magnitude of 800 N.

a)   Find the rate of work of the engine.

(4 marks)

When the van passes a point A, still travelling at 16 ms⁻¹, the engine is switched off and the van comes to rest without braking, a distance x m from A. If all resistance to motion remains constant, find:

b)   the distance x,

(5 marks)

c)   the time taken for the van to come to rest.

(4 marks)

7   A stone of mass 0.3 kg is dropped down a well.
The stone hits the surface of the water in the well with a speed of 20 ms⁻¹.

a)   Calculate the kinetic energy of the stone as it hits the water.

(2 marks)

b)   By modelling the stone as a particle and using conservation of energy, find the height above the surface of the water from which the stone was dropped.

(3 marks)

When the stone hits the water, it begins to sink vertically and experiences a constant resistive force of 23 N.

c)   Use the work-energy principle to find the depth the stone has sunk to when the speed of the stone has been reduced to 1 ms⁻¹.

(5 marks)

8

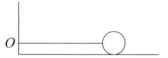

A particle of weight 10 N is attached to one end of a light elastic string, the other end of which is attached to O, a point on a vertical wall. The particle is placed on a rough horizontal surface, as shown, where the coefficient of friction between the particle and the surface is $\mu = 0.5$. The string has natural length 5 m and modulus of elasticity 50 N.

a)   The particle is held a horizontal distance d m from O, where $d > 5$.
Find an expression for the elastic potential energy of the system in terms of d.

(2 marks)

The particle is released from rest d m from O. The subsequent motion results in the particle coming to rest just as it reaches O.

b)   Assuming that the string does not interfere with the motion of the particle when it is slack, find d.

(7 marks)

Chapter 4

Uniform Circular Motion

1. Horizontal Circular Motion

Things often move in circular paths — think satellites in orbit, fairground carousel horses and conkers on strings being twirled dangerously. It's a whole new world of motion to sink your teeth into.

Circular motion

Linear speed and angular speed

- There are two ways of describing the speed of a body moving on a **circular path**.

- As you know from M1, if a body is moving at a constant speed, this speed is given by the formula **speed = $\dfrac{\text{distance}}{\text{time}}$**.

- This formula can also be used to give the **linear speed** of a body moving on a **circular path**. This tells you the body's 'straight-line' speed in the direction of the **tangent** to the circle at a particular point.

- Another way of describing the speed of a body moving on a circular path is using its **angular speed**. This is a measure of how quickly the **radius** of the circle is **turning**, or the **rate of change** of the angle through which the radius has moved with respect to **time**.

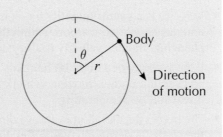

Consider a body moving in a circular path of radius *r* metres.
The radius moves through an angle **θ radians** in time *t* **seconds**.
The body's **angular speed**, ω, is given by the formula:

$$\omega = \frac{\theta}{t}$$

- If θ is measured in **radians** and *t* is measured in **seconds**, then ω is measured in **radians per second (rad s⁻¹)**.

- The relationship between a body's **linear speed** and its **angular speed** can be derived as follows:

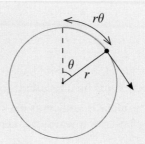

Using the formula for arc length, when the radius moves through an angle **θ**, the body moves a distance **rθ**.

So using the formula 'speed = $\dfrac{\text{distance}}{\text{time}}$',
the body's **linear speed**, *v*, is given by:

$$v = \frac{r\theta}{t} \quad \text{or} \quad v = r\omega$$

Learning Objectives:

- Be able to find the angular speed of a body moving in a circle with constant speed.

- Know and be able to use the formulas for linear speed, angular speed and radial acceleration.

- Be able to solve problems involving conical pendulums.

Tip: Radians are a unit of angular measurement. A full circle has angle 2π radians at its centre, so one full revolution corresponds to $\theta = 2\pi$ rad.

Tip: You need to learn the formula for angular speed.

Tip: Linear speed is usually measured in metres per second, ms⁻¹.

Tip: You need to learn the formula for linear speed too.

Example

A particle moves in a horizontal circle of radius 1.2 m. It completes 600 revolutions per minute.

a) Find the particle's angular speed.

- The particle makes 600 revolutions of the circle, so it moves through an angle $\theta = 600 \times 2\pi$ rad $= 1200\pi$ rad.
- It moves through this angle in a time of 60 seconds.
- So using the formula for angular speed:

$$\omega = \frac{\theta}{t} = \frac{1200\pi}{60}$$

$$= 20\pi \text{ rad s}^{-1}$$

b) Find the particle's linear speed.

$$v = r\omega = 1.2 \times 20\pi$$

$$= 24\pi \text{ ms}^{-1}$$

Tip: Make sure you convert time to seconds.

Tip: It's best to give exact values — so leave your answers in terms of π if you can.

Radial acceleration

- As you saw on the previous page, if a body is travelling on a circular path, then at any point on the circle, its motion will be parallel to the direction of the **tangent** to the circle at that point.
- This means that as the body moves around the circle, its **direction of motion** is constantly **changing**.
- Velocity is a **vector quantity** (i.e. it has both magnitude and direction). So if a body's **direction** is constantly **changing**, then its **velocity** is also constantly **changing**.
- If the velocity of a body is changing, then the body is **accelerating**. So even if a body is moving in a circle with **constant speed**, it will still be **accelerating**.
- The body's acceleration is always directed to the **centre of the circle** — **perpendicular** to the **direction of motion**.
- This acceleration is known as **radial acceleration**, and there are a couple of formulas for you to learn:

Tip: This is a bit of a weird concept — make sure you take some time to get your head around it.

Tip: The proof of these two formulas is pretty tricky. But don't worry — you don't need to know it. You do need to learn the formulas though — you won't be given them in the exam.

$$a = r\omega^2$$
$$a = \frac{v^2}{r}$$

Where a is the body's **radial acceleration**, ω is its **angular speed**, v is its **linear speed** and r is the **radius** of the circle.

- By Newton's second law, $F = ma$, for the body to accelerate, there must be a **resultant force** acting on it.
- This force is known as the **centripetal force**, and it always acts **towards** the **centre of the circle**.

Example 1

A particle moves with an angular speed of 20π rad s^{-1} around a horizontal circle of radius 0.25 m.

a) Find the magnitude of its acceleration.

$$a = r\omega^2 = 0.25 \times (20\pi)^2$$
$$= 100\pi^2 \text{ ms}^{-2}$$

b) A string connects the particle to the centre of the circle. Find the tension in the string, given that the particle's mass is 3 kg.

Tip: The tension in the string provides the centripetal force.

- Resolving horizontally for the particle, perpendicular to the direction of motion, and using $F_{net} = ma$:

$$T = ma$$
$$= 3 \times 100\pi^2 = 300\pi^2 \text{ N}$$

Example 2

A bike travels around a horizontal circular track of radius 18 m with linear speed 12 ms^{-1}. The bike and its rider have a combined mass of 86 kg. The bike experiences no resistance to motion.

Find the least value of the coefficient of friction between the bike and the track that would keep the bike on the track.

- First find the bike's acceleration:

$$a = \frac{v^2}{r} = \frac{12^2}{18} = 8 \text{ ms}^{-2}$$

- Now resolving horizontally for the bike, perpendicular to the direction of motion, and using $F_{net} = ma$:

$$F = 86 \times 8 = 688 \text{ N}$$

- Resolving vertically for the bike:

$$R = mg = 86 \times 9.8 = 842.8 \text{ N}$$

Tip: F is the frictional force between the track and the bike. It acts perpendicular to the direction of motion and provides the centripetal force which keeps the bike moving in a circular path. It's not acting as a resistive force against the motion of the bike to slow it down.

- Now using $F \leq \mu R$:

$$688 \leq \mu \times 842.8$$
$$\Rightarrow \mu \geq 688 \div 842.8$$
$$\Rightarrow \mu \geq 0.82 \text{ (2 d.p.)}$$

- So the least value of μ is 0.82 (2 d.p.)

Exercise 1.1

Q1 Each of the following describes the motion of a particle travelling in a circle. In each case, find the angular speed of the particle. Give your answers in rad s^{-1}, in exact form where appropriate.

a) A particle completes 100 revolutions per minute.

b) A particle takes 3 seconds to complete one revolution.

c) A particle takes 4 minutes to complete ten full circles.

Q2 Each of the following describes the motion of a particle travelling in a circle. In each case, find the linear speed of the particle. Give your answers in ms^{-1}, to 3 significant figures where appropriate.

a) A particle travels in a circle of radius 2 m with an angular speed of 5 rad s^{-1}.

b) A particle takes 20 seconds to complete seven revolutions of a circle of radius 50 cm.

c) A particle completes 300 revolutions per minute of a horizontal circle of radius 2 m.

Q3 An object of mass 2 kg is attached to one end of a light, inextensible string, the other end of which is fixed in position. The object moves in a horizontal circle of radius 0.5 m with linear speed 10 ms^{-1}.

a) Find the magnitude of the object's acceleration.

b) Find the magnitude of the tension in the string.

Q4 A particle moves along a horizontal circular path with linear speed 20 ms^{-1}. It completes 10 revolutions per second. Find the circle's radius in metres to 3 significant figures.

Q5 The horses on a circular carousel are 5 m from the circle's centre. They travel with linear speed 8 ms^{-1}. How long does the carousel take to complete one revolution?

Q6 Hint: The child is playing on a playground roundabout — not in the middle of a road.

Q6 A child of mass 40 kg is on the outside edge of a roundabout of radius 4 m. The child travels in a horizontal circle with linear speed 5 ms^{-1}. Find:

a) the child's acceleration,

b) the centripetal force experienced by the child.

The child moves 2.5 m closer to the centre of the roundabout. The roundabout's angular speed remains the same.

c) Find the child's new linear speed.

Q7 A body of mass 250 kg travels in a horizontal circle of radius 8 m on the inside of a spherical surface. The centripetal force acting on the body has magnitude 400 N. Find the time taken for the body to complete a single revolution.

Q8 Hint: Friction between the particle and the plane provides the centripetal force that keeps the particle moving in a circle.

Q8 A particle of mass 0.35 kg moves in a circle of radius 0.95 m on a rough horizontal plane. The coefficient of friction between the particle and the plane is 0.45. Given that friction is limiting, find the particle's angular speed.

Q9 A car of mass 800 kg travels around a rough, horizontal, circular track of radius 40 m with angular speed 0.2 rad s^{-1}. Find the least value of the coefficient of friction between the car and the track that would keep the car on the track.

Conical pendulums

- If you dangle a body on the end of a string, the other end of which is fixed in place, then twirl it round so the body moves in a horizontal circle, you've made a **conical pendulum**.
- There are only two forces acting on the body — its **weight** (*mg*) and the **tension** in the string (*T*).
- The **vertical component** of the **tension** in the string supports the body's **weight**, and the **horizontal component** is the **centripetal force** causing the **radial acceleration**.

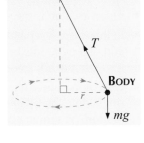

Tip: The centre of the circle must be vertically below the point where the string is fixed.

- You can solve problems involving conical pendulums by **resolving forces horizontally** and **vertically**, and using the **formulas** for linear speed, angular speed, radial acceleration and centripetal force.

Example

One end of a light, inextensible string is attached to a fixed point X. The other end is attached to a particle of mass 5 kg. The particle moves in a horizontal circle centred directly below X with an angular speed of 4π rad s^{-1}. The string makes an angle of 40° with the vertical.

a) Find the magnitude of the tension in the string.

- Draw a diagram to show the forces acting on the particle:

- Resolving vertically for the particle, taking up as positive:

$$F_{net} = ma$$
$$T\cos 40° - 5g = 5 \times 0$$
$$\Rightarrow T = (5 \times 9.8) \div \cos 40°$$
$$= 63.964... = \boxed{64.0 \text{ N (3 s.f.)}}$$

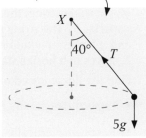

Tip: Be careful with the units of angular measurement in these questions — the angle of the string is given in degrees, but the angular speed is given in radians per second. So make sure you have your calculator set to the right mode (it should be in degrees for this question).

b) Find the radius of the circle.

- Resolving horizontally for the particle, taking left as positive:

$$F_{net} = ma$$
$$T\sin 40° = mr\omega^2$$
$$(63.964...)\sin 40° = 5 \times r \times (4\pi)^2$$
$$\Rightarrow r = 41.115... \div 789.568...$$
$$= 0.05207... \text{ m} = \boxed{5.21 \text{ cm (3 s.f.)}}$$

Tip: You're given the particle's angular speed, so use the formula $a = r\omega^2$.

c) Find the length of the string.

- Call the length of the string l.
- Using trigonometry:

$$\sin 40° = \frac{0.05207...}{l}$$
$$\Rightarrow l = \frac{0.05207...}{\sin 40°} = 0.08101... \text{ m}$$
$$= \boxed{8.10 \text{ cm (3 s.f.)}}$$

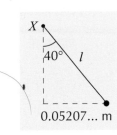

The single string through a ring

- Don't be put off by variations in conical pendulum questions — the maths is basically the same.
- One variation is the **single string through a ring**.
- In this case, a separate body is attached to either end of a light, inextensible string, which passes through a fixed, smooth ring.
- One of the bodies **hangs vertically** below the ring, while the other is set into **horizontal circular motion**, as shown.
- The thing to remember here is that the magnitude of the **tension** in **both parts** of the string is **the same**.

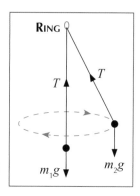

Tip: The magnitude of the tension in both parts of the string is only the same if the string is inextensible and the ring is smooth.

Example

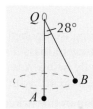

A particle, A, of mass 1.8 kg, is attached to one end of a light, inextensible string, the other end of which is attached to a second particle, B. The string passes through a fixed, smooth ring, Q, and A hangs in equilibrium vertically below Q, as shown.
B moves in a horizontal circle of radius 2.4 m.
Find the linear speed of B.

- Draw a diagram to show the forces acting on the particles:

- Resolving vertically for A ($\uparrow$):
$$T - 1.8g = 0 \implies T = 1.8g$$

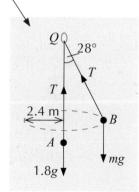

- Resolving vertically for B ($\uparrow$):
$$T\cos 28° - mg = 0$$
$$\implies 1.8g\cos 28° = mg$$
$$m = 1.8\cos 28° \text{ kg}$$

Tip: Remember, the magnitude of T is the same for both parts of the string.

- Resolving horizontally for B ($\leftarrow$):
$$F_{net} = ma$$
$$T\sin 28° = \frac{mv^2}{r}$$
$$1.8g\sin 28° = \frac{1.8\cos 28° \times v^2}{2.4}$$
$$v^2 = \frac{2.4 \times 1.8g\sin 28°}{1.8\cos 28°}$$
$$= 12.505...$$
$$\implies v = 3.54 \text{ ms}^{-1} \text{ (3 s.f.)}$$

The two-string pendulum

- Another common variation of the conical pendulum is the **two-string pendulum**.
- In this case, two light and inextensible strings are attached to a body. The other ends of the strings are then fixed in place, with one fixed vertically below the other.
- The body is set into **horizontal circular motion**, as shown.
- Each string will have a **separate tension** — you'll have to consider the **horizontal** and **vertical components** of **both strings** when resolving forces.

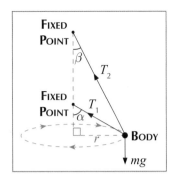

Tip: One of the strings might be horizontal — which makes life a bit easier, as there's no vertical component of tension to worry about for that string.

Example

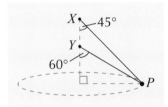

Two light, inextensible strings are fixed at one end to a particle, *P*, of mass 14 kg. The other ends of the strings are fixed at the points *X* and *Y*, where *X* is vertically above *Y*. The two strings are taut and inclined at angles of 45° and 60° to the vertical, as shown, and *P* moves in a horizontal circle of radius 0.8 m.

Given that the tension in the string *XP* has magnitude 120 N, find the angular speed of *P*.

- Draw a diagram to show the forces acting on *P*:

- Resolving vertically for *P* (↑):

$$T\cos 60° + 120\cos 45° - 14g = 0$$

$$\Rightarrow T = \frac{14g - 120\cos 45°}{\cos 60°}$$

$$= 104.694... \text{ N}$$

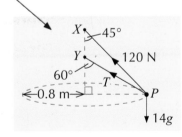

- Resolving horizontally for *P* (←):

$$F_{\text{net}} = ma$$

$$T\sin 60° + 120\sin 45° = mr\omega^2$$

$$(104.694...)\sin 60° + 120\sin 45° = 14 \times 0.8 \times \omega^2$$

$$175.5208 = 11.2\omega^2$$

$$\omega^2 = 15.6715$$

$$\Rightarrow \omega = 3.96 \text{ rad s}^{-1} \text{ (3 s.f.)}$$

Q1

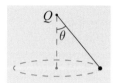

One end of a light, inextensible string of length 3 m is attached to a particle of mass 2 kg. The other end of the string is fixed at point Q, as shown. The particle moves in a horizontal circle centred vertically below Q. It moves with angular speed π rad s^{-1}. Find:

Q1 a) Hint: Find the radius of the circle first.

a) the magnitude of the tension in the string,

b) the angle, θ, that the string makes with the downward vertical.

Q2 A particle is attached to one end of a light, inextensible string, the other end of which is attached to a fixed point, Q. The particle moves in a horizontal circle of radius 0.9 m centred directly below Q. The string makes an angle of 50° with the downward vertical and has tension of magnitude 40 N.

a) Draw a diagram showing the forces acting on the particle.

b) Find the length of the string.

c) Find the mass of the particle.

d) Calculate the number of full revolutions the particle makes in one minute.

Q3 A light, inextensible string of length 1.6 m is attached at one end to a fixed point, Q. The other end of the string is attached to a body of mass 1.2 kg. The body and string form a conical pendulum with the body moving in a horizontal circle centred vertically below Q and the string making an angle of 25° with the downward vertical. Find:

a) the body's acceleration,

b) the body's angular speed,

c) the body's linear speed.

Q4

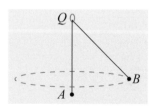

A light, inextensible string passes through a fixed, smooth ring, Q. An object, A, of mass 6 kg, is attached to one end of the string and hangs vertically below Q, as shown. A second object, B, of mass 4 kg, is attached to the other end of the string and moves in a horizontal circle of radius 0.6 m. Find:

a) tension in the string,

b) the angular speed of B,

c) the number of full revolutions B completes each minute.

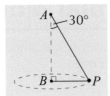

Two light, inextensible strings each have one end attached to a particle, P, of mass 3 kg. The other ends of the strings are fixed at the points A and B, where A is 1.5 m vertically above B. P is set into horizontal circular motion centred at B. AP makes an angle of 30° with the downward vertical and BP is horizontal, as shown.
The magnitude of the tension in each string is the same. Show that:

a) the magnitude of the tension in each string is $2\sqrt{3}\,g$ N,

b) the particle's linear speed is $\sqrt{1.5g}$ ms^{-1}.

Q6 A light, inextensible string passes through a fixed, smooth ring, Q. A ball, X, of mass 0.5 kg, is attached to one end of the string and hangs vertically below Q. A second ball, Y, of mass 0.2 kg, is attached to the other end of the string and moves in horizontal circles centred directly below Q, completing 40 revolutions per minute.

a) Find the magnitude of the acceleration of Y.

b) Calculate the radius of the horizontal circle.

Q7

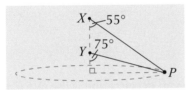

Two light, inextensible strings are fixed at one end to a particle, P, of mass 0.25 kg. The other ends of the strings are fixed at the points X and Y, where X is vertically above Y. The strings are taut and inclined at angles of 55° and 75° to the vertical, as shown. P moves in a horizontal circle centred vertically below X and Y with linear speed 2.25 ms^{-1}. Given that the tension in the string YP has magnitude 1 N, find the radius of the horizontal circle.

Q8

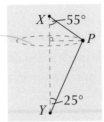

Two light, inextensible strings are fixed at one end to a particle, P, of mass 0.3 kg. The other ends of the strings are fixed at the points X and Y, where X is vertically above Y. The strings are taut and inclined at angles of 55° and 25° to the vertical, as shown, and XP has length 0.8 m. P moves in a horizontal circle centred vertically below X. Given that the magnitude of the tension in string XP is twice the magnitude of the tension in string YP, find the angular speed of P.

2. Vertical Circular Motion

Learning Objectives:

- Be able to solve problems involving bodies moving with vertical circular motion.
- Be able to find the speed of a body at a particular point on the circular path.
- Be able to find the forces acting on a body at a particular point on the circular path.
- Be able to determine whether or not a body will complete a full circle.
- Be able to find the point at which a body leaves the circular path.

So far you've only seen bodies moving in horizontal circles — now it's time to look at vertical circles.

Vertical circular motion

- The speed of a body moving in a vertical circle **isn't** the same all the way around.
- As the body moves **downwards**, from its **highest point** at the top of the circle to its **lowest point** at the bottom of the circle, the effect of **gravity** will cause it to **speed up**.
- As the body then moves **upwards**, back to the top of the circle, the effect of **gravity** will cause it to **slow down**.
- At the **bottom** of the circle, the body will be moving at its **maximum speed**.
- At the **top** of the circle, it will be moving at its **minimum speed**.

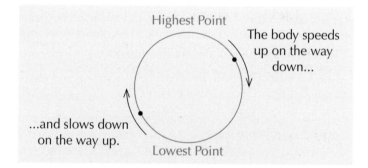

- This **acceleration** and **deceleration** is the rate of change of the body's **linear speed** with respect to time — it acts in the **direction of motion**, at a **tangent** to the circle.
- Don't get it confused with the body's **radial acceleration** — the acceleration of the body due to its **constantly changing direction** — which is still directed towards the **centre of the circle**.

Vertical circular motion and energy

- Remember, the **centripetal force** that keeps a body moving in a circle always acts **perpendicular** to the **direction of motion**.
- This means that the force does **no work** in the direction of motion.
- So you can use the **principle of conservation of mechanical energy** from page 86:

> If there is no resultant external force acting on a body, the total mechanical energy of the body will remain constant.

Tip: Remember — Work done = Force × Distance moved in the direction of the force. See page 70 for a reminder.

- So, for a body moving in a **vertical circle**:

> The sum of a body's gravitational potential energy (G.P.E.) and kinetic energy (K.E.) is the same at any point on the circle.

- You can use this fact to find out all sorts of information about a body's motion at **different points on the circle**.

Example 1

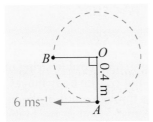

A particle of mass m kg is attached to a light, inextensible string of length 0.4 m. The other end of the string is attached to a fixed point, O, and the particle moves in a vertical circle about O. It has speed $v_A = 6$ ms^{-1} when it passes through point A, the lowest point on the circle.

Find v_B, the particle's speed when it reaches point B, shown.

- Take the level of point A as the base level — the point where the particle has no gravitational potential energy.

- At this point, the particle's total mechanical energy is given by only its kinetic energy:

$$\text{G.P.E.} + \text{K.E.} = 0 + \frac{1}{2}mv_A^2$$
$$= \frac{1}{2} \times m \times 6^2$$
$$= 18m \text{ J}$$

> **Tip:** Always use linear speed to calculate kinetic energy — if you're given a body's angular speed, you'll have to work out its linear speed first.

- At point B, the particle's height above the base level is 0.4 m, so it now has gravitational potential energy as well as kinetic energy. Its total mechanical energy at B is given by:

$$\text{G.P.E.} + \text{K.E.} = mgh + \frac{1}{2}mv_B^2$$
$$= (m \times 9.8 \times 0.4) + (\frac{1}{2} \times m \times v_B^2)$$
$$= (3.92 + \frac{1}{2}v_B^2)m \text{ J}$$

- Using the principle of conservation of mechanical energy:

Total mechanical energy at A = Total mechanical energy at B

$$18m = (3.92 + \frac{1}{2}v_B^2)m$$
$$18 = 3.92 + \frac{1}{2}v_B^2$$
$$v_B^2 = 28.16$$
$$\Rightarrow v_B = 5.31 \text{ ms}^{-1} \text{ (3 s.f.)}$$

Example 2

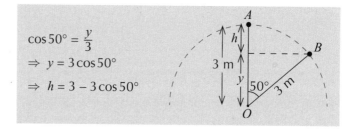

A body is attached to a light, inextensible string of length 3 m, the other end of which is fixed at point O. The body moves with vertical circular motion about O. It passes through point A, the highest point on the circle, with speed $v_A = 0.5$ ms^{-1}. Find v_B, the body's speed when it has moved through an angle of 50° to point B, shown.

Tip: You could take any point as the base level — pick the one you think will make the calculations easiest. If you take A as the base level, then the body will have zero G.P.E. at A and negative G.P.E. at B — so be careful with minus signs.

- Take the level of B as the base level — the point where the body has no gravitational potential energy.

- At this point, the body's total mechanical energy is given by:

$$\text{G.P.E.} + \text{K.E.} = 0 + \frac{1}{2}mv_B^2$$
$$= \frac{1}{2}mv_B^2$$

- To find the body's total mechanical energy at A, you first need to find the vertical height of A above B:

$$\cos 50° = \frac{y}{3}$$
$$\Rightarrow y = 3\cos 50°$$
$$\Rightarrow h = 3 - 3\cos 50°$$

- So the body's total mechanical energy at A is given by:

$$\text{G.P.E.} + \text{K.E.} = mgh + \frac{1}{2}mv_A^2$$
$$= (m \times 9.8 \times (3 - 3\cos 50°)) + (\frac{1}{2} \times m \times 0.5^2)$$
$$= (29.4(1 - \cos 50°) + 0.125)m$$
$$= (10.627...)m$$

- Using the principle of conservation of mechanical energy:

  Total mechanical energy at A = Total mechanical energy at B
  $$(10.627...)m = \frac{1}{2}mv_B^2$$
  $$v_B^2 = 21.254...$$
  $$\Rightarrow v_B = 4.61 \text{ ms}^{-1} \text{ (3 s.f.)}$$

Vertical circular motion and forces

Remember — the **weight** of a body always acts **vertically downwards**, and the **centripetal force** acting on a body moving in a circle always acts **towards the centre** of the circle.

When a body is moving in a **horizontal circle**, these two forces are always at **right angles** to each other.

However, when a body is moving in a **vertical** circle, the angle between the lines of action of the two forces is **constantly changing**.

Consider a body attached to the end of a light, inextensible string, moving in a vertical circle about a fixed point:

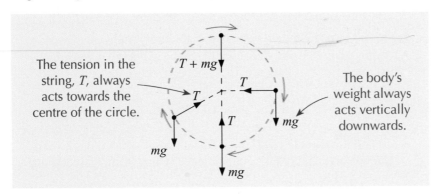

The tension in the string, T, always acts towards the centre of the circle.

The body's weight always acts vertically downwards.

Tip: As the body moves around the circle, the angle of the string will change, and so the line of action of the tension in the string, and hence the resultant force acting on the body, will also change.

To find the **centripetal force** acting on the body at a particular point on the circle, you'll need to **resolve forces perpendicular** to the **direction of motion**. This is often referred to as 'resolving radially'.

Example

A particle of mass 2.5 kg is attached to a light, inextensible string of length 1.6 m. The other end of the string is attached to a fixed point, O, and the particle moves in a vertical circle about O.
It passes through the lowest point on the circle with speed 4 ms⁻¹.

a) Find the magnitude of the tension in the string when the particle is at its lowest point on the circle.

- Draw a diagram to show the forces acting on the particle:

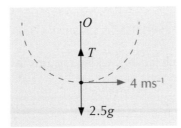

- Resolving vertically, taking up as positive:

$$F_{net} = ma$$
$$T - 2.5g = \frac{mv^2}{r}$$
$$T = \frac{2.5 \times 4^2}{1.6} + (2.5 \times 9.8)$$
$$= 49.5 \text{ N}$$

b) Find the magnitude of the tension in the string when the particle has moved through an angle of 60° from the lowest point on the circle.

- Again, draw a diagram to show what's going on:

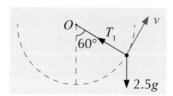

- First, you'll need to find the particle's linear speed at this point by using the principle of conservation of mechanical energy.
- Set the lowest point on the circle as the base level.
- At this point, the particle's total mechanical energy is given by:

$$\text{G.P.E.} + \text{K.E.} = 0 + \frac{1}{2}mv_B^2$$

$$= \frac{1}{2} \times 2.5 \times 4^2 = 20 \text{ J}$$

- To find the particle's total mechanical energy when it has moved through an angle of 60°, you first need to find its increase in height:

$$\cos 60° = \frac{y}{1.6}$$
$$\Rightarrow y = 1.6\cos 60°$$
$$\Rightarrow h = 1.6 - 1.6\cos 60°$$

- So the particle's total mechanical energy at this point is given by:

$$\text{G.P.E.} + \text{K.E.} = mgh + \frac{1}{2}mv^2$$

$$= (2.5 \times 9.8 \times (1.6 - 1.6\cos 60°)) + (\frac{1}{2} \times 2.5 \times v^2)$$

$$= (19.6 + 1.25v^2) \text{ J}$$

- Using the principle of conservation of mechanical energy:

$$20 = 19.6 + 1.25v^2$$

$$\Rightarrow v^2 = 0.32 \text{ m}^2\text{s}^{-2}$$

Tip: You'll need v^2 in the next step, so don't bother square-rooting.

- Now resolving radially, taking towards the centre of the circle as positive:

$$F_{net} = ma$$

$$T_1 - 2.5g\cos 60° = \frac{mv^2}{r}$$

$$T_1 - 12.25 = \frac{2.5 \times 0.32}{1.6}$$

$$\Rightarrow T_1 = 12.75 \text{ N}$$

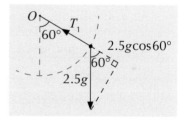

Q1

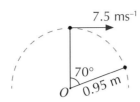

A body moves in a vertical circle of radius 0.95 m about a fixed point O. The body's speed when it is at the highest point on the circle is 7.5 ms⁻¹. Find the body's speed when it has moved through an angle of 70° from the upward vertical, as shown above.

Q2 A particle moves in a vertical circle of radius 0.6 m about a fixed point O. It passes vertically below O with speed 5 ms⁻¹. Find:

a) the speed of the particle when it is vertically level with O,

b) the speed of the particle when it is vertically above O,

c) the speed of the particle when the string makes an angle of 20° with the upward vertical.

Q3 An object of mass 3 kg is attached to one end of a light, inextensible string of length 0.8 m. The other end of the string is attached to a fixed point, O. The object is held so that the string is taut and horizontal. The object is released, and begins to move in a vertical circle about O. It passes through the point A when the string has moved through an angle of 40° from the horizontal.

a) Draw a diagram showing the forces acting on the object when it passes through A.

b) Find the speed of the object when it passes through A.

c) Find the magnitude of the tension in the string at the instant the object passes through A.

Q4

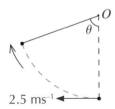

An object of mass 0.75 kg is attached to one end of a light, inextensible string of length 0.4 m. The other end of the string is fixed at point O. The object hangs in equilibrium vertically below O, and is then set into motion with horizontal speed 2.5 ms⁻¹. The object first comes to rest when the string has moved through an angle θ from the lowest point on the circle, as shown. Find:

a) the value of θ,

b) the tension in the string at the point the object first comes to rest.

Q5

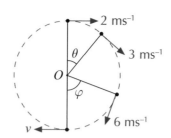

A particle is attached to one end of a light, inextensible string of length 1.2 m, the other end of which is held at the fixed point O. The particle moves in a vertical circle about O, passing through the highest point on the circle with speed 2 ms^{-1}, as shown. Find:

a) the particle's speed, v, when it is at the lowest point on the circle,

b) the angle, θ, the string makes with the upward vertical when the particle's speed is 3 ms^{-1},

c) the angle, φ, the string makes with the downward vertical when the particle's speed is 6 ms^{-1}.

Q6 A body of mass m kg is attached to one end of a light, inextensible string of length 2 m. The other end of the string is attached to the fixed point O, and the body moves in a vertical circle about this point. When the body is at the lowest point on the circle, its speed is twice that when it is at the highest point on the circle. Find:

a) the body's speed at the highest point on the circle,

b) the body's speed at the lowest point on the circle,

c) the body's speed when the string is horizontal,

d) the magnitude of the tension in the string, in terms of m, when the body is at the highest point on the circle,

e) the magnitude of the tension in the string, in terms of m, when the string is horizontal.

Q7

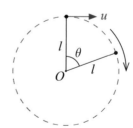

A particle of mass m kg is attached to a light, inextensible string of length l m, the other end of which is held at the fixed point O. The particle moves in a vertical circle about O, passing vertically above O with speed u. As the particle moves in the circle, the string makes an angle θ with the upward vertical, as shown. Find:

a) an expression for the particle's speed, in terms of u, g and l, when:

    (i) $\theta = 60°$,   (ii) $\theta = 150°$,   (iii) $\theta = 180°$.

b) an expression for the magnitude of the tension in the string, in terms of m, u, g and l, when:

    (i) $\theta = 60°$,   (ii) $\theta = 150°$,   (iii) $\theta = 180°$.

Circular wires and surfaces

Beads moving on circular wires

- A body attached to the end of a string isn't the only circular motion set-up you'll see in M2.

- You'll also come across **beads** sliding around **smooth circular wires**.

- There's no tension force here — instead, there's the **normal reaction** of the wire on the bead.

- The thing to remember here is that the **normal reaction** doesn't always act towards the centre of the circle — sometimes it'll act **outwards**, **directly away** from the circle's centre.

Tip: Remember — a bead is a particle with a hole in it which a wire or string can pass through.

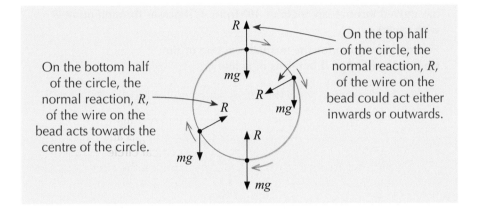

On the bottom half of the circle, the normal reaction, R, of the wire on the bead acts towards the centre of the circle.

On the top half of the circle, the normal reaction, R, of the wire on the bead could act either inwards or outwards.

Tip: If the normal reaction acts outwards, then the centripetal force causing the bead's radial acceleration is equal to the component of its weight acting towards the centre of the circle minus the reaction force.

- It may seem odd that the reaction force could act in either one of two directions, but if you look closely, you can see why:

  - In the first diagram, the bead is 'sitting on' the wire as it slides along, so the wire '**pushes upwards**' on the bead.

  - In the second diagram, the particle is moving fast enough that it 'pushes upwards' on the wire, so the wire '**pushes back down**' on the bead. In effect, the wire is preventing the bead from 'flying off' and **leaving the circle**.

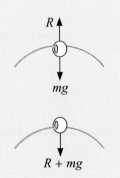

- Solving problems involving a bead on a wire is pretty much the same as for a particle on a string — just **resolve forces perpendicular** to the **direction of motion** to find the magnitude of the centripetal force.

- When the bead is on the **top half** of the circle, you'll have to **guess** whether the normal reaction acts **inwards** or **outwards**. If you guess wrong, then the reaction will just pop out of your calculations as a **negative value**.

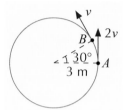

A bead of mass m moves around a smooth vertical circular ring of radius 3 m, as shown. The bead passes through the point A, horizontally level with the centre of the ring, with speed $2v$. When it has moved through an angle of 30° from A, it passes through point B with speed v.

Find an expression for the normal reaction of the ring on the bead at B in terms of m and g.

- Draw a diagram to show the forces acting on the bead at B:

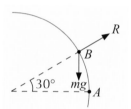

Tip: The diagram assumes that the reaction force acts outwards — you could've drawn it acting inwards instead.

- Resolving radially, taking towards the centre of the circle as positive:

$$F_{net} = ma$$
$$mg\sin 30° - R = \frac{mv^2}{r}$$
$$R = \frac{mg}{2} - \frac{mv^2}{3}$$

- You're asked for an expression in terms of m and g, so you need to get rid of the v.

- Using the principle of conservation of mechanical energy, taking the level of A as the base level:

$$\frac{1}{2}m(2v)^2 = \frac{1}{2}mv^2 + (mg \times 3\sin 30°)$$
$$4v^2 = v^2 + 3g \qquad \longleftarrow \quad \text{Dividing throughout by } \frac{m}{2}$$
$$\Rightarrow v^2 = g \qquad\qquad\qquad \text{— remember that } \sin 30° = \frac{1}{2}.$$

- You can now eliminate v^2 from your expression:

$$R = \frac{mg}{2} - \frac{mv^2}{3}$$
$$= \frac{mg}{2} - \frac{mg}{3}$$
$$\Rightarrow R = \frac{mg}{6}$$

Bodies moving on circular surfaces

- You might also have to answer questions involving bodies moving on **circular surfaces**.

- For example, you might be asked about a body moving on the **inside** of a **horizontal cylinder**, or on the **outside** of a **sphere** or **hemisphere**.

- Answer these questions in the same way as with a bead on a wire — **resolve forces perpendicular** to the **direction of motion**.

- The thing to remember here is that the **normal reaction** of the surface on the body will always act **inwards** if the body is moving on the **inside** of the surface, and always act **outwards** if it is moving on the **outside** of the surface:

On the inside of the surface, the normal reaction, R, acts inwards, towards the centre of the circle.

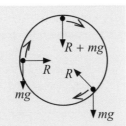

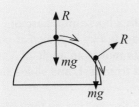

On the outside of the surface, the normal reaction, R, acts outwards, away from the centre.

Example 1

A particle of mass 1.8 kg moves on the inside surface of a smooth horizontal cylinder of radius 0.6 m. It passes through the lowest point on the circle with speed 8.5 ms⁻¹. The magnitude of the normal reaction of the surface on the particle is R_1 when the particle is at the lowest point on the circle, and R_2 when it is at the highest point on the circle. Find the values of R_1 and R_2.

- Draw a force diagram:

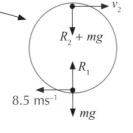

- Resolving vertically at the lowest point on the circle, taking up as positive:

$$F_{net} = ma$$

$$R_1 - mg = \frac{mv_1^2}{r}$$

$$\Rightarrow R_1 = \frac{1.8 \times 8.5^2}{0.6} + (1.8 \times 9.8)$$

$$= 234.39 \text{ N}$$

- Now, using the principle of conservation of mechanical energy, taking the lowest point on the circle as the base level:

$$\frac{1}{2} \times 1.8 \times (8.5)^2 = (\frac{1}{2} \times 1.8 \times v_2^2) + (1.8 \times 9.8 \times 1.2)$$

$$\Rightarrow v_2^2 = 43.875 \div 0.9 = 48.73$$

- Resolving vertically at the highest point on the circle, taking down as positive:

$$F_{net} = ma$$

$$R_2 + mg = \frac{mv_2^2}{r}$$

$$\Rightarrow R_2 = \frac{1.8 \times 48.73}{0.6} - (1.8 \times 9.8)$$

$$= \boxed{128.55 \text{ N}}$$

Example 2

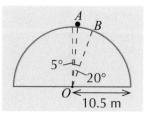

Tip: The diagram shows a cross-section of the hemisphere.

The diagram shows a smooth hemisphere with a horizontal base of radius 10.5 m, centred at O. An object of mass 0.4 kg is placed at point A on the surface of the hemisphere, where OA makes an angle of 5° with the vertical, as shown. The object is released from rest, and slides along the smooth outside surface of the hemisphere.

Find the magnitude of the normal reaction of the surface on the object when it is at point B, where OB makes an angle of 20° with the vertical.

- Draw a force diagram:

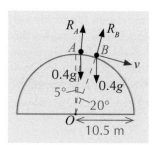

- First find the vertical distance, h, between A and B:

Tip: This diagram isn't drawn accurately, but it makes it easier to see what's going on.

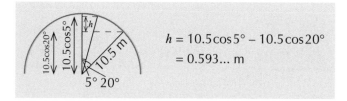

$$h = 10.5 \cos 5° - 10.5 \cos 20°$$

$$= 0.593... \text{ m}$$

Tip: At A, the object has G.P.E., but no K.E. (it is released from rest). At B, it has K.E., but no G.P.E. (B is the base level).

- Now use the principle of conservation of mechanical energy, taking the level of B as the base level:

$$mgh = \frac{1}{2}mv^2$$

$$\Rightarrow v^2 = 2gh$$

- Resolving radially at B, taking 'inwards' as positive:

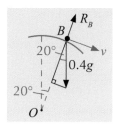

$F_{net} = ma$

$0.4g\cos 20° - R_B = \dfrac{mv^2}{r}$

$\Rightarrow R_B = (0.4 \times 9.8 \times \cos 20°) - \dfrac{0.4 \times (2 \times 9.8 \times 0.593...)}{10.5}$

$= 3.24 \text{ N (3 s.f.)}$

Substituting in $v^2 = 2gh$.

Exercise 2.2

Q1

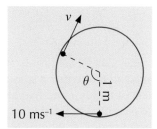

A particle of mass 3 kg moves in a vertical circle on the smooth inside surface of a cylinder of radius 1 m. At the lowest point on the circle, the particle has speed 10 ms⁻¹. As the particle moves around the circle, it makes an angle θ with the downward vertical, as shown.

a) Find the particle's speed, v, when:

(i) $\theta = 45°$,   (ii) $\theta = 75°$,   (iii) $\theta = 135°$.

b) Find the magnitude of the reaction of the cylinder on the particle when:

(i) $\theta = 45°$,   (ii) $\theta = 75°$,   (iii) $\theta = 135°$.

Q2   A bead of mass m kg moves on a smooth circular ring which is fixed in a vertical plane. The bead's speed at the highest point on the circle is $\sqrt{3gr}$ ms⁻¹, where r is the radius of the ring. Find:

a) an expression for the bead's speed at the lowest point on the ring, in terms of g and r,

b) an expression for the normal reaction of the ring on the bead at the highest point on the circle, in terms of m,

c) an expression for the normal reaction of the ring on the bead at the lowest point on the circle, in terms of m.

Q3

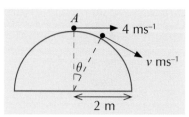

A body of mass m kg is placed at point A, at the top of a hemisphere of radius 2 m. The base of the hemisphere is horizontal. The body is set into motion with horizontal speed 4 ms^{-1}, and slides along the smooth surface of the hemisphere, reaching speed v ms^{-1} when the radius has moved through an angle θ, as shown.

a) Show that $v^2 = 16 + 4g(1 - \cos\theta)$.

b) Find an expression for the normal reaction of the surface on the body when the body's speed is v ms^{-1}, in terms of m, g and θ.

c) Find the value of θ for which the magnitude of the normal reaction of the surface on the body is half that at A.

Q4

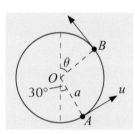

A bead of mass m is threaded onto a smooth wire, which is then formed into a circle of radius a and fixed in a vertical plane. The circle's centre is at O. The bead is set into motion around the ring. It passes through point A, where OA makes an angle of 30° with the downward vertical, with speed u. It goes on to pass through the point B, where OB is inclined at an angle θ to the upward vertical, as shown. Show that the magnitude of the normal reaction of the wire on the bead at B is:

$$\left| mg(3\cos\theta + \sqrt{3}) - \frac{mu^2}{a} \right|$$

Completing the circle

In some vertical circular motion set-ups — like a body at the end of a string or on the inside surface of a cylinder — the body will **leave the circular path** if its speed is **too low**.

In these cases, the body will only complete the circle if:

- It has enough **kinetic energy** to **reach the top** of the circle (i.e. it has enough mechanical energy so that when it is at the **highest point** on the circle, and its **gravitational potential energy** is at its **maximum**, it still has **positive kinetic energy**).

Tip: If you get a negative value for the tension, then the body will have left the circle and the string will be slack (i.e. not taut).

- When the body is at the top of the circle, the **tension** in the string or the **reaction** from the cylinder wall is **greater than or equal to zero** (i.e. acting towards the centre of the circle). If the force is equal to zero, the body will **only just** complete the circle.

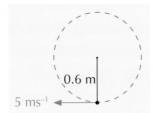

A particle is attached to the end of a light, inextensible string of length 0.6 m, the other end of which is held at a fixed point. The particle is set into vertical circular motion. It passes through the lowest point on the circle with speed 5 ms⁻¹, as shown. Will it complete a full circle?

- Draw a diagram showing the particle at the highest point on the circle:

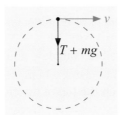

- First, check to see whether the particle has enough kinetic energy to reach the top.

- Taking the lowest point on the circle as the base level:

    Total mechanical energy of the particle at the lowest point

    $$= \frac{1}{2} \times m \times 5^2$$

    $$= 12.5m$$

    Total mechanical energy of the particle at the top of the circle

    $$= (m \times 9.8 \times 1.2) + (\frac{1}{2} \times m \times v^2)$$

    $$= m(11.76 + \frac{1}{2}v^2)$$

- Assuming the particle reaches the top, using the principle of conservation of mechanical energy:

    $$12.5m = m(11.76 + \frac{1}{2}v^2)$$

    $$12.5 = 11.76 + \frac{1}{2}v^2$$

    $$v^2 = 1.48$$

    $$\Rightarrow v = 1.22 \text{ ms}^{-1} \text{ (3 s.f.)}$$

Tip: If you'd ended up with a negative value for v^2, then you'd know that the particle didn't have enough kinetic energy to reach the top of the circle.

- So the particle has enough kinetic energy to reach the top, and it will have speed 1.22 ms⁻¹ (3 s.f.) when it is at the top.

- Now check the tension in the string.

- Resolving vertically at the top of the circle, taking down as positive:

$$F_{net} = ma$$

$$T + mg = \frac{mv^2}{r}$$

$$\Rightarrow T = \frac{1.48m}{0.6} - 9.8m = -7.33m \text{ N (3 s.f.)}$$

- The tension in the string is negative, so the particle will not complete a full circle.

Tip: Use the value of v^2 that you've just found.

Finding where the body leaves the circle

At the point where the body **leaves the circular path**, the **tension** in the string, or the **normal reaction** of the surface on the body, will be **zero**.

So the only force causing the radial acceleration is the **component** of the body's **weight** acting towards the **centre** of the circle.

It's important to remember that in some situations the body **can't leave the circular path** — a **bead on a wire**, for example.

However, the body can still **fail to complete a full circle**.

In these cases, you only need to check whether or not the body has **enough kinetic energy** to **reach the top** of the circle — you don't need to worry about whether the forces are positive or negative.

Example

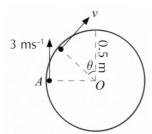

A particle is held in place on the inside surface of a horizontal circular pipe of radius 0.5 m. It is held at the point A, horizontally level with the centre of the circle, O. The particle is projected vertically upwards with speed 3 ms⁻¹ and begins to move in a circle along the smooth inside surface of the pipe.

Find the value of θ (shown) for which the particle leaves the pipe wall.

- Using the principle of conservation of mechanical energy, taking OA as the base level:

$$\frac{1}{2} \times m \times 3^2 = \frac{1}{2}mv^2 + (m \times g \times 0.5\cos\theta)$$

$$9 = v^2 + g\cos\theta$$

$$\Rightarrow v^2 = 9 - g\cos\theta$$

- When the particle leaves the wall, the normal reaction of the wall on the particle will be zero — i.e. the only force acting on the particle will be its weight.

- So, resolving radially, taking inwards as positive:

$$mg\cos\theta = \frac{mv^2}{r}$$

$$mg\cos\theta = \frac{m(9 - g\cos\theta)}{0.5}$$

$$0.5g\cos\theta = 9 - g\cos\theta$$

$$1.5g\cos\theta = 9$$

$$\cos\theta = 9 \div (1.5 \times 9.8) = 0.612...$$

$$\Rightarrow \boxed{\theta = 52.2° \text{ (3 s.f.)}}$$

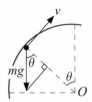

Exercise 2.3

Q1

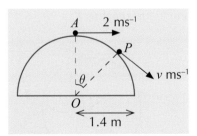

A particle, P, of mass m kg, is placed at point A, the highest point of a hemisphere of radius 1.4 m, whose base has midpoint O. The base is placed on a horizontal plane. P is given an initial horizontal speed of 2 ms^{-1}, and it begins to slide along the smooth surface of the hemisphere. When OP makes an angle θ with OA, as shown, the speed of P is v ms^{-1}. Find:

a) an expression for the normal reaction of the hemisphere on P, in terms of m, g and θ,

b) the value of θ for which P leaves the surface of the hemisphere,

c) the speed of P at the instant it leaves the surface of the hemisphere.

Q2 A body of mass m kg is attached to one end of a light, inextensible string of length 0.8 m, the other end of which is held at a fixed point, O. The body hangs in equilibrium, vertically below O.
The body is given an initial horizontal speed of 5 ms^{-1}, and begins to move in a vertical circle about O. As the body moves, the string makes an angle θ with the downward vertical.

a) Find an expression, in terms of θ, for the body's speed as it moves around the circle.

b) Show that when the string is first horizontal, it is taut.

c) Show that the body will not complete the circle.

d) Find the value of θ for which the body leaves the circle.

e) Find the body's speed when it leaves the circle.

Q3

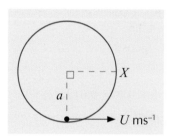

A particle moves anticlockwise in a vertical circle of radius a on the inside surface of a smooth cylinder. At the lowest point on the circle, the particle has speed U ms^{-1}, as shown. Find:

a) the value of U for which the particle just completes a full circle,

b) the value of U for which the particle just reaches point X, vertically level with the centre of the circle,

c) the normal reaction of the cylinder on the particle at X if the particle just reaches X.

Q4

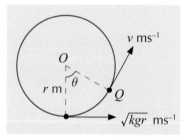

A bead, Q, of mass m kg, moves on a smooth circular wire of radius r m which is fixed in a vertical plane and centred at O. The bead's speed at the lowest point on the circle is $\sqrt{kgr}$ ms^{-1}, where k is a positive constant. When OQ makes an angle θ measured anticlockwise from the downward vertical, as shown, the speed of Q is v ms^{-1}.

a) Show that the bead will complete a full circle if $k \geq 4$.

b) When $k = 3$, find the maximum vertical height that the bead reaches above the lowest point on the circle.

c) When $k = 1$, show that $R = 0$ when $\cos\theta = \dfrac{1}{3}$.

Review Exercise — Chapter 4

Q1   A particle attached to a light, inextensible string moves in a horizontal circle of radius 3 m. Find the particle's angular speed and acceleration given that:

     a)   the particle takes 1.5 seconds to complete 1 revolution,

     b)   the particle completes 15 revolutions in one minute,

     c)   the string moves through 160° in one second,

     d)   the linear speed of the particle is 10 ms⁻¹.

Q2   A particle of mass 2 kg moves in a horizontal circle of radius 0.4 m. Find the centripetal force acting on the particle if:

     a)   the particle's angular speed is 10π rad s⁻¹,

     b)   the particle's linear speed is 4 ms⁻¹.

Q3

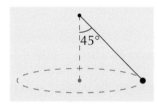

A body of mass 4 kg is attached to one end of a light, inextensible string, the other end of which is held at a fixed point. The body moves in a horizontal circle centred directly below the fixed end of the string, and the string makes an angle of 45° with the vertical, as shown.

     a)   Calculate the magnitude of the tension in the string.

     b)   Find the radius of the circle, giving your answer in terms of v, the linear speed of the body.

Q4

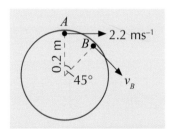

A particle of mass m kg is set into vertical circular motion on the inside surface of a smooth horizontal pipe. The particle is initially at point A, vertically above the circle's centre. At this point, it has speed 2.2 ms⁻¹.

     a)   Draw a force diagram for the particle when it is at point B, shown in the diagram.

     b)   Find v_B, the particle's speed at point B.

     c)   Find, in terms of m, the normal reaction of the pipe on the particle at point B.

Q5   A body is set into vertical circular motion with a horizontal speed of 9 ms⁻¹ from the lowest point of the circle. The circular path has a 2 m radius.

     a)   Show that the body will complete the circle if it is a bead on a smooth wire, but not if it is a particle at the end of a light, inextensible string.

     b)   Assuming that the body is a particle at the end of a light, inextensible string, find the angle the string makes with the upward vertical when the particle leaves the circular path.

1

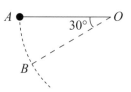

A particle of mass 2 kg is attached to one end of a light, inextensible string of length 0.5 m. The other end of the string is attached to a fixed point, O. The particle is released from rest at point A, where AO is horizontal, as shown, and moves in a circular path in a vertical plane.

Find, in terms of g:

a)   the particle's speed at point B, where $\angle AOB = 30°$,

(3 marks)

b)   the tension in the string when the particle is at point B,

(3 marks)

c)   the angular speed of the particle at point B.

(2 marks)

2

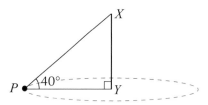

Particle P is attached to one end of two light, inextensible strings. The other end of each string is attached to a vertical rod, XY, as shown in the diagram. The tension in string PX has magnitude 55 N, and the tension in string PY has magnitude 80 N.
The particle moves in a horizontal circle about Y with a constant speed of 3 ms^{-1}.
Find:

a)   the mass of particle P,

(2 marks)

b)   the length of string PY,

(3 marks)

c)   the number of complete revolutions the particle will make in one minute.

(3 marks)

3

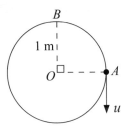

A bead of mass m kg moves with vertical circular motion about a fixed point O on a smooth ring of radius 1 m. At point A, shown on the diagram, the bead has speed u.

a) When $u = \sqrt{20}$ ms^{-1}, show that the bead's speed at the highest point of the circle, B, is $\sqrt{0.4}$ ms^{-1}.

(3 marks)

b) When $u = \sqrt{20}$ ms^{-1}, find the normal reaction of the ring on the bead at point B. Give your answer in terms of m.

(3 marks)

c) Find the minimum value of u that will result in a complete circle being made.

(3 marks)

4   A quad bike and its rider, of combined mass 500 kg, are travelling with constant speed around a horizontal circular track with a radius of 30 m. A frictional force acts towards the centre of the track, and there is no resistance to motion.

If the coefficient of friction between the quad bike and the track is 0.5, find the greatest speed the quad bike can go round the track without slipping.

(5 marks)

5

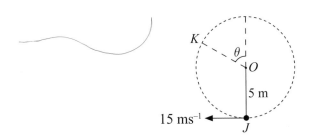

A particle at the end of a light, inextensible string of length 5 m is set into vertical circular motion about a fixed point O. The particle's initial speed is 15 ms^{-1}, and it starts from J, the lowest point on the circle. When the particle reaches point K, it has speed v ms^{-1} and the string makes an angle of θ with the upward vertical, as shown.

a) Show that $v^2 = 225 - 10g(1 + \cos\theta)$.

(4 marks)

b) Show that the particle will not complete the circle.

(4 marks)

c) Find the value of θ when the string first becomes slack.

(4 marks)

Answers

Chapter 1: Moments and Centres of Mass

1. Moments

Exercise 1.1 — Moments

Q1 a) Moment = Force × Perpendicular Distance
= 3 × 2.5 = 7.5 Nm anticlockwise

b) Moment = 6sin30° × 4 = 12 Nm clockwise

c) Moment = 23 × 0.8cos18°
= 17.5 Nm (3 s.f.) clockwise

Q2 a) Taking clockwise as positive:
(2 × 9) – (7 × 2) = 4 Nm clockwise

b) Taking clockwise as positive:
(19 × 1.5) – (14 × 2) = 0.5 Nm clockwise

c) Taking clockwise as positive:
(12.6 × 5) – (4.5 × 2) – (6 × 9) = 0
(i.e. There is no moment about X.)

d) Taking clockwise as positive:
(3 × 2) + (12 × 4) – (22 × 2.5) = –1 Nm
i.e. 1 Nm anticlockwise.

e) Taking clockwise as positive:
(7sin30° × 3) – (15 × 1.5) = –12 Nm
i.e. 12 Nm anticlockwise

f) Taking clockwise as positive:
(10sin30° × 3) + (8sin45° × 4) = $(15 + 16\sqrt{2})$ Nm
= 37.6 Nm (3 s.f.) clockwise

g) Taking clockwise as positive:
(18sin25° × 13) – (24sin32° × 13)
= –66.4 Nm (3 s.f.), i.e. 66.4 Nm anticlockwise

h) Taking clockwise as positive:
(6sin105° × 10) + (2sin50° × 8)
– (3sin28° × 10) – (1 × 8)
= 48.1 Nm (3 s.f.) clockwise.

Q3 Find the sum of the moments about O, taking clockwise as positive:
(13 × 3) + (X × 1) – (21 × 3) = X – 24
For the rod to rotate clockwise, the sum of the moments must be positive:
X – 24 > 0
$\Rightarrow X > 24$

Q4 Find the sum of the moments about O, taking clockwise as positive:
4(d + 1) + (38 × 2) – (25 × 1) –
(24sin150° × 5) = 4d – 5
For the rod to rotate anticlockwise, the sum of the moments must be negative:
4d – 5 < 0
$\Rightarrow d < 1.25$
Also, d must be greater than or equal to zero, otherwise the 25 N force will be applied to a point which isn't on the rod, and so the rod will rotate clockwise. So:
$0 \leq d < 1.25$

Q5 Find the sum of the moments about O, taking anticlockwise as positive:
$(4\sqrt{3}\sin60° × 3) + 5l – (8 × 1)$
$- (4\sqrt{2}\sin45° × [3 + l]) = l – 2$
Sum of moments is 0.5 Nm, so:
0.5 = l – 2
$\Rightarrow l = 2.5$ m

Q6 Find the sum of moments about O, taking clockwise as positive, and resolving forces perpendicular to the rod:
(27sinθ × 3) + (9sinθ × 1) – (7 × 6)
= 90sinθ – 42
Sum of moments is 3 Nm, so:
3 = 90sinθ – 42
45 = 90sinθ
0.5 = sinθ
$\Rightarrow \theta = 30°$

Exercise 1.2 — Moments in equilibrium

Q1 Taking moments about A:
Moments clockwise = Moments anticlockwise
1.5S + (2 × 8) = 16 × 5.5
1.5S = 72
S = 48 N
Resolving vertically:
R + 16 = S + 2
R = 50 – 16 = 34 N

Q2 Resolving vertically:
10 + 6 = 13 + M
M = 3 N
Taking moments about C:
10l + 2M = 6 × 5
10l = 30 – 6
l = 2.4 m

Q3 a) Mass acts at centre of rod, i.e. 2.5 m from A, 1 m from C and 0.5 m from D.
Taking moments about the midpoint:
0.5R_D = 49 × 1
R_D = 98 N

b) Resolving vertically:
Mg = 49 + R_D
M = (49 + 98) ÷ 9.8 = 15 kg

Q4 When the rod is about to tilt about D, $T_C = 0$.
The rod is uniform, so its mass acts at its midpoint, x m from D.
Taking moments about D:
$3g \times 1.5 = 9g \times x$
$x = 44.1 \div 88.2 = 0.5$
So the distance from B to the midpoint is $1.5 + 0.5 = 2$ m, and so the length of the rod is $2 \times 2 = 4$ m

Q5 **a)**

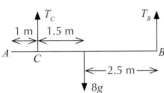

Taking moments about C:
$8g \times 1.5 = 4T_B$
$T_B = 117.6 \div 4 = 29.4$ N
Resolving vertically:
$T_C + T_B = 8g$
$T_C = 78.4 - 29.4 = 49$ N

b) When the beam is about to tilt about C, $T_B = 0$.
Taking moments about C:
$8g \times 1.5 = 16g \times x$
$x = 117.6 \div 156.8 = 0.75$
So the distance of the particle from A is $1 - 0.75 = 0.25$ m

Q6 **a)** Resolving vertically:
$T_C + T_D = 240$
$T_C = 2T_D$
$\Rightarrow 2T_D + T_D = 240$
$3T_D = 240$
$T_D = 80$ N
$\Rightarrow T_C = 2 \times 80 = 160$ N

b) Taking moments about A:
$(T_C \times 1) + (T_D \times 8) = 240x$
$160 + 640 = 240x$
$\Rightarrow x = 3.33$ m (3 s.f.)

Q7 **a)**

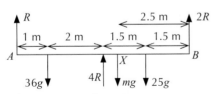

b) Taking moments about X:
$(4R \times 0.5) + 3.5R + (25g \times 1) =$
$(36g \times 2.5) + (2R \times 2.5)$
$\Rightarrow 2R + 3.5R + 25g = 90g + 5R$
$\Rightarrow 0.5R = 65g$
$R = 1274$ N
Resolving vertically:
$R + 2R + 4R = 36g + 25g + mg$
$\Rightarrow 7 \times 1274 = 597.8 + 9.8m$
$\Rightarrow m = 849$ kg

c) The plank is modelled as a non-uniform rod, the children are modelled as particles, the reaction forces act perpendicular to the plank, there are no other external forces acting on the plank, the plank is horizontal, acceleration due to gravity is constant at 9.8 ms⁻².

Q8 **a)** The painter stands at the plank's COM, so the weight acting at this point is his weight plus the plank's weight, i.e. $80g + 20g = 100g$.

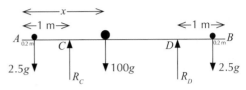

The reaction at C is 4 times the reaction at D, i.e. $R_C = 4R_D$
Resolving vertically:
$2.5g + 100g + 2.5g = R_C + R_D$
$105g = 4R_D + R_D$
$105g = 5R_D$
$\Rightarrow R_D = 21g$ N $\Rightarrow R_C = 84g$ N
Taking moments about A:
$(2.5g \times 0.2) + (100g \times x) + (2.5g \times 3.8) = R_C + 3R_D$
$10g + 100gx = 84g + 63g$
$10g + 100gx = 147g$
$x = (147 - 10) \div (100) = 1.37$ m

b) The distance between the plank's COM and the point D is $4 - 1 - 1.37 = 1.63$ m

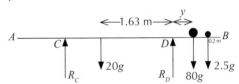

When the plank is about to tilt about D, $R_C = 0$.
Taking moments about D:
$20g \times 1.63 = (80g \times y) + (2.5g \times 0.8)$
$y = (319.48 - 19.6) \div 784 = 0.3825$
So the distance from B is:
$1 - 0.3825 = 0.6175$ m

Exercise 1.3 — Friction and limiting equilibrium

Q1 a)

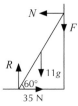

Resolving horizontally:
$N = 35$ N

b) Resolving vertically:
$F + 11g = R$
Taking moments about top of ladder:
$(11g\cos 60° × 3.5) + (35\sin 60° × 7) =$
$R\cos 60° × 7$
$\Rightarrow R = 400.826... ÷ 3.5 = 114.521...$ N
So $F = 114.521... - 11g = 6.721...$
$= 6.72$ N (3 s.f.)

c) $F = \mu N$
$6.721... = \mu × 35$
$\Rightarrow \mu = 0.19$ (2 d.p.)

Q2 a)

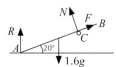

Taking moments about A:
$1.6g\cos 20° × 0.75 = N × 1.1$
$\Rightarrow N = 10.046... = 10.0$ N (3 s.f.)

b) Taking moments about C:
$1.6g\cos 20° × (1.1 - 0.75) = R\cos 20° × 1.1$
$\Rightarrow R = 5.157... ÷ 1.033... = 4.989...$
$= 4.99$ N (3 s.f.)

c) Resolving horizontally:
$F\cos 20° = N\sin 20°$
$\Rightarrow F = (10.046...)\tan 20° = 3.656...$
$= 3.66$ N (3 s.f.)

d) $F = \mu N$
$3.656... = \mu × 10.046...$
$\Rightarrow \mu = 0.36$ (2 d.p.)

Q3

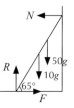

Resolving vertically:
$R = 10g + 50g = 60g$
Resolving horizontally:
$F = N$
If the ladder is on the point of slipping, then $F = \mu R$.
$\Rightarrow \mu R = N$
$\Rightarrow N = 0.3 × 60g = 176.4$ N
Let x be the girl's distance up the ladder from the base.
Taking moments about base of ladder:
$176.4\sin 65° × 6 = (10g\cos 65° × 3) + (50g\cos 65° × x)$
$\Rightarrow x = 834.986... ÷ 207.082... = 4.03$ m (3 s.f.)

Q4 a)

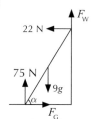

Resolving horizontally:
$F_G = 22$ N
Resolving vertically:
$75 + F_W = 9g$
$\Rightarrow F_W = 13.2$ N
Taking moments about base of ladder:
$9g\cos\alpha × 2.4 = (22\sin\alpha × 4.8)$
$+ (13.2\cos\alpha × 4.8)$
$148.32\cos\alpha = 105.6\sin\alpha$
$\tan\alpha = 1.4045...$
$\Rightarrow \alpha = 54.550...° = 54.6°$ (3 s.f.)

b) $F = \mu R$
$F_W = \mu_W × 22$
$\Rightarrow \mu_W = 13.2 ÷ 22 = 0.6$

c) $F_G = \mu_G × 75$
$\Rightarrow \mu_G = 22 ÷ 75 = 0.29$ (2 d.p.)

2. Centres of Mass — Particles

Exercise 2.1 — Particles in a line

Q1 $\sum mx = \bar{x}\sum m$
$(4 \times 3) + (6 \times 5) + (10 \times 7) = \bar{x}(4 + 6 + 10)$
$112 = 20\bar{x}$
$\Rightarrow \bar{x} = 5.6$
i.e. the centre of mass is at the point $(5.6, 0)$

Q2 $\sum mx = \bar{x}\sum m$
$(8 \times -3) + (4 \times 1) + (M \times 13) = 5(8 + 4 + M)$
$8M = 80$
$\Rightarrow M = 10$

Q3 $\sum mx = \bar{x}\sum m$
$(2 \times 1) + (1 \times 2.5) + (1.5 \times 3) = \bar{x}(2 + 1 + 1.5)$
$9 = 4.5\bar{x}$
$\Rightarrow \bar{x} = 2$ m

Q4 $\sum mx = \bar{x}\sum m$
$(1 \times 0.5) + (4 \times 1.4) + (3 \times 2) = \bar{x}(1 + 4 + 3)$
$12.1 = 8\bar{x}$
$\Rightarrow \bar{x} = 1.5125$ m

Q5 $\sum my = \bar{y}\sum m$
$(0.8 \times -2) + (1.2 \times -2.6) + (1.8 \times -3.5) + (2.1 \times -3.8)$
$= \bar{y}(0.8 + 1.2 + 1.8 + 2.1)$
$-19 = 5.9\bar{y}$
$\Rightarrow \bar{y} = -3.220...$
So the centre of mass is at $(0, -3.22)$ (3 s.f.)

Q6 $\sum my = \bar{y}\sum m$
$(3 \times -7) + (2 \times -5) + (4 \times -1) + (1 \times 0) + (4 \times 6)$
$+ (6 \times 8) = \bar{y}(3 + 2 + 4 + 1 + 4 + 6)$
$37 = 20\bar{y}$
$\Rightarrow \bar{y} = 1.85$
So the centre of mass is at $(0, 1.85)$

Q7 The particles will be placed at the points:
$(0, 0)$, $(3, 0)$, $(6, 0)$, $(9, 0)$ and $(12, 0)$.
$\sum mx = \bar{x}\sum m$
$(1 \times 0) + (2 \times 3) + (3 \times 6) + (4 \times 9) + (5 \times 12)$
$= \bar{x}(1 + 2 + 3 + 4 + 5)$
$120 = 15\bar{x}$
$\Rightarrow \bar{x} = 8$
So the centre of mass is at $(8, 0)$

Q8 $\sum my = \bar{y}\sum m$
$(M \times -3) + (2M \times 1) + (5 \times 2) = 0(M + 2M + 5)$
$-M + 10 = 0$
$\Rightarrow M = 10$

Q9 For string P:
$\sum my = \bar{y}\sum m$, where y is the distance of each point from the top of the string:
$(5 \times 1) + (4 \times 2) = \bar{y}_P(5 + 4)$
$13 = 9\bar{y}_P$
$\Rightarrow \bar{y}_P = 1.444...$
For string Q:
$\sum my = \bar{y}\sum m$
$(4 \times 1) + (5 \times 2) = \bar{y}_Q(4 + 5)$
$14 = 9\bar{y}_Q$
$\Rightarrow \bar{y}_Q = 1.555...$
$\bar{y}_Q - \bar{y}_P = 1.555... - 1.444... = 0.111...$
So the required distance is 0.111 m (3 s.f.)

Q10 $\sum mx = \bar{x}\sum m$, where x is the distance of each point from A:
$(1.5 \times 0) + (0.5 \times 1) + (2 \times 0.5) + (0.2 \times AC)$
$= AC(1.5 + 0.5 + 2 + 0.2)$
$1.5 + 0.2AC = 4.2AC$
$1.5 = 4AC$
$AC = 0.375$ m

Exercise 2.2 — Particles in two dimensions

Q1 $\sum m\mathbf{r} = \bar{\mathbf{r}}\sum m$
$2\binom{3}{1} + 3\binom{2}{4} + 5\binom{5}{2} = \bar{\mathbf{r}}(2 + 3 + 5)$
$\binom{37}{24} = 10\bar{\mathbf{r}}$
$\Rightarrow \bar{\mathbf{r}} = \binom{3.7}{2.4}$
So the coordinates are $(3.7, 2.4)$

Q2 $\sum m\mathbf{r} = \bar{\mathbf{r}}\sum m$
$2\binom{1}{2} + 8\binom{2}{3} + 6\binom{6}{4} = \bar{\mathbf{r}}(2 + 8 + 6)$
$\binom{54}{52} = 16\bar{\mathbf{r}}$
$\Rightarrow \bar{\mathbf{r}} = \binom{3.375}{3.25}$
So the coordinates are $(3.375, 3.25)$

Q3 $\sum m\mathbf{r} = \bar{\mathbf{r}}\sum m$
$3\binom{1}{2} + 4\binom{5}{1} + 5\binom{3}{6} + M\binom{0}{1} = (3 + 4 + 5 + M)\binom{1.9}{2.4}$
$\binom{38}{40 + M} = \binom{22.8 + 1.9M}{28.8 + 2.4M}$
Using the top row:
$38 = 22.8 + 1.9M$
$\Rightarrow M = 15.2 \div 1.9 = 8$ kg
You can check your answer using the bottom row.

Q4 a) $\sum m\mathbf{r} = \bar{\mathbf{r}}\sum m$
$3\binom{2}{1} + 4\binom{4}{0} + M_1\binom{-4}{0} + M_2\binom{0}{-5}$
$= (3 + 4 + M_1 + M_2)\binom{0}{0}$
$\binom{22 - 4M_1}{3 - 5M_2} = \binom{0}{0}$
Using the top row:
$22 - 4M_1 = 0$
$\Rightarrow M_1 = 5.5$ kg

b) Using the bottom row:
$3 - 5M_2 = 0$
$\Rightarrow M_2 = 0.6$ kg

Q5

0.25 kg B —— 10 cm —— C 0.3 kg

8 cm

0.2 kg A ———————— D 0.25 kg

Taking A as the origin:
$\sum m\mathbf{r} = \bar{\mathbf{r}}\sum m$
$0.2\binom{0}{0} + 0.25\binom{0}{8} + 0.3\binom{10}{8} + 0.25\binom{10}{0}$
$= (0.2 + 0.25 + 0.3 + 0.25)\bar{\mathbf{r}}$
$\binom{5.5}{4.4} = 1\bar{\mathbf{r}}$
$\Rightarrow \bar{\mathbf{r}} = \binom{5.5}{4.4}$
Using Pythagoras' theorem:
Distance from $A = |\bar{\mathbf{r}}| = \sqrt{5.5^2 + 4.4^2} = 7.04$ cm (3 s.f.)

Q6 $\Sigma m\mathbf{r} = \bar{\mathbf{r}}\Sigma m$

$2.5\binom{-3}{1} + 2\binom{-2}{-4} + 3\binom{4}{-3} + 1.5\binom{2}{3} + 1\mathbf{r}_5$

$= (2.5 + 2 + 3 + 1.5 + 1)\binom{0.65}{-0.8}$

$\binom{3.5}{-10} + \mathbf{r}_5 = \binom{6.5}{-8}$

$\Rightarrow \mathbf{r}_5 = \binom{6.5}{-8} - \binom{3.5}{-10} = \binom{3}{2}$

So the particle should be placed at (3, 2).

Q7 a)

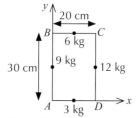

$\Sigma m\mathbf{r} = \bar{\mathbf{r}}\Sigma m$

$9\binom{0}{15} + 6\binom{10}{30} + 12\binom{20}{15} + 3\binom{10}{0}$

$= (9 + 6 + 12 + 3)\bar{\mathbf{r}}$

$\binom{330}{495} = 30\bar{\mathbf{r}}$

$\Rightarrow \bar{\mathbf{r}} = \binom{11}{16.5}$

So the coordinates of the COM are (11, 16.5).

b) The x-coordinate of the centre of mass of the system is now $x = 10$.

$\Sigma mx = \bar{x}\Sigma m$

From part a), the x-coordinate of the centre of mass of the system without the M kg particle is 11, and its mass is 30 kg, so:

$(30 \times 11) + (M \times 0) = (30 + M) \times 10$

$330 = 300 + 10M$

$30 = 10M$

$\Rightarrow M = 3$ kg

You could also answer part b) using symmetry —
for the new centre of mass to lie on EF, the sum of the
masses of the particles on AB must equal the mass of
the particle on CD. i.e. 9 + M = 12 ⇒ M = 3 kg.

Q8 a) E is the midpoint of $A(0, 0)$ and $C(0.8, 0.6)$.
So E has coordinates (0.4, 0.3).
F is the midpoint of $B(0, 0.6)$ and $D(1.2, 0)$.
So F has coordinates (0.6, 0.3).

b) $\Sigma m\mathbf{r} = \bar{\mathbf{r}}\Sigma m$

$0.5\binom{0.4}{0.3} + 0.75\binom{0.6}{0.3} + 0.25\binom{0.8}{0.6} + 1\binom{1.2}{0}$

$= (0.5 + 0.75 + 0.25 + 1)\bar{\mathbf{r}}$

$\binom{2.05}{0.525} = 2.5\bar{\mathbf{r}}$

$\Rightarrow \bar{\mathbf{r}} = \binom{0.82}{0.21}$

So the coordinates of the COM are (0.82, 0.21).

c) Let the new COM have coordinates $\binom{p}{q}$.

$\Sigma m\mathbf{r} = \bar{\mathbf{r}}\Sigma m$

$2.5\binom{0.82}{0.21} + M\binom{0}{0.6} = (2.5 + M)\binom{p}{q}$

$\binom{2.05}{0.525 + 0.6M} = (2.5 + M)\binom{p}{q}$

Using the top row:
$2.05 = p(2.5 + M)$ **eqn1**
Using the bottom row:
$0.525 + 0.6M = q(2.5 + M)$ **eqn2**
The gradient of AC is $\frac{0.6}{0.8} = \frac{3}{4}$, so the equation of the line AC is $y = \frac{3}{4}x$.

$\binom{p}{q}$ lies on this line, so $q = \frac{3}{4}p$, or $\frac{p}{q} = \frac{4}{3}$.

Dividing **eqn1** by **eqn2**:

$\dfrac{2.05}{0.525 + 0.6M} = \dfrac{p(2.5 + M)}{q(2.5 + M)}$

$\dfrac{2.05}{0.525 + 0.6M} = \dfrac{4}{3}$

$6.15 = 2.1 + 2.4M$

$\Rightarrow M = 1.6875$ kg

d) Using **eqn1**:

$2.05 = p(2.5 + M)$

$p = 2.05 \div (2.5 + 1.6875) = 0.4895...$

$q = \frac{3}{4}p = 0.3671...$

So the COM has coordinates (0.490, 0.367) (3 s.f.)

3. Centres of Mass — Laminas

Exercise 3.1 — Uniform laminas

Q1 The centre of mass is at the square's centre.
$\bar{x}$ is the x-coordinate of the midpoint of AD (or BC):
$\bar{x} = (1 + 4) \div 2 = 2.5$
$\bar{y}$ is the y-coordinate of the midpoint of AB (or CD):
$\bar{y} = (2 + 5) \div 2 = 3.5$
So the coordinates of the COM are (2.5, 3.5).

Q2 COM is at centre of circle — i.e. at midpoint of AB.
$(-5 + 1) \div 2 = -2$
$(-5 + 3) \div 2 = -1$
So coordinates of COM are (−2, −1).

Q3

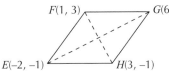

$F(1, 3)$ $G(6, 3)$
$E(-2, -1)$ $H(3, -1)$

The centre of mass of the parallelogram is the point that the diagonals intersect — i.e. the midpoint of EG or the midpoint of FH.
Midpoint of EG is at $\left(\dfrac{-2 + 6}{2}, \dfrac{-1 + 3}{2}\right) = (2, 1)$
So the COM is at (2, 1).

Q4

2.5 cm   6.5 cm $\bar{x}$ 5 cm

Using Pythagoras' theorem:
$2.5^2 + x^2 = 6.5^2$
$x^2 = 36$
$x = 6$ cm
So the length of the longer side is 12 cm.

Exercise 3.2 — Loaded laminas and composite shapes

Q1 By symmetry, the centre of mass of the lamina is at
$\left(\dfrac{1 + 7}{2}, \dfrac{1 + 7}{2}\right) = (4, 4)$
$\sum m\mathbf{r} = \bar{\mathbf{r}}\sum m$
$4.5\binom{4}{4} + 4\binom{5}{4} + 1.5\binom{2}{2} = \bar{\mathbf{r}}(4.5 + 4 + 1.5)$
$\binom{41}{37} = 10\bar{\mathbf{r}}$
$\Rightarrow \bar{\mathbf{r}} = \binom{4.1}{3.7}$
So the coordinates of the COM are (4.1, 3.7).

Q2 $\sum m\mathbf{r} = \bar{\mathbf{r}}\sum m$
$8\binom{10}{8} + 7\binom{4}{3} + 10\binom{2}{0} + 6\binom{1}{6} = \bar{\mathbf{r}}(8 + 7 + 10 + 6)$
$\binom{134}{121} = 31\bar{\mathbf{r}}$
$\Rightarrow \bar{\mathbf{r}} = \binom{4.322...}{3.903...}$
So the coordinates of the COM are:
(4.32, 3.90) (3 s.f.)

Q3 $\sum m\mathbf{r} = \bar{\mathbf{r}}\sum m$
$0.8\binom{-1}{2} + 1.2\binom{1}{-1} = \bar{\mathbf{r}}(0.8 + 1.2)$
$\binom{0.4}{0.4} = 2\bar{\mathbf{r}}$
$\Rightarrow \bar{\mathbf{r}} = \binom{0.2}{0.2}$
So the coordinates of the COM are (0.2, 0.2).

Q4 Call the larger rectangle A and the smaller rectangle B. By symmetry, the COM of A is at (2, 2.5) cm and the COM of B is at (5, 3.5) cm.
The area of A is $5 \times 4 = 20$ cm² and the area of B is $3 \times 2 = 6$ cm². The rectangles are made from the same material, so their areas are proportional to their masses.
$\sum m\mathbf{r} = \bar{\mathbf{r}}\sum m$
$20\binom{2}{2.5} + 6\binom{5}{3.5} = \bar{\mathbf{r}}(20 + 6)$
$\binom{70}{71} = 26\bar{\mathbf{r}}$
$\Rightarrow \bar{\mathbf{r}} = \binom{2.692...}{2.730...}$ cm
So the coordinates of the COM are (2.69, 2.73) cm (3 s.f.)

Q5 a) Call the rectangle P and the circle Q.
By symmetry, the COM of P is at $\left(\dfrac{1 + 7}{2}, \dfrac{2 + 7}{2}\right)$
$= (4, 4.5)$ and its area is $(7 - 1) \times (7 - 2) = 30$.
By symmetry, the COM of Q is at (4, 5) and its area is $(\pi \times 1^2) = \pi$. The shapes are made from the same material, so the masses of P and Q are proportional to their areas.
$\sum m\mathbf{r} = \bar{\mathbf{r}}\sum m$
$m_P r_P + m_Q r_Q = (m_P + m_Q)\bar{\mathbf{r}}$
$30\binom{4}{4.5} + \pi\binom{4}{5} = (30 + \pi)\bar{\mathbf{r}}$
$\binom{120 + 4\pi}{135 + 5\pi} = (30 + \pi)\bar{\mathbf{r}}$
$\Rightarrow \bar{\mathbf{r}} = \binom{4}{4.547...}$
So the coordinates of the centre of mass of the resulting shape are (4, 4.55) (3 s.f.)
The line $x = 4$ is a line of symmetry here — the COM of both shapes has an x-coordinate of 4, so you could've used symmetry to find the x-coordinate of the resultant shape, rather than performing any calculations.

b) Using coordinates found in part a), as well as $A(1, 2)$, $C(7, 7)$ and $D(1, 7)$:
$\sum m\mathbf{r} = \bar{\mathbf{r}}\sum m$
$6.5\binom{4}{4.547...} + 2\binom{1}{2} + 2.5\binom{7}{7} + 3\binom{1}{7}$
$= \bar{\mathbf{r}}(6.5 + 2 + 2.5 + 3)$
$\binom{48.5}{72.058...} = 14\bar{\mathbf{r}}$
$\Rightarrow \bar{\mathbf{r}} = \binom{3.464...}{5.147...}$
So the coordinates of the COM are:
(3.46, 5.15) (3 s.f.).

Q6 Split the letter up as shown:

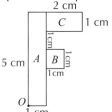

Taking O as the origin, by symmetry, A has COM (0.5, 2.5) and area 5 cm². Similarly, B has COM (1.5, 2.5) and area 1 cm², and C has COM (2, 4.5) and area 2 cm². The whole shape is cut from one sheet of card, so the masses of A, B and C are proportional to their areas.

$\Sigma m\mathbf{r} = \bar{\mathbf{r}}\Sigma m$

$5\binom{0.5}{2.5} + 1\binom{1.5}{2.5} + 2\binom{2}{4.5} = \bar{\mathbf{r}}(5 + 1 + 2)$

$\binom{8}{24} = 8\bar{\mathbf{r}}$

$\Rightarrow \bar{\mathbf{r}} = \frac{1}{8}\binom{8}{24} = \binom{1}{3}$

This is the position vector of the COM of the letter relative to O. You need to find the distance of the COM from O. Using Pythagoras' theorem:

$|\bar{\mathbf{r}}| = \sqrt{1^2 + 3^2} = 3.16$ cm (3 s.f.)

You can split the shape up any way you like — it doesn't have to be in the way shown here.

Q7 Let K be the larger disc and L be the smaller disc which is added. Let A be the origin.

By symmetry, the COM of K is a horizontal distance of 12 cm from A.

The area of K is $\pi \times 12^2 = 144\pi$ cm².

By symmetry, the COM of L is a horizontal distance of 8 cm from A:

The area of L is $\pi \times 4^2 = 16\pi$ cm².

K and L are made from the same material, so the masses of K and L are proportional to their areas.

$\Sigma mx = \bar{x}\Sigma m$

$m_K x_K + m_L x_L = \bar{x}(m_K + m_L)$

$(144\pi \times 12) + (16\pi \times 8) = AC(144\pi + 16\pi)$

$1856\pi = 160\pi AC$

$\Rightarrow AC = 11.6$ cm

Placing the smaller disc to the left of P will 'move' the COM of the whole body to the left of P. So AC is bound to be less than 12 cm.

4. Centres of Mass — Frameworks

Exercise 4.1 — Frameworks

Q1 a) Using the fact that all sides are made of the same uniform wire, the mass of each side is proportional to its length. By symmetry, the COM of each side is at its midpoint.

Let x be the distance of the COM of each side from AB.

$\Sigma mx = \bar{x}\Sigma m$

$m_{AB}x_{AB} + m_{BC}x_{BC} + m_{CD}x_{CD} + m_{DE}x_{DE} + m_{EF}x_{EF} + m_{AF}x_{AF} = \bar{x}(m_{AB} + m_{BC} + m_{CD} + m_{DE} + m_{EF} + m_{AF})$

$(5 \times 0) + (4 \times 2) + (1 \times 4) + (3 \times 2.5) + (4 \times 1) + (1 \times 0.5) = \bar{x}(5 + 4 + 1 + 3 + 4 + 1)$

$24 = 18\bar{x}$

$\Rightarrow \bar{x} = 1.33$ cm (3 s.f.)

b) Let y be the distance of the COM of each side from AF.

$\Sigma my = \bar{y}\Sigma m$

$m_{AB}y_{AB} + m_{BC}y_{BC} + m_{CD}y_{CD} + m_{DE}y_{DE} + m_{EF}y_{EF} + m_{AF}y_{AF} = \bar{y}(m_{AB} + m_{BC} + m_{CD} + m_{DE} + m_{EF} + m_{AF})$

$(5 \times 2.5) + (4 \times 5) + (1 \times 4.5) + (3 \times 4) + (4 \times 2) + (1 \times 0) = \bar{y}(5 + 4 + 1 + 3 + 4 + 1)$

$57 = 18\bar{y}$

$\Rightarrow \bar{y} = 3.17$ cm (3 s.f.)

Q2

The rods are uniform, so you can use symmetry to say that the COM of each rod is at its midpoint.

Using Pythagoras' theorem, the height of the triangle is $\sqrt{10^2 - 6^2} = 8$ cm, so $y_{AB} = y_{BC} = 4$ cm, where y_{AB} and y_{BC} are the vertical distances of the midpoints of AB and BC from AC.

$\Sigma my = \bar{y}\Sigma m$

$m_{AB}y_{AB} + m_{BC}y_{BC} + m_{AC}y_{AC} = \bar{y}(m_{AB} + m_{BC} + m_{AC})$

$(1 \times 4) + (2 \times 4) + (1.5 \times 0) = \bar{y}(1 + 2 + 1.5)$

$12 = 4.5\bar{y}$

$\Rightarrow \bar{y} = 2.67$ cm (3 s.f.)

Q3 a) The rods are uniform, so you can use symmetry to say that the COM of each rod is at its midpoint.

$\Sigma mx = \bar{x}\Sigma m$

$m_{AB}x_{AB} + m_{BC}x_{BC} + m_{CD}x_{CD} + m_{AD}x_{AD} = \bar{x}(m_{AB} + m_{BC} + m_{CD} + m_{AD})$

$(M \times 0.12) + (2M \times 0.24) + (1.5M \times 0.12) + (m_{AD} \times 0) = 0.15 \times (M + 2M + 1.5M + m_{AD})$

$0.78M = 0.15 \times (4.5M + m_{AD})$

$0.105M = 0.15m_{AD}$

$\Rightarrow m_{AD} = 0.7M$ kg

b) $\Sigma my = \bar{y}\Sigma m$

$m_{AB}y_{AB} + m_{BC}y_{BC} + m_{CD}y_{CD} + m_{AD}y_{AD} = \bar{y}(m_{AB} + m_{BC} + m_{CD} + m_{AD})$

$(M \times 0) + (2M \times 0.09) + (1.5M \times 0.18) + (0.7M \times 0.09) = \bar{y}(M + 2M + 1.5M + 0.7M)$

$0.513 = 5.2\bar{y}$

$\Rightarrow \bar{y} = 0.0987$ m (3 s.f.)

Q4 a) The mass of each rod is proportional to its length. The rods are uniform, so, by symmetry, the COM of each rod is at its midpoint.

You need to find length of EF, so, using Pythagoras' theorem:

$EF = \sqrt{12^2 + 9^2} = 15$ cm

Let $\mathbf{r}$ be the position vector of the COM of each side of the framework relative to A.

$\mathbf{r}_{AC} = \begin{pmatrix} 0 \\ -7.5 \end{pmatrix}$; $\mathbf{r}_{AB} = \begin{pmatrix} 10 \\ 0 \end{pmatrix}$; $\mathbf{r}_{EF} = \mathbf{r}_{AF} = \begin{pmatrix} 6 \\ -4.5 \end{pmatrix}$;

$\mathbf{r}_{BD} = \begin{pmatrix} 20 \\ -2 \end{pmatrix}$

$\sum m\mathbf{r} = \bar{\mathbf{r}} \sum m$

$m_{AC}\mathbf{r}_{AC} + m_{AB}\mathbf{r}_{AB} + m_{EF}\mathbf{r}_{EF} + m_{BD}\mathbf{r}_{BD} = \bar{\mathbf{r}}(m_{AC} + m_{AB} + m_{EF} + m_{BD})$

$15\begin{pmatrix} 0 \\ -7.5 \end{pmatrix} + 20\begin{pmatrix} 10 \\ 0 \end{pmatrix} + 15\begin{pmatrix} 6 \\ -4.5 \end{pmatrix} + 4\begin{pmatrix} 20 \\ -2 \end{pmatrix}$

$= \bar{\mathbf{r}}(15 + 20 + 15 + 4)$

$\begin{pmatrix} 370 \\ -188 \end{pmatrix} = 54\bar{\mathbf{r}}$

$\Rightarrow \bar{\mathbf{r}} = \frac{1}{54}\begin{pmatrix} 370 \\ -188 \end{pmatrix} = \begin{pmatrix} 6.851... \\ -3.481... \end{pmatrix}$ cm

This is the position vector of the COM of the bracket relative to A. The distance from A can be found using Pythagoras' theorem:

distance $= \sqrt{(6.851...)^2 + (-3.481...)^2}$

$= 7.69$ cm (3 s.f.)

b) Let the mass of the bracket be 1 and the mass of the basket be 2.

$\sum m\mathbf{r} = \bar{\mathbf{r}} \sum m$

$m_{\text{bracket}}\mathbf{r}_{\text{bracket}} + m_{\text{basket}}\mathbf{r}_{\text{basket}} = \bar{\mathbf{r}}(m_{\text{bracket}} + m_{\text{basket}})$

$1\begin{pmatrix} 6.851... \\ -3.481... \end{pmatrix} + 2\begin{pmatrix} 20 \\ -4 \end{pmatrix} = \bar{\mathbf{r}}(1 + 2)$

$\begin{pmatrix} 46.851... \\ -11.481... \end{pmatrix} = 3\bar{\mathbf{r}}$

$\Rightarrow \bar{\mathbf{r}} = \frac{1}{3}\begin{pmatrix} 46.851... \\ -11.481... \end{pmatrix} = \begin{pmatrix} 15.617... \\ -3.827... \end{pmatrix}$ cm

$\Rightarrow$ distance $= \sqrt{(15.617...)^2 + (-3.827...)^2}$

$= 16.1$ cm (3 s.f.)

5. Laminas in Equilibrium

Exercise 5.1 — Laminas suspended from a point

Q1 a) Let A be the rectangle and B be the square.

By symmetry, the COM of A is at (3, 2.5) and the COM of B is at (4, 2). The area of A is $6 \times 5 = 30$ and the area of B is $2 \times 2 = 4$.

$\sum m\mathbf{r} = \bar{\mathbf{r}} \sum m$

$m_A\mathbf{r}_A + m_B\mathbf{r}_B = \bar{\mathbf{r}}(m_A + m_B)$

$30\begin{pmatrix} 3 \\ 2.5 \end{pmatrix} + 4\begin{pmatrix} 4 \\ 2 \end{pmatrix} = \bar{\mathbf{r}}(30 + 4)$

$\begin{pmatrix} 106 \\ 83 \end{pmatrix} = 34\bar{\mathbf{r}}$

$\Rightarrow \bar{\mathbf{r}} = \begin{pmatrix} 3.117... \\ 2.441... \end{pmatrix}$

So the COM is at (3.12, 2.44) (3 s.f.)

b)

$\theta = \tan^{-1}\left(\frac{2.441...}{3.117...}\right) = 38.1°$ (3 s.f.)

Q2 a) The wire is uniform, so, by symmetry, the COM of each side is at its midpoint. The framework is made from a single wire, so the mass of each side is proportional to its length.

$\sum m\mathbf{r} = \bar{\mathbf{r}} \sum m$

$4\begin{pmatrix} 0 \\ 2 \end{pmatrix} + 2\begin{pmatrix} 1 \\ 4 \end{pmatrix} + 2\begin{pmatrix} 2 \\ 3 \end{pmatrix} + 4\begin{pmatrix} 4 \\ 2 \end{pmatrix} + 2\begin{pmatrix} 6 \\ 1 \end{pmatrix} + 6\begin{pmatrix} 3 \\ 0 \end{pmatrix}$

$= \bar{\mathbf{r}}(4 + 2 + 2 + 4 + 2 + 6)$

$\begin{pmatrix} 52 \\ 32 \end{pmatrix} = 20\bar{\mathbf{r}}$

$\Rightarrow \bar{\mathbf{r}} = \begin{pmatrix} 2.6 \\ 1.6 \end{pmatrix}$ So the COM is at (2.6, 1.6)

b)

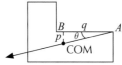

$p = 2 - 1.6 = 0.4$

$q = 6 - 2.6 = 3.4$

$\theta = \tan^{-1}\left(\frac{0.4}{3.4}\right) = 6.71°$ (3 s.f.)

c)

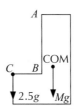

Taking moments about A,
moments clockwise = moments anticlockwise:

$(Mg \times 0.4) = (2.5g \times 2)$

$M = 5 \div 0.4 = 12.5$ kg

Q3

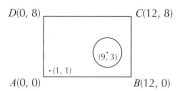

Let P be the rectangle and Q be the circle. By symmetry, the COM of P is at $(6, 4)$ and the COM of Q is at $(9, 3)$. The area of P is $12 \times 8 = 96$ and the area of Q is $\pi \times 2^2 = 4\pi$.

$\Sigma m\mathbf{r} = \bar{\mathbf{r}}\Sigma m$

$m_P\mathbf{r}_P + m_Q\mathbf{r}_Q = \bar{\mathbf{r}}(m_P + m_Q)$

$96\binom{6}{4} + 4\pi\binom{9}{3} = \bar{\mathbf{r}}(96 + 4\pi)$

$\binom{576 + 36\pi}{384 + 12\pi} = \bar{\mathbf{r}}(96 + 4\pi)$

$\Rightarrow \bar{\mathbf{r}} = \binom{6.347...}{3.884...}$

So the COM has coordinates $(6.347..., 3.884...)$.
Draw an arrow from the pivot point $(1, 1)$ to the COM, and form a right-angled triangle. You can find the horizontal and vertical side lengths of the triangle using the coordinates of the pivot point and COM:

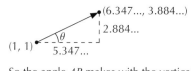

So the angle AB makes with the vertical is:

$\theta = \tan^{-1}\left(\frac{2.884...}{5.347...}\right) = 28.3°$ (3 s.f.)

Q4 a) Let P be the larger rectangle and Q be the smaller rectangle. By symmetry, the COM of each lamina is at its midpoint. P and Q are made from the same material, so their masses are proportional to their areas.

$x_P = 4$, $m_P = 8 \times 9 = 72$;

$x_Q = 8 + 2 = 10$, $m_Q = 4 \times 3 = 12$.

$\Sigma mx = \bar{x}\Sigma m$

$(72 \times 4) + (12 \times 10) = \bar{x}(72 + 12)$

$\Rightarrow \bar{x} = 4.857... = 4.86$ cm (3 s.f.)

b) $y_P = 4.5$; $y_Q = 1.5$.

$\Sigma my = \bar{y}\Sigma m$

$(72 \times 4.5) + (12 \times 1.5) = \bar{x}(72 + 12)$

$\Rightarrow \bar{y} = 4.071... = 4.07$ cm (3 s.f.)

c)

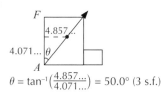

$\theta = \tan^{-1}\left(\frac{4.857...}{4.071...}\right) = 50.0°$ (3 s.f.)

d)

F
d
α
$4.857...$
A

$d = 9 - 4.071... = 4.928...$

$\alpha = \tan^{-1}\left(\frac{4.857...}{4.928...}\right) = 44.6°$ (3 s.f.)

Q5 a) Let P be the 10-unit radius circle, and Q be the 2-unit radius circle.
By symmetry, the COM of each circle is at its centre.
P has area $\pi \times 10^2 = 100\pi$ and Q has area $\pi \times 2^2 = 4\pi$.

$\Sigma m\mathbf{r} = \bar{\mathbf{r}}\Sigma m$

$m_P\mathbf{r}_P + m_Q\mathbf{r}_Q = \bar{\mathbf{r}}(m_P + m_Q)$

$100\pi\binom{0}{0} + 4\pi\binom{2}{-4} = \bar{\mathbf{r}}(100\pi + 4\pi)$

$\binom{8\pi}{-16\pi} = 104\pi\bar{\mathbf{r}}$

$\Rightarrow \bar{\mathbf{r}} = \binom{0.076...}{-0.153...}$

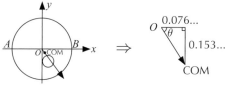

$\theta = \tan^{-1}\left(\frac{0.153...}{0.076...}\right) = 63.4°$ (3 s.f.)

b) $\Sigma m\mathbf{r} = \bar{\mathbf{r}}\Sigma m$

$m_{lamina}\mathbf{r}_{lamina} + m_{particle}\mathbf{r}_{particle} = \bar{\mathbf{r}}(m_{lamina} + m_{particle})$

$0.7\binom{0.076...}{-0.153...} + 0.9\binom{10}{0} = \bar{\mathbf{r}}(0.7 + 0.9)$

$\binom{9.053...}{-0.107...} = 1.6\bar{\mathbf{r}}$

$\Rightarrow \bar{\mathbf{r}} = \binom{5.658...}{-0.067...}$

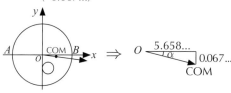

$\alpha = \tan^{-1}\left(\frac{0.067...}{5.658...}\right) = 0.681°$ (3 s.f.)

Q6 First find the length of side BC:

$\tan 25° = \frac{BC}{50}$

$\Rightarrow BC = 50\tan 25° = 23.315...$ cm

Take D as the origin. The COM of the unloaded lamina is at its centre, i.e. at $\left(\frac{50}{2}, \frac{23.315...}{2}\right)$
$= (25, 11.657...)$
So, finding $\bar{\mathbf{r}}$, the COM of the loaded lamina:

$\Sigma m\mathbf{r} = \bar{\mathbf{r}}\Sigma m$

$0.5\binom{25}{11.657...} + 0.2\binom{0}{0} = \bar{\mathbf{r}}(0.5 + 0.2)$

$\binom{12.5}{5.828...} = 0.7\bar{\mathbf{r}}$

$\Rightarrow \bar{\mathbf{r}} = \binom{17.857...}{8.326...}$

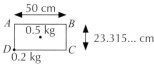

$d = 23.315... - 8.326... = 14.988...$

$\theta = \tan^{-1}\left(\frac{14.988...}{17.857...}\right) = 40.0°$ (3 s.f.)

Review Exercise — Chapter 1

Q1 Taking moments about D:
$(21 \times 10) = 14P$
$\Rightarrow P = 210 \div 14 = 15$ N
Resolving vertically:
$21 + 25 = P + Q$
$Q = 46 - 15 = 31$ N

Q2 a) Resolving vertically:
$70.16 = 12 + mg + 17$
$\Rightarrow m = 41.16 \div 9.8 = 4.2$ kg

b) Taking moments about midpoint:
$17 \times 6.5 = mgl + (12 \times 6.5)$
$4.2gl = 32.5$
$\Rightarrow l = 32.5 \div 41.16 = 0.7896...$
$= 0.790$ m (3 s.f.)

Q3

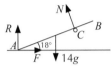

Taking moments about A:
$14g\cos18° \times 7.5 = N \times 13$
$\Rightarrow N = 75.279...$ N
Resolving vertically:
$R + (75.279...)\cos18° = 14g$
$\Rightarrow R = 65.604...$ N
Resolving horizontally:
$F = N\sin18° = (75.279...)\sin18° = 23.262...$ N
Friction is limiting, so, using $F = \mu R$:
$23.262... = \mu \times 65.604...$
$\Rightarrow \mu = 0.35$ (2 d.p.)

Q4 a)

Let l be the length of the ladder.
Taking moments about base of ladder:
$20g\cos60° \times 0.5l = N\sin60° \times l$
$49l = \frac{\sqrt{3}}{2}Nl$
$\Rightarrow N = \frac{98}{\sqrt{3}}$ N
Resolving vertically:
$R = 20g = 196$ N
Resolving horizontally:
$F = N$
Using $F = \mu R$:
$\frac{98}{\sqrt{3}} = \mu \times 196$
$\Rightarrow \mu = \frac{98}{196\sqrt{3}} = \frac{1}{2\sqrt{3}} = \frac{\sqrt{3}}{2(\sqrt{3})^2}$
$= \frac{\sqrt{3}}{6}$, as required.

b)

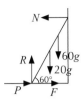

Let P be the horizontal force applied at the base of the ladder. P will be at its minimum value when friction is limiting (i.e. when F is at its greatest value).
Taking moments about base of ladder:
$(20g\cos60° \times 0.5l) + (60g\cos60° \times 0.75l)$
$\qquad = N\sin60° \times l$
$269.5l = \frac{\sqrt{3}}{2}Nl$
$\Rightarrow N = \frac{539}{\sqrt{3}}$ N
Resolving vertically:
$R = 60g + 20g = 80g = 784$ N
Resolving horizontally:
$P + F = \frac{539}{\sqrt{3}}$
$P + \mu R = \frac{539}{\sqrt{3}}$
$P + (\frac{\sqrt{3}}{6} \times 784) = \frac{539}{\sqrt{3}}$
$\Rightarrow P = \frac{539}{\sqrt{3}} - \frac{392\sqrt{3}}{3} = \frac{147\sqrt{3}}{3} = 49\sqrt{3}$ N
$= 84.9$ N (3 s.f.)

Q5 a) $\Sigma mx = \bar{x}\Sigma m$
$m_1x_1 + m_2x_2 + m_3x_3 = \bar{x}(m_1 + m_2 + m_3)$
$(1 \times 1) + (2 \times 2) + (3 \times 3) = \bar{x}(1 + 2 + 3)$
$\Rightarrow 14 = 6\bar{x} \Rightarrow \bar{x} = 14 \div 6 = 2.333...$
So the coordinates are (2.33, 0) (3 s.f.)

b) $\Sigma my = \bar{y}\Sigma m$
$m_1y_1 + m_2y_2 + m_3y_3 = \bar{y}(m_1 + m_2 + m_3)$
$(1 \times 3) + (2 \times 2) + (3 \times 1) = \bar{y}(1 + 2 + 3)$
$\Rightarrow 10 = 6\bar{y} \Rightarrow \bar{y} = 10 \div 6 = 1.666...$
So the coordinates are (0, 1.67) (3 s.f.)

c) $\Sigma m\mathbf{r} = \bar{\mathbf{r}}\Sigma m$
$m_1\mathbf{r}_1 + m_2\mathbf{r}_2 + m_3\mathbf{r}_3 = \bar{\mathbf{r}}(m_1 + m_2 + m_3)$
$1\binom{3}{4} + 2\binom{3}{1} + 3\binom{1}{0} = \bar{\mathbf{r}}(1 + 2 + 3)$
$\binom{12}{6} = 6\bar{\mathbf{r}}$
$\Rightarrow \bar{\mathbf{r}} = \binom{12}{6} \div 6 = \binom{2}{1}$
So the coordinates are (2, 1).

Q6 $\Sigma m\mathbf{r} = \bar{\mathbf{r}}\Sigma m$
$m\binom{0}{0} + 2m\binom{0}{4} + 3m\binom{5}{4} + 12\binom{5}{0}$
$= (m + 2m + 3m + 12)\binom{3.5}{2}$
$\binom{15m + 60}{20m} = \binom{21m + 42}{12m + 24}$
Using the bottom row:
$20m = 12m + 24$
$8m = 24$
$\Rightarrow m = 24 \div 8 = 3$ kg

Q7 a) Split the shape up into a 2 × 3 rectangle and a 1 × 1 square. The rectangle (1) has area 2 × 3 = 6, so $m_1 = 6$.
By symmetry, the COM of the rectangle is at its centre, so $x_1 = 2$ and $y_1 = 2.5$.
The square (2) has area 1 × 1 = 1, so $m_2 = 1$.
Again by symmetry, the COM of the square is at its centre, so $x_2 = 3.5$ and $y_2 = 1.5$.
Combined shape has:
$m_1x_1 + m_2x_2 = \bar{x}(m_1 + m_2)$
$(6 \times 2) + (1 \times 3.5) = (6 + 1)\bar{x}$
$\Rightarrow 15.5 = 7\bar{x} \Rightarrow \bar{x} = 15.5 \div 7 = 2.21$ (3 s.f.).
and:
$m_1y_1 + m_2y_2 = \bar{y}(m_1 + m_2)$
$\Rightarrow (6 \times 2.5) + (1 \times 1.5) = (6 + 1)\bar{y}$
$\Rightarrow 16.5 = 7\bar{y} \Rightarrow \bar{y} = 16.5 \div 7 = 2.36$ (3 s.f.).
So coordinates are (2.21, 2.36).
You could also have used the formula in 2D to find this.

b) The circle (1) has area $\pi \times 1^2 = \pi$, so $m_1 = \pi$.
By symmetry, the COM of the circle is at its centre, so $x_1 = 8$ and $y_1 = 3$.
The rectangle (2) has area 4 × 3 = 12, so $m_2 = 12$.
Again by symmetry, the COM of the rectangle is at its centre, so $x_2 = 8$ and $y_2 = 2.5$.
The combined shape has $x = 8$ as a line of symmetry, so $\bar{x} = 8$.
$m_1y_1 + m_2y_2 = \bar{y}(m_1 + m_2)$
$\Rightarrow (\pi \times 3) + (12 \times 2.5) = (\pi + 12)\bar{y}$
$\Rightarrow 39.42... = (15.14...)\bar{y}$
$\Rightarrow \bar{y} = 2.60$ (3 s.f.).
So coordinates are (8, 2.60).

c) The circle (1) has area $\pi \times 2^2 = 4\pi$, so $m_1 = 4\pi$.
By symmetry, the COM of the circle is at its centre, so $x_1 = 14$ and $y_1 = 2$.
The square (2) has area 1 × 1 = 1, so $m_2 = 1$.
Again by symmetry, the COM of the square is at its centre, so $x_2 = 14.5$ and $y_2 = 2.5$.
$\Sigma m\mathbf{r} = \bar{\mathbf{r}}\Sigma m$
$m_1\mathbf{r}_1 + m_2\mathbf{r}_2 = \bar{\mathbf{r}}(m_1 + m_2)$
$4\pi\binom{14}{2} + 1\binom{14.5}{2.5} = \bar{\mathbf{r}}(4\pi + 1)$
$\binom{56\pi + 14.5}{8\pi + 2.5} = \bar{\mathbf{r}}(4\pi + 1)$
$\Rightarrow \bar{\mathbf{r}} = \binom{14.036...}{2.036...}$
So coordinates are (14.0, 2.04) (3 s.f.)

Q8 a) $m_1y_1 + m_2y_2 + m_3y_3 + m_4y_4$
$= \bar{y}(m_1 + m_2 + m_3 + m_4)$
$(7 \times 0) + (12 \times 5) + (10 \times 5) + (6 \times 0)$
$= \bar{y}(7 + 12 + 10 + 6)$
$110 = 35\bar{y}$
$\Rightarrow \bar{y} = 3.142... = 3.14$ cm (3 s.f.).
The framework is 'light' so it has no mass.

b) $m_1x_1 + m_2x_2 + m_3x_3 + m_4x_4$
$= \bar{x}(m_1 + m_2 + m_3 + m_4)$
$(7 \times 0) + (12 \times 0) + (10 \times 5) + (6 \times 5)$
$= \bar{x}(7 + 12 + 10 + 6)$
$80 = 35\bar{x}$
$\Rightarrow \bar{x} = 2.285... = 2.29$ cm (3 s.f.)

Q9 a) (i)

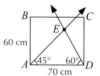

The COM is the point at which the two arrows intersect, marked E on the diagram.
Angle $AED = 180° - 45° - 60° = 75°$.
By the sine rule:
$\dfrac{AE}{\sin 60°} = \dfrac{70}{\sin 75°}$
$\Rightarrow AE = 62.76...$ cm
So, using trigonometry, the distance of the COM from AD is $(62.76...)\sin 45° = 44.37...$
$= 44.4$ cm (3 s.f.)

(ii) Again using trigonometry, the distance of the COM from AB is $(62.76...)\cos 45° = 44.37...$
$= 44.4$ cm (3 s.f.)

b)

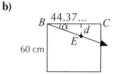

$d = 60 - 44.37... = 15.62...$ cm
$\alpha = \tan^{-1}\left(\dfrac{15.62...}{44.37...}\right) = 19.4°$ (3 s.f.)

Q10

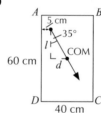

The COM is at the centre of the rectangle, i.e. 20 cm from AD and 30 cm from AB.
$d = 20 - 5 = 15$ cm
$\tan 35° = \dfrac{d}{l}$
$\Rightarrow l = \dfrac{15}{\tan 35°} = 21.42...$ cm
So the distance of the pivot from AB is:
$30 - 21.42... = 8.58$ cm (3 s.f.)

Exam-Style Questions — Chapter 1

Q1 a)

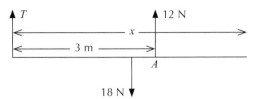

Taking moments about left-hand end of beam:

$12 \times 3 = 18 \times \frac{x}{2}$

$36 = 9x$

$x = 4$ m

[2 marks available in total]:
- *1 mark for taking moments*
- *1 mark for showing that x = 4 m*

b) Resolving vertically:

$T + 12 = 18$

$\Rightarrow T = 6$ N *[1 mark]*

Q2 a)

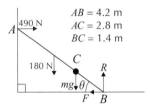

$AB = 4.2$ m
$AC = 2.8$ m
$BC = 1.4$ m

Taking moments about B:

$(mg\cos\theta \times 1.4) + (180\cos\theta \times 2.1)$
$= (490\sin\theta \times 4.2)$

Dividing throughout by $\cos\theta$:

$1.4mg + 378 = 2058\tan\theta = 2058 \times \frac{8}{11}$

$1.4mg = 1496.7... - 378 = 1118.7...$

$m = \frac{1118.7...}{13.72} = 81.539... = 82$ kg (to nearest kg)

[3 marks available in total]:
- *1 mark for taking moments about B*
- *1 mark for correct workings*
- *1 mark for the correct value of m*

b) Resolving horizontally:

$F = 490$ N

Resolving vertically:

$R = 180 + (81.539...)g = 979.090...$ N

As equilibrium is limiting, $F = \mu R$

so $(979.090...)\mu = 490$ N

$\Rightarrow \mu = 0.50$ (2 d.p.)

[5 marks available in total]:
- *1 mark for resolving horizontally*
- *1 mark for resolving vertically*
- *1 mark for using F = μR*
- *1 mark for correct workings*
- *1 mark for correct value of μ*

Q3 a) Using the formula $\Sigma my = \bar{y}\Sigma m$

$m_1 y_1 + m_2 y_2 + m_3 y_3 = \bar{y}(m_1 + m_2 + m_3)$

$\Rightarrow (4 \times 3) + (3 \times 1) + (2 \times y) = 2 \times (4 + 3 + 2)$

[1 mark]

$\Rightarrow 15 + 2y = 18$ *[1 mark]*

$\Rightarrow y = (18 - 15) \div 2 = 1.5$ *[1 mark]*.

b) Using the formula $\Sigma mx = \bar{x}\Sigma m$

$m_1 x_1 + m_2 x_2 + m_3 x_3 = \bar{x}(m_1 + m_2 + m_3)$

$\Rightarrow (4 \times 1) + (3 \times 5) + (2 \times 4) = \bar{x}(4 + 3 + 2)$

[1 mark]

$\Rightarrow 27 = 9\bar{x}$ *[1 mark]*

$\Rightarrow \bar{x} = 27 \div 9 = 3$ *[1 mark]*.

c) Centre of mass of the lamina is at (3.5, 2.5), due to the symmetry of the shape, and $m_{lamina} = 6$ kg. Centre of mass of the group of particles is (3, 2) (from b)) and $m_{particles} = 4 + 3 + 2 = 9$ kg.

$\Sigma m\mathbf{r} = \bar{\mathbf{r}}\Sigma m$

$m_{lamina}\mathbf{r}_{lamina} + m_{particles}\mathbf{r}_{particles} = \bar{\mathbf{r}}(m_{lamina} + m_{particles})$

$6\binom{3.5}{2.5} + 9\binom{3}{2} = \bar{\mathbf{r}}(6 + 9)$

$\binom{21 + 27}{15 + 18} = 15\bar{\mathbf{r}}$

$\Rightarrow \bar{\mathbf{r}} = \binom{48}{33} \div 15 = \binom{3.2}{2.2}$,

So the coordinates are (3.2, 2.2).

[6 marks available — 1 mark for the correct x_{lamina}, 1 mark for the correct y_{lamina}, 1 mark for correct entry of horizontal positions in the formula, 1 mark for correct entry of vertical positions in the formula, 1 mark for x coordinate of 3.2, 1 mark for y coordinate of 2.2.]

d)

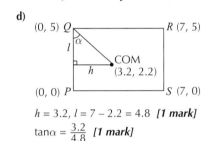

$h = 3.2, l = 7 - 2.2 = 4.8$ *[1 mark]*

$\tan\alpha = \frac{3.2}{4.8}$ *[1 mark]*

$\Rightarrow \alpha = 33.7°$ (3 s.f.) *[1 mark]*

Q4 a) Splitting up the shape into a circle (1), large square (2) and small square (3) and taking the point A as the origin, the position vectors of the centres of mass of each shape are as follows:
Circle:
$x_1 = 25$ and $y_1 = 50 + (40 - 35) = 55$
(by symmetry) so $\mathbf{r}_1 = \binom{25}{55}$.
Large Square:
$x_2 = 25$ and $y_2 = 25$ (by symmetry) so $\mathbf{r}_2 = \binom{25}{25}$.
Small Square:
$x_3 = 50 + 5 = 55$ and $y_3 = 5$ (by symmetry)
so $\mathbf{r}_3 = \binom{55}{5}$.
$\sum m\mathbf{r} = \bar{\mathbf{r}}\sum m$
$m_1\mathbf{r}_1 + m_2\mathbf{r}_2 + m_3\mathbf{r}_3 = \bar{\mathbf{r}}(m_1 + m_2 + m_3)$
$5\binom{25}{55} + 4\binom{25}{25} + 1\binom{55}{5} = \bar{\mathbf{r}}(5 + 4 + 1)$
$\binom{125 + 100 + 55}{275 + 100 + 5} = 10\bar{\mathbf{r}}$
$\Rightarrow \bar{\mathbf{r}} = \binom{280}{380} \div 10 = \binom{28}{38}$.
The centre of mass of the sign is 28 cm from AB and 38 cm from AF.
[5 marks available — 1 mark for each individual centre of mass entered correctly into the formula, 1 mark for correct distance from AB, 1 mark for correct distance from AF.]

b) For the sign to hang with AF horizontal, the centre of mass of the whole system (sign + particle) must be vertically below C, i.e. $\bar{x}$ must be 25 (taking A as the origin again).
Given that $m_{\text{sign}} = 10$ kg and $x_{\text{sign}} = 28$ (from a)), and $x_{\text{particle}} = 0$ (since it's attached at the origin):
$\sum mx = \bar{x}\sum m$
$m_{\text{sign}}x_{\text{sign}} + m_{\text{particle}}x_{\text{particle}} = \bar{x}(m_{\text{sign}} + m_{\text{particle}})$
$(10 \times 28) + 0 = 25(10 + m_{\text{particle}})$
$280 \div 25 = 10 + m_{\text{particle}}$
$11.2 - 10 = m_{\text{particle}}$
$\Rightarrow m_{\text{particle}} = 1.2$ kg
You could have done this by taking moments about C and using 'clockwise moments = anticlockwise moments'.

[3 marks available — 1 mark for stating the correct required value of $\bar{x}$, 1 mark for correct entry of values into the formula, 1 mark for correct final answer.]

Chapter 2: Kinematics

1. Variable Acceleration in 1 Dimension

Exercise 1.1 — Differentiating to find velocity and acceleration

Q1 a) $v = \dfrac{dx}{dt} = (9t^2 + 10t)$ ms^{-1}

b) $a = \dfrac{dv}{dt} = (18t + 10)$ ms^{-2}

c) When $t = 3$, $a = 18(3) + 10 = 64$ ms^{-2}
Using $F = ma$:
$480 = 64m$
$\Rightarrow m = 480 \div 64 = 7.5$ kg

Q2 a) $v = \dfrac{dx}{dt} = (2bt + 6)$ ms^{-1}
When $t = 3$, $v = 18$, so:
$18 = 6b + 6$
$\Rightarrow b = 2$

b) $a = \dfrac{dv}{dt} = \dfrac{d}{dt}(4t + 6) = 4$ ms^{-2}, i.e. constant

Q3 a) $v = \dfrac{ds}{dt} = (6t^2 - 42t + 60)$ ms^{-1}

b) When the object is at rest, $v = 0$:
$6t^2 - 42t + 60 = 0$
$t^2 - 7t + 10 = 0$
$(t - 2)(t - 5) = 0$
$\Rightarrow t = 2$ s and $t = 5$ s

c) $a = \dfrac{dv}{dt} = (12t - 42)$ ms^{-2}

d) When $t = 0$, $a = 12(0) - 42 = -42$ ms^{-2}

Q4 a) When $t = 0$, $x = 12(0)^2 + 60(0) - (0)^3 = 0$ m
i.e. the particle is initially at the origin.

b) $a = \dfrac{d^2x}{dt^2} = \dfrac{d}{dt}(24t + 60 - 3t^2) = (24 - 6t)$ ms^{-2}
$24 - 6t = 0$
$\Rightarrow t = 4$ s

c) When $t = 0.5$, $a = 24 - 6(0.5) = 21$ ms^{-2}
Using $F = ma$:
$F = 1.4 \times 21 = 29.4$ N

d) When the particle reaches its maximum displacement from the origin, $v = 0$:
$24t + 60 - 3t^2 = 0$
$t^2 - 8t - 20 = 0$
$(t - 10)(t + 2) = 0$
$\Rightarrow t = 10$ or $t = -2$
You can't have a negative time, so ignore $t = -2$.
When $t = 10$, $x = 12(10)^2 + 60(10) - (10)^3$
$= 800$ m

Q5 **a)** $v = \dfrac{ds}{dt} = (12 - 30t + 12t^2)$ kmh^{-1}
$12 - 30t + 12t^2 = 0$
$2t^2 - 5t + 2 = 0$
$(2t - 1)(t - 2) = 0$
$\Rightarrow t = 0.5$ h and $t = 2$ h

b) When $t = 0.5$:
$s = 12(0.5) - 15(0.5)^2 + 4(0.5)^3 = 2.75$ km
When $t = 2$:
$s = 12(2) - 15(2)^2 + 4(2)^3 = -4$ km
So the vehicle travels 2.75 km – –4 km = 6.75 km
between these two times.
The negative displacement means the particle is 4 km
from its starting point, but in the negative direction
(i.e. when t = 2, the particle is on the 'other side' of its
starting point to when t = O.5).

Q6 **a)** Find the times that the train is at rest:
$v = \dfrac{ds}{dt} = (180t - 135t^2)$ ms^{-1}
$180t - 135t^2 = 0$
$4t - 3t^2 = 0$
$t(4 - 3t) = 0$
$\Rightarrow t = 0$ h and $t = \dfrac{4}{3}$ h
So the time taken to travel between the two
stations is $\dfrac{4}{3}$ hours, or 1 hour and 20 minutes.

b) When $t = 0$, $s = 90(0)^2 - 45(0)^3 = 0$ km
and when $t = \dfrac{4}{3}$, $s = 90\left(\dfrac{4}{3}\right)^2 - 45\left(\dfrac{4}{3}\right)^3 = 53\dfrac{1}{3}$ km
So the distance between the two stations is
53.3 km (3 s.f.)

c) $a = \dfrac{dv}{dt} = (180 - 270t)$ ms^{-2}
When train reaches its maximum speed,
its acceleration will be zero:
$180 - 270t = 0$
$\Rightarrow t = \dfrac{2}{3}$ h
When $t = \dfrac{2}{3}$, $v = 180\left(\dfrac{2}{3}\right) - 135\left(\dfrac{2}{3}\right)^2 = 60$ kmh^{-1}

Exercise 1.2 — Integrating to find velocity and displacement

Q1 **a)** **(i)** $v = \int a\, dt = \int 5\, dt = 5t + C$
When $t = 0$, $v = 10$, so:
$10 = 5(0) + C$
$\Rightarrow C = 10$
So $v = (5t + 10)$ ms^{-1}

   (ii) When $t = 6$, $v = 5(6) + 10 = 40$ ms^{-1}

b) **(i)** $x = \int v\, dt = \int (5t + 10)\, dt = \dfrac{5}{2}t^2 + 10t + D$
When $t = 0$, $x = 0$, so:
$0 = \dfrac{5}{2}(0)2 + 10(0) + D$
$\Rightarrow D = 0$
So $x = (\dfrac{5}{2}t^2 + 10t)$ m

   (ii) When $t = 6$, $x = \dfrac{5}{2}(6)^2 + 10(6) = 150$ m

Q2 **a)** $x = \int v\, dt = \int (3t^2 - 14t + 8)\, dt$
$= t^3 - 7t^2 + 8t + C$
When $t = 1$, $x = 8$, so:
$8 = (1)^3 - 7(1)^2 + 8(1) + C$
$\Rightarrow C = 6$
So $x = (t^3 - 7t^2 + 8t + 6)$ m

b) The object is at rest when $v = 0$:
$3t^2 - 14t + 8 = 0$
$(3t - 2)(t - 4) = 0$
$\Rightarrow t = \dfrac{2}{3}$ or $t = 4$
So the object is at rest when $t = 0.667$ s (3 s.f.)
and when $t = 4$ s.

c) When $t = \dfrac{2}{3}$, $x = \left(\dfrac{2}{3}\right)^3 - 7\left(\dfrac{2}{3}\right)^2 + 8\left(\dfrac{2}{3}\right) + 6$
$= 8.518...$ m
and when $t = 4$, $x = 4^3 - 7(4)^2 + 8(4) + 6$
$= -10$ m
So the distance between the two points is
$8.518... - -10 = 18.5$ m (3 s.f.)

Q3 **a)** $v = \int a\, dt = \int (2t - 6)\, dt = t^2 - 6t + C$
When $t = 0$, $v = 6$, so:
$6 = (0)^2 - 6(0) + C$
$\Rightarrow C = 6$
So $v = (t^2 - 6t + 6)$ ms^{-1}

b) $x = \int v\, dt = \int (t^2 - 6t + 6)\, dt$
$= \dfrac{1}{3}t^3 - 3t^2 + 6t + D$
When $t = 0$, $x = 0$, so:
$0 = \dfrac{1}{3}(0)^3 - 3(0)^2 + 6(0) + D$
$\Rightarrow D = 0$
So $x = (\dfrac{1}{3}t^3 - 3t^2 + 6t)$ m

c) The particle passes through the origin when $x = 0$:
$\dfrac{1}{3}t^3 - 3t^2 + 6t = 0$
$t^3 - 9t^2 + 18t = 0$
$t(t^2 - 9t + 18) = 0$
$\Rightarrow t = 0$ and $t^2 - 9t + 18 = 0$
$t^2 - 9t + 18 = 0$
$(t - 3)(t - 6) = 0$
So the particle passes through the origin when
$t = 3$ s and $t = 6$ s.

Q4 **a)** $v = \int a\, dt = \int (2t - 4)\, dt = t^2 - 4t + C$
When $t = 0$, $v = 0$, so:
$0 = 0^2 - 4(0) + C$
$\Rightarrow C = 0$
So $v = (t^2 - 4t)$ ms^{-1}
When $t = 5$, $v = 5^2 - 4(5) = 5$ ms^{-1}

b) $x = \int v\, dt = \int (t^2 - 4t)\, dt = \dfrac{1}{3}t^3 - 2t^2 + D$
When $t = 0$, $x = 0$, so:
$0 = \dfrac{1}{3}(0)^3 - 2(0)^2 + D$
$\Rightarrow D = 0$
So $x = (\dfrac{1}{3}t^3 - 2t^2)$ m
When $t = 5$, $x = \dfrac{1}{3}(5)^3 - 2(5)^2 = -\dfrac{25}{3}$
$= -8.33$ m (3 s.f.)

c) When the object reverses its direction, it will stop
momentarily (i.e. $v = 0$):
$t^2 - 4t = 0$
$t(t - 4) = 0$
$\Rightarrow t = 0$ and $t = 4$
So the object reverses its direction at $t = 4$ s.

d) The object returns to O when $x = 0$:
$$\tfrac{1}{3}t^3 - 2t^2 = 0$$
$$t^3 - 6t^2 = 0$$
$$t^2(t - 6) = 0$$
$$\Rightarrow t = 0 \text{ and } t = 6$$
So the object returns to O at $t = 6$ s.

Q5 a) $v = \int a \, dt = \int (k - 18t^2) \, dt = kt - 6t^3 + C$
When $t = 0$, $v = 7$, so:
$7 = k(0) - 6(0)^3 + C$
$\Rightarrow C = 7$
So $v = (kt - 6t^3 + 7)$ ms^{-1}
When $t = 1$, $v = 9$, so:
$9 = k(1) - 6(1)^3 + 7$
$\Rightarrow k = 8$

b) $x = \int v \, dt = \int (8t - 6t^3 + 7) \, dt$
$= 4t^2 - \tfrac{3}{2}t^4 + 7t + D$
When $t = 0$, $x = 0$, so:
$0 = 4(0)^2 - \tfrac{3}{2}(0)^4 + 7(0) + D$
$\Rightarrow D = 0$
So $x = (4t^2 - \tfrac{3}{2}t^4 + 7t)$ m
When $t = 1$, $x = 4(1)^2 - \tfrac{3}{2}(1)^4 + 7(1) = 9.5$ m
So Q is 9.5 m from O.

Exercise 1.3 — Using the chain rule to find velocity and acceleration

Q1 a) Let $u = 4t$, then $x = 3\sin u$.
$\dfrac{du}{dt} = 4$, $\dfrac{dx}{du} = 3\cos u$
$v = \dfrac{dx}{dt} = \dfrac{dx}{du} \times \dfrac{du}{dt} = 3\cos u \times 4$
$= 12\cos 4t$

b) Let $u = 2t$, then $x = 4e^u$.
$\dfrac{du}{dt} = 2$, $\dfrac{dx}{du} = 4e^u$
$v = \dfrac{dx}{dt} = \dfrac{dx}{du} \times \dfrac{du}{dt} = 4e^u \times 2$
$= 8e^{2t}$

c) First differentiate $-2\cos 3t$.
Let $u_1 = 3t$, then $x_1 = -2\cos u_1$.
$\dfrac{du_1}{dt} = 3$, $\dfrac{dx_1}{du_1} = 2\sin u_1$
$v_1 = \dfrac{dx_1}{dt} = \dfrac{dx_1}{du_1} \times \dfrac{du_1}{dt} = 2\sin u_1 \times 3$
$= 6\sin 3t$
Differentiating $3t^2 + 6t - 7$ gives $6t + 6$, so:
$v = 6\sin 3t + 6t + 6 = 6(\sin 3t + t + 1)$

d) First differentiate $2\sin 3t$.
Let $u_1 = 3t$, then $x_1 = 2\sin u_1$.
$\dfrac{du_1}{dt} = 3$, $\dfrac{dx_1}{du_1} = 2\cos u_1$
$v_1 = \dfrac{dx_1}{dt} = \dfrac{dx_1}{du_1} \times \dfrac{du_1}{dt} = 2\cos u_1 \times 3$
$= 6\cos 3t$
Now differentiate $-4e^{-t}$.
Let $u_2 = -t$, then $x_2 = -4e^{u_2}$.
$\dfrac{du_2}{dt} = -1$, $\dfrac{dx_2}{du_2} = -4e^{u_2}$
$v_2 = \dfrac{dx_2}{dt} = \dfrac{dx_2}{du_2} \times \dfrac{du_2}{dt} = -4e^{u_2} \times -1$
$= 4e^{-t}$
So $v = 6\cos 3t + 4e^{-t}$

In Q2-5, you can go through the whole substitution method (as shown in Q1) if you like. But if you can differentiate the whole thing in one step, then go for it.

Q2 a) $v = \dfrac{dx}{dt} = (12\cos 4t + 48t)$ ms^{-1}

b) Substitute $t = \dfrac{\pi}{8}$ into your expression from a):
$v = 12\cos\dfrac{4\pi}{8} + \dfrac{48\pi}{8} = 6\pi = 18.8$ ms^{-1} (3 s.f.)
t is given in terms of π here, so make sure you've got your calculator set to work in radians.

c) Differentiate your expression from a):
$a = \dfrac{dv}{dt} = -48\sin 4t + 48$
Substitute in $t = \dfrac{\pi}{8}$:
$a = -48\sin\dfrac{4\pi}{8} + 48 = -48 + 48 = 0$, as required.

Q3 a) When $t = 0$, $x = 3\cos 0 + e^0 = 4$
So the particle is initially at the point $(4, 0)$.

b) $v = \dfrac{dx}{dt} = (-12\sin 4t - 2e^{-2t})$ ms^{-1}
When $t = 0.7$, $v = -12\sin(4 \times 0.7) - 2e^{(-2 \times 0.7)}$
$= -4.513...$ ms^{-1}
When $t = 0.8$, $v = -12\sin(4 \times 0.8) - 2e^{(-2 \times 0.8)}$
$= 0.296...$ ms^{-1}
When $t = 0.7$, v is negative, and when $t = 0.8$, v is positive, so the particle must change direction in this interval.

Q4 a) When $t = 3$, $v = 6 + 20(3) - 0.1e^{2(3)} = 25.657...$
When $t = 4$, $v = 6 + 20(4) - 0.1e^{2(4)} = -212.095...$
The body's speed at $t = 3$ is positive, and its speed at $t = 4$ is negative, so the body has changed direction between these times. This means that it must have been at rest at some point in this interval.

b) $a = \dfrac{dv}{dt} = (20 - 0.2e^{2t})$ ms^{-2}
$20 - 0.2e^{2t} = 0$
$20 = 0.2e^{2t}$
$100 = e^{2t}$
$2t = \ln 100$
$\Rightarrow t = 2.30$ s (3 s.f.)

c) $x = \int v \, dt = \int (6 + 20t - 0.1e^{2t}) \, dt$
$= 6t + 10t^2 - 0.05e^{2t} + C$
When $t = 0$, $x = 0$, so:
$0 = 6(0) + 10(0)^2 - 0.05e^{2(0)} + C$
$\Rightarrow C = 0.05$
So $x = (6t + 10t^2 - 0.05e^{2t} + 0.05)$ m
When $t = 2$:
$x = 6(2) + 10(2)^2 - 0.05e^{2(2)} + 0.05$
$= 49.3$ m (3 s.f.)

Q5 a) $v = \dfrac{dx}{dt} = (6t + 4e^{-t} + 2)$ ms^{-1}

b) $a = \dfrac{dv}{dt} = (6 - 4e^{-t})$ ms^{-2}

c) t must be ≥ 0. When $t = 0$:
$a = 6 - 4e^0 = 2$ ms^{-2}
As $t \to \infty$, $e^{-t} \to 0$, so $a \to 6$ ms^{-2}
So: 2 ms$^{-2} \leq a < 6$ ms^{-2}.

2. Variable Acceleration in 2 and 3 Dimensions

Exercise 2.1 — Using vectors

Q1 a) (i) $\mathbf{v} = \dot{\mathbf{r}} = [(3t^2 - 3\cos t)\mathbf{i} + (2t - 2e^{-t})\mathbf{j}]$ ms^{-1}

(ii) When $t = 3$:
$\mathbf{v} = (3(3)^2 - 3\cos 3)\mathbf{i} + (2(3) - 2e^{-3})\mathbf{j}$
$= (29.969...\mathbf{i} + 5.900...\mathbf{j})$ ms^{-1}
Using Pythagoras' theorem:
speed $= \sqrt{29.969...^2 + 5.900...^2}$
$= 30.5$ ms^{-1} (3 s.f.)
Using trigonometry:
$\theta = \tan^{-1}\left(\dfrac{5.900...}{29.969...}\right)$
$= 11.1°$ (3 s.f.) above $\mathbf{i}$.

b) (i) $\mathbf{a} = \dot{\mathbf{v}} = ((6t + 3\sin t)\mathbf{i} + (2 + 2e^{-t})\mathbf{j})$ ms^{-2}

(ii) When $t = 4$, $\mathbf{a} = (6(4) + 3\sin 4)\mathbf{i} + (2 + 2e^{-4})\mathbf{j}$
$= (21.729...\mathbf{i} + 2.036...\mathbf{j})$ ms^{-2}
Using Pythagoras' theorem:
magnitude $= \sqrt{21.729...^2 + 2.036...^2}$
$= 21.8$ ms^{-2} (3 s.f.)

Q2 $\mathbf{a} = \dot{\mathbf{v}} = (3t^2 - 12t - 36)\mathbf{i}$ ms^{-2}
$3t^2 - 12t - 36 = 0$
$t^2 - 4t - 12 = 0$
$(t + 2)(t - 6) = 0$
$\Rightarrow t = -2$ and $t = 6$
Ignore the negative time.
When $t = 6$, $\mathbf{v} = [(6)^3 - 6(6)^2 - 36(6)]\mathbf{i} + 14\mathbf{j}$
$= (-216\mathbf{i} + 14\mathbf{j})$ ms^{-1}

Q3 a) $\mathbf{v} = \int \mathbf{a}\, dt = \int (3t\mathbf{i} + 6\mathbf{j})\, dt$
$= \frac{3}{2}t^2\mathbf{i} + 6t\mathbf{j} + \mathbf{C}$
When $t = 2$, $\mathbf{v} = (4\mathbf{i} + 6\mathbf{j})$, so:
$4\mathbf{i} + 6\mathbf{j} = \frac{3}{2}(2)^2\mathbf{i} + 6(2)\mathbf{j} + \mathbf{C}$
$4\mathbf{i} + 6\mathbf{j} = 6\mathbf{i} + 12\mathbf{j} + \mathbf{C}$
$\Rightarrow \mathbf{C} = -2\mathbf{i} - 6\mathbf{j}$
So $\mathbf{v} = [(\frac{3}{2}t^2 - 2)\mathbf{i} + (6t - 6)\mathbf{j}]$ ms^{-1}

b) $\mathbf{r} = \int \mathbf{v}\, dt = \int [(\frac{3}{2}t^2 - 2)\mathbf{i} + (6t - 6)\mathbf{j}]\, dt$
$= (\frac{1}{2}t^3 - 2t)\mathbf{i} + (3t^2 - 6t)\mathbf{j} + \mathbf{D}$
When $t = 2$, $\mathbf{r} = (2\mathbf{i} - 9\mathbf{j})$, so:
$2\mathbf{i} - 9\mathbf{j} = (\frac{1}{2}(2)^3 - 2(2))\mathbf{i} + (3(2)^2 - 6(2))\mathbf{j} + \mathbf{D}$
$2\mathbf{i} - 9\mathbf{j} = 0\mathbf{i} + 0\mathbf{j} + \mathbf{D}$
$\Rightarrow \mathbf{D} = 2\mathbf{i} - 9\mathbf{j}$
So $\mathbf{r} = [(\frac{1}{2}t^3 - 2t + 2)\mathbf{i} + (3t^2 - 6t - 9)\mathbf{j}]$ m

c) (i) When the body is due east of O, the $\mathbf{j}$-component of its position vector is zero:
$3t^2 - 6t - 9 = 0$
$t^2 - 2t - 3 = 0$
$(t + 1)(t - 3) = 0$
$\Rightarrow t = -1$ and $t = 3$
When $t = 3$, the $\mathbf{i}$-component of $\mathbf{r}$ is:
$\frac{1}{2}(3)^3 - 2(3) + 2 = 9.5 > 0$
So the body is due east of O at time $t = 3$ s.
Remember to check that the $\mathbf{i}$-component of $\mathbf{r}$ is greater than zero, otherwise you can't be sure that the body isn't at O or due west of O.

(ii) From c)(i), the $\mathbf{i}$-component of $\mathbf{r}$ at this time is 9.5, so the body's distance from O is 9.5 m.

Q4 a) $\mathbf{a} = \dot{\mathbf{v}} = [(2t - 6)\mathbf{i} + 4\mathbf{j}]$ ms^{-2}

b) $\mathbf{r} = \int \mathbf{v}\, dt = \int [(t^2 - 6t)\mathbf{i} + (4t + 5)\mathbf{j}]\, dt$
$= (\frac{1}{3}t^3 - 3t^2)\mathbf{i} + (2t^2 + 5t)\mathbf{j} + \mathbf{C}$
When $t = 0$, $\mathbf{r} = \mathbf{0}$, so:
$\mathbf{0} = (\frac{1}{3}(0)^3 - 3(0)^2)\mathbf{i} + (2(0)^2 + 5(0))\mathbf{j} + \mathbf{C}$
$\Rightarrow \mathbf{C} = \mathbf{0}$
So $\mathbf{r} = [(\frac{1}{3}t^3 - 3t^2)\mathbf{i} + (2t^2 + 5t)\mathbf{j}]$ m

c) When the particle is travelling parallel to $\mathbf{j}$, the $\mathbf{i}$-component of its velocity is zero:
$t^2 - 6t = 0$
$t(t - 6) = 0$
$\Rightarrow t = 0$ and $t = 6$
When $t = 0$, the $\mathbf{j}$-component of $\mathbf{v}$ is:
$(4(0) + 5) = 5 \neq 0$
and when $t = 6$, the $\mathbf{j}$-component of $\mathbf{v}$ is:
$(4(6) + 5) = 29 \neq 0$
So the particle is travelling parallel to $\mathbf{j}$ at time $t = 0$ s and time $t = 6$ s.

d) $(\frac{1}{3}t^3 - 3t^2)\mathbf{i} + (2t^2 + 5t)\mathbf{j} = b\mathbf{i} + 12\mathbf{j}$
Equating $\mathbf{j}$-components:
$2t^2 + 5t = 12$
$2t^2 + 5t - 12 = 0$
$(2t - 3)(t + 4) = 0$
$\Rightarrow t = 1.5$ and $t = -4$
The time can't be negative, so the particle passes through the point $(b\mathbf{i} + 12\mathbf{j})$ m at time $t = 1.5$ s.
Equating $\mathbf{i}$-components and substituting $t = 1.5$:
$\frac{1}{3}t^3 - 3t^2 = b$
$\frac{1}{3}(1.5)^3 - 3(1.5)^2 = b$
$\Rightarrow b = -5.625$

Q5 a) $\mathbf{r} = \int \mathbf{v}\, dt = \int [6t\mathbf{i} + 2\mathbf{j} + (3t^2 - 4)\mathbf{k}]\, dt$
$= 3t^2\mathbf{i} + 2t\mathbf{j} + (t^3 - 4t)\mathbf{k} + \mathbf{C}$
When $t = 0$, $\mathbf{r} = 4\mathbf{i}$, so:
$4\mathbf{i} = 3(0)^2\mathbf{i} + 2(0)\mathbf{j} + ((0)^3 - 4(0))\mathbf{k} + \mathbf{C}$
$\Rightarrow \mathbf{C} = 4\mathbf{i}$
So $\mathbf{r} = [(3t^2 + 4)\mathbf{i} + 2t\mathbf{j} + (t^3 - 4t)\mathbf{k}]$ m

b) When $t = 3$:
$\mathbf{r} = (3(3)^2 + 4)\mathbf{i} + 2(3)\mathbf{j} + ((3)^3 - 4(3))\mathbf{k}$
$= (31\mathbf{i} + 6\mathbf{j} + 15\mathbf{k})$ m

c) $\mathbf{a} = \dot{\mathbf{v}} = (6\mathbf{i} + 6t\mathbf{k})$ ms^{-2}

d) When $t = 4$, $\mathbf{a} = (6\mathbf{i} + 24\mathbf{k})$ ms^{-2}
So the magnitude is:
$\sqrt{6^2 + 24^2} = 24.7$ ms^{-2} (3 s.f.)

Q6 a) $\mathbf{v} = \dot{\mathbf{r}} = [2t\mathbf{i} + (3t^2 - 4)\mathbf{j} + (6t - 3)\mathbf{k}]$ ms^{-1}
When $t = 0$:
$\mathbf{v} = 2(0)\mathbf{i} + (3(0)^2 - 4)\mathbf{j} + (6(0) - 3)\mathbf{k}$
$= (-4\mathbf{j} - 3\mathbf{k})$ ms^{-1}
So initial speed $= \sqrt{(-4)^2 + (-3)^2} = 5$ ms^{-1}
— as required.

b) $\mathbf{a} = \dot{\mathbf{v}} = (2\mathbf{i} + 6t\mathbf{j} + 6\mathbf{k})$ ms^{-2}
When $t = 3$, $\mathbf{a} = (2\mathbf{i} + 18\mathbf{j} + 6\mathbf{k})$ ms^{-2}

Q7 a) $\mathbf{v} = \int \mathbf{a}\, dt = \int (12t\mathbf{i} + 6\mathbf{j})\, dt$
$= 6t^2\mathbf{i} + 6t\mathbf{j} + \mathbf{C}$
When $t = 0$, $\mathbf{v} = -6\mathbf{i} - 6\mathbf{j} + 5\mathbf{k}$, so:
$-6\mathbf{i} - 6\mathbf{j} + 5\mathbf{k} = 6(0)^2\mathbf{i} + 6(0)\mathbf{j} + \mathbf{C}$
$\Rightarrow \mathbf{C} = -6\mathbf{i} - 6\mathbf{j} + 5\mathbf{k}$
So $\mathbf{v} = [(6t^2 - 6)\mathbf{i} + (6t - 6)\mathbf{j} + 5\mathbf{k}]$ ms^{-1}

b) When $t = 1$:
$\mathbf{v} = (6(1)^2 - 6)\mathbf{i} + (6(1) - 6)\mathbf{j} + 5\mathbf{k} = 5\mathbf{k}$ ms^{-1}
The only non-zero term is the $\mathbf{k}$ term, so the particle is travelling parallel to $\mathbf{k}$ at this time.

c) $\mathbf{r} = \int \mathbf{v}\, dt = \int [(6t^2 - 6)\mathbf{i} + (6t - 6)\mathbf{j} + 5\mathbf{k}]\, dt$
$= (2t^3 - 6t)\mathbf{i} + (3t^2 - 6t)\mathbf{j} + 5t\mathbf{k} + \mathbf{D}$
When $t = 0$, $\mathbf{r} = 2\mathbf{k}$, so:
$2\mathbf{k} = [2(0)^3 - 6(0)]\mathbf{i} + [3(0)^2 - 6(0)]\mathbf{j} + 5(0)\mathbf{k} + \mathbf{D}$
$\Rightarrow 2\mathbf{k} = \mathbf{D}$
So $\mathbf{r} = [(2t^3 - 6t)\mathbf{i} + (3t^2 - 6t)\mathbf{j} + (5t + 2)\mathbf{k}]$ m

d) Set $4\mathbf{i} + 12\mathbf{k} = (2t^3 - 6t)\mathbf{i} + (3t^2 - 6t)\mathbf{j} + (5t + 2)\mathbf{k}$
Equating $\mathbf{k}$ terms:
$12 = 5t + 2$
$\Rightarrow t = 2$
Now substituting $t = 2$ into the position vector:
$[2(2)^3 - 6(2)]\mathbf{i} + [3(2)^2 - 6(2)]\mathbf{j} + [5(2) + 2]\mathbf{k}$
$= 4\mathbf{i} + 12\mathbf{k}$
Therefore, the particle does pass through the point $(4\mathbf{i} + 12\mathbf{k})$ m, and does so at time $t = 2$.

Q8 $\mathbf{r} = \int \mathbf{v}\, dt = \int (12\cos 4t\mathbf{i} - 12\sin 4t\mathbf{j})\, dt$
$= 3\sin 4t\mathbf{i} + 3\cos 4t\mathbf{j} + \mathbf{C}$
When $t = 0$, $\mathbf{r} = 3\mathbf{j}$, so:
$3\mathbf{j} = 3\sin 0\mathbf{i} + 3\cos 0\mathbf{j} + \mathbf{C}$
$3\mathbf{j} = 3\mathbf{j} + \mathbf{C}$
$\Rightarrow \mathbf{C} = 0$
So $\mathbf{r} = (3\sin 4t\mathbf{i} + 3\cos 4t\mathbf{j})$ m
The object's distance from O is therefore:
$\sqrt{(3\sin 4t)^2 + (3\cos 4t)^2} = \sqrt{9\sin^2 4t + 9\cos^2 4t}$
$= \sqrt{9(\sin^2 4t + \cos^2 4t)} = \sqrt{9} = 3$ m
So the object's distance from O is constant at 3 m.
This means that the object's path lies on a circle of radius 3 m, centred at O.
It's always useful to remember your trig identities — here, $\sin^2 x + \cos^2 x = 1$ has been used.

Q9 a) $\mathbf{v}_A = \dot{\mathbf{r}}_A = [(3t^2 - 2t - 4)\mathbf{i} + (3t^2 - 4t + 3)\mathbf{j}]$ ms^{-1}
$(3t^2 - 2t - 4)\mathbf{i} + (3t^2 - 4t + 3)\mathbf{j} = -3\mathbf{i} + 2\mathbf{j}$
Equating $\mathbf{i}$-components:
$3t^2 - 2t - 4 = -3$
$3t^2 - 2t - 1 = 0$
$(3t + 1)(t - 1) = 0$
$\Rightarrow t = -\frac{1}{3}$ and $t = 1$
When $t = 1$, the $\mathbf{j}$-component of $\mathbf{v}_A$ is:
$3(1)^2 - 4(1) + 3 = 2$
So the particle's velocity is $(-3\mathbf{i} + 2\mathbf{j})$ ms^{-1} at time $t = 1$ second.

b) When the particle's direction of motion is 45° above $\mathbf{i}$, the horizontal and vertical components of the particle's velocity will be equal.
A good way to picture this is that if the particle was moving relative to a pair of coordinate axes, it would be moving along the line y = x (for positive x and y).
$3t^2 - 2t - 4 = 3t^2 - 4t + 3$
$2t = 7 \Rightarrow t = 3.5$ s
This is the value of t for which the horizontal and vertical components of velocity are equal.
You need to check that the particle is moving at 45° above $\mathbf{i}$, not 45° below $-\mathbf{i}$ at this time.
(The components will also be equal if the particle is moving along a path 45° below $-\mathbf{i}$.)
From part a),
$\mathbf{v}_A = [(3t^2 - 2t - 4)\mathbf{i} + (3t^2 - 4t + 3)\mathbf{j}]$ ms^{-1}.
When $t = 3.5$, $\mathbf{v}_A = [(3(3.5)^2 - 2(3.5) - 4)\mathbf{i} + (3(3.5)^2 - 4(3.5) + 3)\mathbf{j}]$
$= (25.75\mathbf{i} + 25.75\mathbf{j})$ ms^{-1}
Both components are positive, so the particle is moving along a path 45° above $\mathbf{i}$ when $t = 3.5$ s.
You don't actually need to check that both components are positive — if one is, the other one will be too.

c) $\mathbf{v}_B = \int \mathbf{a}_B\, dt = \int (6t\mathbf{i} + 6t\mathbf{j})\, dt$
$= 3t^2\mathbf{i} + 3t^2\mathbf{j} + \mathbf{C}$
When $t = 1$, $\mathbf{v}_B = (4\mathbf{i} - \mathbf{j})$, so:
$4\mathbf{i} - \mathbf{j} = 3(1)^2\mathbf{i} + 3(1)^2\mathbf{j} + \mathbf{C}$
$4\mathbf{i} - \mathbf{j} = 3\mathbf{i} + 3\mathbf{j} + \mathbf{C}$
$\Rightarrow \mathbf{C} = \mathbf{i} - 4\mathbf{j}$
So $\mathbf{v}_B = [(3t^2 + 1)\mathbf{i} + (3t^2 - 4)\mathbf{j}]$ ms^{-1}
$\mathbf{r}_B = \int \mathbf{v}_B\, dt = \int [(3t^2 + 1)\mathbf{i} + (3t^2 - 4)\mathbf{j}]\, dt$
$= (t^3 + t)\mathbf{i} + (t^3 - 4t)\mathbf{j} + \mathbf{D}$
When $t = 1$, $\mathbf{r}_B = (2\mathbf{i} + 3\mathbf{j})$, so:
$2\mathbf{i} + 3\mathbf{j} = (1^3 + 1)\mathbf{i} + (1^3 - 4(1))\mathbf{j} + \mathbf{D}$
$2\mathbf{i} + 3\mathbf{j} = 2\mathbf{i} - 3\mathbf{j} + \mathbf{D}$
$\Rightarrow \mathbf{D} = 6\mathbf{j}$
So $\mathbf{r}_B = [(t^3 + t)\mathbf{i} + (t^3 - 4t + 6)\mathbf{j}]$ m

d) $\mathbf{r}_B - \mathbf{r}_A = [(t^3 + t)\mathbf{i} + (t^3 - 4t + 6)\mathbf{j}] - [(t^3 - t^2 - 4t + 3)\mathbf{i} + (t^3 - 2t^2 + 3t - 7)\mathbf{j}]$
$= [(t^2 + 5t - 3)\mathbf{i} + (2t^2 - 7t + 13)\mathbf{j}]$ m

e) When $t = 4$, $\mathbf{r}_B - \mathbf{r}_A =$
$(4^2 + 5(4) - 3)\mathbf{i} + (2(4)^2 - 7(4) + 13)\mathbf{j}$
$= (33\mathbf{i} + 17\mathbf{j})$ m
Using Pythagoras' theorem:
distance $= \sqrt{33^2 + 17^2} = 37.1$ m (3 s.f.)

Exercise 2.2 — Forces

Q1 $a = \dot{v} = (3t^2i - 8tj)$ ms^{-2}
When $t = 5$, $a = 3(5)^2i - 8(5)j = (75i - 40j)$ ms^{-2}
Using $F = ma$:
$15i - 8j = m(75i - 40j)$
Equating **i**-components:
$15 = 75m \Rightarrow m = 0.2$ kg

Q2 $a = \ddot{r} = \dfrac{d}{dt}[-2ti + (6t + 1)j - 2tk] = (-2i + 6j - 2k)$ ms^{-2}
So **a** doesn't depend on t, and as $F = ma$, and m is constant, **F** doesn't depend on t either, so **F** is constant.

Q3 **a)** $v = \dot{r} = [(2t - 4)i + (2t - 4)j]$ ms^{-1}
The object is at rest when $2t - 4 = 0$,
i.e. at time $t = 2$ seconds.

b) When $t = 2$:
$r = ((2)^2 - 4(2) - 5)i + ((2)^2 - 4(2) + 3)j + 5k$
$= (-9i - j + 5k)$ m
Using Pythagoras' theorem:
distance $= \sqrt{(-9)^2 + (-1)^2 + (5)^2} = 10.3$ m (3 s.f.)

c) $a = \dot{v} = \dfrac{d}{dt}[(2t - 4)i + (2t - 4)j] = (2i + 2j)$ ms^{-2}
$F = ma = 14(2i + 2j) = (28i + 28j)$ N

Q4 **a)** When $t = 1$, $F = 3i + 6j$
Using $F = ma$:
$3i + 6j = 3a$
$\Rightarrow a = (i + 2j)$ ms^{-2}
Using Pythagoras' theorem:
magnitude $= \sqrt{1^2 + 2^2} = 2.24$ ms^{-2} (3 s.f.)

b) Using $F = ma$:
$3i + 6tj = 3a \Rightarrow a = (i + 2tj)$ ms^{-2}
$v = \int a\, dt = \int (i + 2tj)\, dt = (ti + t^2j) + C$
When $t = 0$, $v = -2i + 5j$, so:
$-2i + 5j = (0)i + (0)^2j + C$
$\Rightarrow C = -2i + 5j$
So $v = [(t - 2)i + (t^2 + 5)j]$ ms^{-1}

c) The particle is moving parallel to **j** when the **i**-component of velocity is zero:
$t - 2 = 0 \Rightarrow t = 2$ s
When $t = 2$, the **j**-component of velocity is:
$2^2 + 5 = 9 \neq 0$, so the particle is moving parallel to **j** when $t = 2$.
Substitute this into the expression for **F**:
$F = 3i + 6(2)j = (3i + 12j)$ N

d) $r = \int v\, dt = \int [(t - 2)i + (t^2 + 5)j]\, dt$
$= (\tfrac{1}{2}t^2 - 2t)i + (\tfrac{1}{3}t^3 + 5t)j + D$
When $t = 0$, $r = 0$, so:
$0 = (\tfrac{1}{2}(0)^2 - 2(0))i + (\tfrac{1}{3}(0)^3 + 5(0))j + D$
$\Rightarrow D = 0$
So $r = [(\tfrac{1}{2}t^2 - 2t)i + (\tfrac{1}{3}t^3 + 5t)j]$ m

e) When $t = 3$, $r = [\tfrac{1}{2}(3)^2 - 2(3)]i + [\tfrac{1}{3}(3)^3 + 5(3)]j$
$= (-1.5i + 24j)$ m
Using Pythagoras' theorem:
distance $= \sqrt{(-1.5)^2 + 24^2} = 24.0$ m (3 s.f.)

Q5 **a)** $a = \dot{v} = (5i + 6tj)$ ms^{-2}
$F = ma = 0.2(5i + 6tj) = (i + 1.2tj)$ N

b) When $t = 2$, $F = i + 1.2(2)j = (i + 2.4j)$ N
Using Pythagoras' theorem:
magnitude $= \sqrt{1^2 + 2.4^2} = 2.6$ N

c) $r = \int v\, dt = \int [(5t - 2)i + 3t^2j]\, dt$
$= (\tfrac{5}{2}t^2 - 2t)i + t^3j + C$
When $t = 1$, $r = -16i - 8j$, so:
$-16i - 8j = (\tfrac{5}{2}(1)^2 - 2(1))i + (1)^3j + C$
$-16i - 8j = 0.5i + j + C$
$\Rightarrow C = -16.5i - 9j$
So $r = [(\tfrac{5}{2}t^2 - 2t - 16.5)i + (t^3 - 9)j]$ m

d) When the particle is directly above O, the **i**-component of its position vector is zero:
$\tfrac{5}{2}t^2 - 2t - 16.5 = 0$
$5t^2 - 4t - 33 = 0$
$(5t + 11)(t - 3) = 0$
$\Rightarrow t = -2.2$ and $t = 3$
When $t = 3$, the **j**-component of **r** is:
$3^3 - 9 = 18 > 0$, so the particle is directly above O at time $t = 3$ seconds.

Q6 **a)** Using $F = ma$:
$(3t - 4)i + (t - 3t^2)j = 0.5a$
$\Rightarrow a = [(6t - 8)i + (2t - 6t^2)j]$ ms^{-2}
$v = \int a\, dt = \int [(6t - 8)i + (2t - 6t^2)j]\, dt$
$= (3t^2 - 8t)i + (t^2 - 2t^3)j + C$
When $t = 0$, $v = -3i + 45j$, so:
$-3i + 45j = [3(0)^2 - 8(0)]i + [0^2 - 2(0)^3]j + C$
$\Rightarrow -3i + 45j = C$
So $v = [(3t^2 - 8t - 3)i + (t^2 - 2t^3 + 45)j]$ ms^{-1}
When $t = 3$:
$v = [3(3)^2 - 8(3) - 3]i + [(3)^2 - 2(3)^3 + 45]j$
$= (0i + 0j)$ ms^{-1}
So the particle is stationary —
i.e. its speed is 0 ms^{-1}.

b) $r = \int v\, dt = \int [(3t^2 - 8t - 3)i + (t^2 - 2t^3 + 45)j]\, dt$
$= (t^3 - 4t^2 - 3t)i + (\tfrac{1}{3}t^3 - \tfrac{1}{2}t^4 + 45t)j + D$
When $t = 0$, $r = 0$, so:
$0 = [0^3 - 4(0)^2 - 3(0)]i + [(\tfrac{1}{3}(0)^3 - \tfrac{1}{2}(0)^4 + 45(0)]j + D$
$\Rightarrow D = 0$
So $r = [(t^3 - 4t^2 - 3t)i + (\tfrac{1}{3}t^3 - \tfrac{1}{2}t^4 + 45t)j]$ m
Substituting in $t = 3$:
$r = [(3)^3 - 4(3)^2 - 3(3)]i + [\tfrac{1}{3}(3)^3 - \tfrac{1}{2}(3)^4 + 45(3)]j$
$= (-18i + 103.5j)$ m
Using Pythagoras' theorem:
distance $= \sqrt{(-18)^2 + 103.5^2} = 105$ m (3 s.f.)

3. Applying Differential Equations

Exercise 3.1 — Applying differential equations

Q1 The body decelerates at a rate of $4\sqrt{v}$ ms^{-2}, so:

$a = -4\sqrt{v} \Rightarrow \dfrac{dv}{dt} = -4\sqrt{v}$

$\Rightarrow \int v^{-0.5} \, dv = \int -4 \, dt$

$2v^{0.5} = -4t + C$

When $t = 0$, $v = 9$, so:

$2(9)^{0.5} = -4(0) + C$

$\Rightarrow C = 6$

So $2v^{0.5} = -4t + 6$

$v^{0.5} = -2t + 3$

$\Rightarrow v = (-2t + 3)^2$

Q2 a) Resolving horizontally, taking the direction of motion as positive, and using $F = ma$:

$-kmv = m\dfrac{dv}{dt}$

$\Rightarrow \dfrac{dv}{dt} = -kv$, as required.

b) $\int \dfrac{1}{v} \, dv = \int -k \, dt$

$\ln|v| = -kt + C$

When $t = 0$, $v = 30$, so:

$\ln 30 = -k(0) + C$

$\Rightarrow C = \ln 30$

So $\ln|v| = -kt + \ln 30$

$\ln\left|\dfrac{v}{30}\right| = -kt$

$\dfrac{v}{30} = e^{-kt}$

$\Rightarrow v = 30e^{-kt}$

You could've done this in the same way as in the example on page 64:

$\ln|v| = -kt + C \Rightarrow |v| = e^{-kt+C} \Rightarrow v = Ae^{-kt}$

When $t = 0$, $v = 30$, so:

$30 = Ae^0 \Rightarrow A = 30 \Rightarrow v = 30e^{-kt}$.

c) When $t = 11$, $v = 10$, so:

$10 = 30e^{-11k}$

$0.333... = e^{-11k}$

$\ln 0.333... = -11k$

$\Rightarrow k = -1.098... \div -11 = 0.0998... = 0.1$ (1 d.p.)

Q3 a) Resolving horizontally, taking the direction of motion as positive, and using $F = ma$:

$-(4 + 2v) = 2\dfrac{dv}{dt}$

$\dfrac{dv}{dt} = -(2 + v)$

$\int \dfrac{1}{2 + v} \, dv = \int -1 \, dt$

$\ln|2 + v| = -t + C$

When $t = 0$, $v = 20$, so:

$\ln 22 = 0 + C$

$\Rightarrow C = \ln 22$

So $\ln|2 + v| = -t + \ln 22$

When $v = 12$:

$\ln 14 = -t + \ln 22$

$\Rightarrow t = \ln 22 - \ln 14 = 0.452$ s (3 s.f.)

b) Using $\ln|2 + v| = -t + \ln 22$, when $t = 1.5$:

$\ln|2 + v| = -1.5 + \ln 22$

$\ln|2 + v| = 1.591...$

$2 + v = e^{1.591...}$

$\Rightarrow v = 2.91$ ms^{-1} (3 s.f.)

Q4 a) Resolving horizontally, taking the direction of motion as positive, and using $F = ma$:

$-20v^{1.5} = 400\dfrac{dv}{dt}$

$\Rightarrow \dfrac{dv}{dt} = -0.05v^{1.5}$, as required.

b) $\int_{25}^{15} v^{-1.5} \, dv = \int_0^T -0.05 \, dt$

$[-2v^{-0.5}]_{25}^{15} = [-0.05t]_0^T$

$[-2(15)^{-0.5} + 2(25)^{-0.5}] = [-0.05T - 0]$

$-0.116... = -0.05T$

$\Rightarrow T = 2.33$ s (3 s.f.)

Q5 a) Resolving horizontally, taking the direction of motion as positive, and using $F = ma$:

$-\dfrac{v^2}{6} = 0.2\dfrac{dv}{dt}$

$\Rightarrow \dfrac{dv}{dt} = -\dfrac{5v^2}{6}$

$\int \dfrac{1}{v^2} \, dv = \int -\dfrac{5}{6} \, dt$

$-\dfrac{1}{v} = -\dfrac{5t}{6} + C$

When $t = 0$, $v = U$, so:

$-\dfrac{1}{U} = 0 + C$

$\Rightarrow C = -\dfrac{1}{U}$

So: $-\dfrac{1}{v} = -\dfrac{5t}{6} - \dfrac{1}{U}$

$\dfrac{1}{v} = \dfrac{5t}{6} + \dfrac{1}{U}$

$\dfrac{1}{v} = \dfrac{5Ut + 6}{6U}$

$\Rightarrow v = \dfrac{6U}{5Ut + 6}$

b) $\dfrac{U}{2} = \dfrac{6U}{5Ut + 6}$

$\dfrac{1}{2} = \dfrac{6}{5Ut + 6}$

$5Ut + 6 = 12$

$5Ut = 6$

$\Rightarrow t = \dfrac{6}{5U}$

Q6 a)

Resolving vertically, taking the direction of motion as positive, and using $F = ma$:

$5g - 4v = 5\dfrac{dv}{dt}$

$\Rightarrow \dfrac{dv}{dt} = g - 0.8v$

$\int \left(\dfrac{1}{g - 0.8v}\right) dv = \int 1 \, dt$

$-\dfrac{1}{0.8} \ln|g - 0.8v| = t + C$

$\Rightarrow -1.25 \ln|g - 0.8v| = t + C$

When $t = 0$, $v = 0$ (as the ball is dropped), so:

$-1.25 \ln g = 0 + C$

$\Rightarrow C = -1.25 \ln g$

So: $-1.25 \ln|g - 0.8v| = t - 1.25 \ln g$

$\ln|g - 0.8v| = -0.8t + \ln g$

$g - 0.8v = e^{(-0.8t + \ln g)}$

$g - 0.8v = ge^{-0.8t}$

$0.8v = g - ge^{-0.8t}$

$\Rightarrow v = 1.25g(1 - e^{-0.8t})$

b) Integrate v between $t = 0.5$ and $t = 1.5$ to find the required distance:

$$s = \int_{0.5}^{1.5} (1.25g - 1.25ge^{-0.8t})\, dt$$

$$= 1.25g \int_{0.5}^{1.5} (1 - e^{-0.8t})\, dt$$

$$= 1.25g[t + 1.25e^{-0.8t}]_{0.5}^{1.5}$$

$$= 1.25g[(1.5 + 1.25e^{-0.8 \times 1.5}) - (0.5 + 1.25e^{-0.8 \times 0.5})]$$

$$= 6.60 \text{ m (3 s.f.)}$$

You don't have to do a definite integral — you could do an indefinite one and find the value of C to form an equation for s. Then you'd just have to find the difference between the values of s when t = 1.5 and t = 0.5.

Review Exercise — Chapter 2

Q1 a) $a = \dfrac{dv}{dt} = (6t + 8\sin 2t)$ ms^{-2}

b) $s = \int v\, dt = t^3 - 2\sin 2t + 8t + C$
When $t = 0$, $s = 0$, so:
$0 = (0)^3 - 2\sin 0 + 8(0) + C$
$\Rightarrow C = 0$
So $s = (t^3 - 2\sin 2t + 8t)$ m

Q2 a) $a = \dfrac{dv}{dt} = (6t - 9)$ ms^{-2}

b) When $t = 3$, $a = 6(3) - 9 = 9$ ms^{-2}
$F = ma = 0.1 \times 9 = 0.9$ N

c) When $F = 0$, $a = 0$:
$6t - 9 = 0$
$\Rightarrow t = 1.5$ s

Q3 a) $\mathbf{a} = \dfrac{d\mathbf{v}}{dt} = (4\mathbf{i} + 2t\mathbf{j})$ ms^{-2}

b) $\mathbf{r} = \int \mathbf{v}\, dt = 2t^2\mathbf{i} + \frac{1}{3}t^3\mathbf{j} + \mathbf{C}$
When $t = 0$, $\mathbf{r} = \mathbf{0}$, so:
$\mathbf{0} = 2(0)^2\mathbf{i} + \frac{1}{3}(0)^3\mathbf{j} + \mathbf{C}$
$\Rightarrow \mathbf{C} = \mathbf{0}$
So $\mathbf{r} = (2t^2\mathbf{i} + \frac{1}{3}t^3\mathbf{j})$ m

Q4 a) When $t = 0$, $\mathbf{r} = (0^2 - 3(0) + 2)\mathbf{i} + (0^2 - 5)\mathbf{j}$
$= (2\mathbf{i} - 5\mathbf{j})$ m

b) When the particle is directly below O, the **i**-component of its position vector will be zero:
$t^2 - 3t + 2 = 0$
$(t - 1)(t - 2) = 0$
$\Rightarrow t = 1$ and $t = 2$
When $t = 1$, the **j**-component of $\mathbf{r}$ is:
$1^2 - 5 = -4 < 0$
When $t = 2$, the **j**-component of $\mathbf{r}$ is:
$2^2 - 5 = -1 < 0$
So the particle is directly below O when $t = 1$ s and $t = 2$ s.

c) $\mathbf{v} = \dot{\mathbf{r}} = [(2t - 3)\mathbf{i} + 2t\mathbf{j}]$ ms^{-1}
When $t = 4$, $\mathbf{v} = [2(4) - 3]\mathbf{i} + 2(4)\mathbf{j} = (5\mathbf{i} + 8\mathbf{j})$ ms^{-1}

Q5 a) $\mathbf{v} = \int \mathbf{a}\, dt = -10t\mathbf{j} + \mathbf{C}$
When $t = 0$, $\mathbf{v} = 15\mathbf{i} + 12\mathbf{j}$, so:
$15\mathbf{i} + 12\mathbf{j} = -10(0)\mathbf{j} + \mathbf{C}$
$\Rightarrow \mathbf{C} = 15\mathbf{i} + 12\mathbf{j}$
So $\mathbf{v} = [15\mathbf{i} + (12 - 10t)\mathbf{j}]$ ms^{-1}

b) $\mathbf{r} = \int \mathbf{v}\, dt = \int [15\mathbf{i} + (12 - 10t)\mathbf{j}]\, dt$
$= 15t\mathbf{i} + (12t - 5t^2)\mathbf{j} + \mathbf{D}$
When $t = 1$, $\mathbf{r} = (15\mathbf{i} + 16\mathbf{j})$, so:
$15\mathbf{i} + 16\mathbf{j} = 15(1)\mathbf{i} + [12(1) - 5(1)^2]\mathbf{j} + \mathbf{D}$
$15\mathbf{i} + 16\mathbf{j} = 15\mathbf{i} + 7\mathbf{j} + \mathbf{D}$
$\Rightarrow \mathbf{D} = 9\mathbf{j}$
So $\mathbf{r} = [15t\mathbf{i} + (12t - 5t^2 + 9)\mathbf{j}]$ m

c) When the body is due east of O, the **j**-component of its position vector will be zero:
$12t - 5t^2 + 9 = 0$
$5t^2 - 12t - 9 = 0$
$(5t + 3)(t - 3) = 0$
$\Rightarrow t = -0.6$ and $t = 3$
When $t = 3$, the **i**-component of $\mathbf{r}$ is:
$15 \times 3 = 45 > 0$, so the body is due east of O at time $t = 3$ seconds.
When $t = 3$, $\mathbf{v} = 15\mathbf{i} + [12 - 10(3)]\mathbf{j}$
$= (15\mathbf{i} - 18\mathbf{j})$ ms^{-1}

Q6 a) $\mathbf{a} = \dot{\mathbf{v}} = [(6t - 8)\mathbf{i} + 4\mathbf{j} - 3t^2\mathbf{k}]$ ms^{-2}
$\mathbf{F} = m\mathbf{a} = 7.5[(6t - 8)\mathbf{i} + 4\mathbf{j} - 3t^2\mathbf{k}]$
$= [(45t - 60)\mathbf{i} + 30\mathbf{j} - 22.5t^2\mathbf{k}]$ N

b) $\mathbf{r} = \int \mathbf{v}\, dt = \int [(3t^2 - 8t)\mathbf{i} + (6 + 4t)\mathbf{j} - t^3\mathbf{k}]\, dt$
$= (t^3 - 4t^2)\mathbf{i} + (6t + 2t^2)\mathbf{j} - \frac{t^4}{4}\mathbf{k} + \mathbf{C}$
When $t = 3$, $\mathbf{r} = -4\mathbf{i} + 32\mathbf{j} - 0.25\mathbf{k}$, so:
$-4\mathbf{i} + 32\mathbf{j} - 0.25\mathbf{k} =$
$\qquad [3^3 - 4(3)^2]\mathbf{i} + [6(3) + 2(3)^2]\mathbf{j} - \frac{3^4}{4}\mathbf{k} + \mathbf{C}$
$-4\mathbf{i} + 32\mathbf{j} - 0.25\mathbf{k} = -9\mathbf{i} + 36\mathbf{j} - 20.25\mathbf{k} + \mathbf{C}$
$\Rightarrow \mathbf{C} = 5\mathbf{i} - 4\mathbf{j} + 20\mathbf{k}$
So:
$\mathbf{r} = [(t^3 - 4t^2 + 5)\mathbf{i} + (6t + 2t^2 - 4)\mathbf{j} + (20 - \frac{t^4}{4})\mathbf{k}]$ m

Q7 a) Resolving horizontally, taking the direction of motion as positive, and using $F = ma$:
$-0.025mv = m\dfrac{dv}{dt}$
$\Rightarrow \dfrac{dv}{dt} = -0.025v$, as required.

b) $\int \frac{1}{v}\, dv = \int -0.025\, dt$
$\ln|v| = -0.025t + C$
When $t = 0$, $v = 15$, so:
$\ln 15 = -0.025(0) + C$
$\Rightarrow C = \ln 15$
So $\ln|v| = -0.025t + \ln 15$
$\ln|v| - \ln 15 = -0.025t$
$\ln|\frac{v}{15}| = -0.025t$
$\frac{v}{15} = e^{-0.025t}$
$\Rightarrow v = 15e^{-0.025t}$
When $t = 60$:
$v = 15e^{(-0.025 \times 60)} = 3.35$ ms^{-1} (3 s.f.)

Exam-Style Questions — Chapter 2

Q1 a) Find v by integrating a with respect to t:

$v = \int a \, dt = \int (8t^2 + 6\sin 2t) \, dt$ *[1 mark]*

$= \frac{8}{3}t^3 - \frac{6}{2}\cos 2t + c = \frac{8}{3}t^3 - 3\cos 2t + c$ *[1 mark]*

When $t = 0$, $v = 0$:

$0 = \frac{8}{3}(0)^3 - 3\cos(2 \times 0) + c \Rightarrow 0 = 0 - 3 + c$

$\Rightarrow c = 3$ *[1 mark]*

So: $v = \frac{8}{3}t^3 - 3\cos 2t + 3$ *[1 mark]*

b) $v = \frac{8}{3}\left(\frac{\pi}{2}\right)^3 - 3\cos 2\left(\frac{\pi}{2}\right) + 3$ *[1 mark]*

$v = \frac{\pi^3}{3} - 3(-1) + 3 = \frac{\pi^3}{3} + 6$ *[1 mark]*

Q2 a) $a = \frac{dv}{dt}$ *[1 mark]*

$a = 2 - 3(-2)e^{-2t} = 2 + 6e^{-2t}$ *[1 mark]*

b) t must be greater than or equal to 0.

When $t = 0$, $a = 2 + 6e^{-2 \times 0} = 8$ *[1 mark]*

As $t \to \infty$, $6e^{-2t} \to 0$, so $a \to 2$ *[1 mark]*

So, $2 \text{ ms}^{-2} < a \leq 8 \text{ ms}^{-2}$ *[1 mark]*

c) $F = ma \Rightarrow 6 = m \times (2 + 6e^{-2 \times 2})$ *[1 mark]*

$m = 2.84$ kg (3 s.f.) *[1 mark]*

d) $s = \int v \, dt$ *[1 mark]*

$s = t^2 + \frac{3}{2}e^{-2t} + 4t + c$ *[1 mark]*

When $t = 0$, the particle is at the origin (i.e. $s = 0$):

$0 = 0 + \frac{3}{2} + c \Rightarrow c = -\frac{3}{2}$ *[1 mark]*

So, $s = t^2 + \frac{3}{2}e^{-2t} + 4t - \frac{3}{2}$ *[1 mark]*

Q3 a) $a = \dot{v} = [(-6\sin 3t + 5)i + 2j)]$ ms⁻²

[2 marks in total — 1 mark for attempting to differentiate the velocity vector, 1 mark for correctly differentiating both components]

b) The **j**-component of the acceleration is constant, so the **i**-component is the only one which can be maximised.

To do this, set $\sin 3t = -1$. *[1 mark]*

The minimum value of sin(anything) is −1

$a_{max} = ((-6 \times -1) + 5)i + 2j = 11i + 2j$ *[1 mark]*

Magnitude $= a = \sqrt{11^2 + 2^2} = \sqrt{121 + 4}$ *[1 mark]*

$a = \sqrt{125} \text{ ms}^{-2} = 5\sqrt{5} \text{ ms}^{-2}$ *[1 mark]*

Q4 a) $v = \dot{r} = [(6t^2 - 14t)i + (6t - 12t^2)j]$ ms⁻¹

[2 marks in total — 1 mark for attempting to differentiate the position vector, 1 mark for correctly differentiating both components]

b) $v = \left(\frac{6}{4} - \frac{14}{2}\right)i + \left(\frac{6}{2} - \frac{12}{4}\right)j$ *[1 mark]*

$= (-5.5i + 0j)$ ms⁻¹

Speed $= \sqrt{(-5.5)^2 + 0^2} = 5.5$ ms⁻¹ *[1 mark]*

The component of velocity in the direction of north is zero, and the component in the direction of east is negative, so the particle is moving due west *[1 mark]*

c) $a = \dot{v}$ *[1 mark]*

$= [(12t - 14)i + (6 - 24t)j]$ ms⁻² *[1 mark]*

At $t = 2$, $a = (10i - 42j)$ ms⁻² *[1 mark]*

d) At $t = 2$, $|a| = a = \sqrt{10^2 + (-42)^2}$

$= 43.174...$ ms⁻² *[1 mark]*

Now use $F = ma$ to find the force at $t = 2$:

$F = (43.174...)m$ N *[1 mark]*

Magnitude of **F** at $t = 2$ is 170 N, so:

$(43.174...)m = 170$

$\Rightarrow m = 3.94$ kg (3 s.f.) *[1 mark]*

e) The vectors **F** and **a** always act in the same direction, so when **F** is acting parallel to **j**, so is **a**. *[1 mark]*

So, when **F** is acting parallel to **j**, the component of **a** in direction of **i** will be zero *[1 mark]*

i.e. $12t - 14 = 0$

$\Rightarrow t = 1.166... = 1.17$ s (3 s.f.) *[1 mark]*

Checking that the **j**-component of **a** is non-zero:

$6 - 24t = 6 - 24(1.166...) = -22 \neq 0$

So **F** is acting parallel to **j** at this time.

Q5 a) Using $F = ma$:

$\frac{10\,000}{v} - 0.1mv^2 = m\frac{dv}{dt}$ *[1 mark]*

Rearranging: $\frac{dv}{dt} = \frac{10\,000}{mv} - 0.1v^2$ *[1 mark]*

b) $\frac{dv}{dt} = -0.1v^2$ *[1 mark]*

Once the engines are switched off, the only force acting horizontally on the plane will be the resistive force.

c) Separate the variables and integrate:

$\int \frac{1}{v^2} dv = \int -0.1 \, dt$ *[1 mark]*

$\Rightarrow -\frac{1}{v} = -0.1t + c$ *[1 mark]*

When $t = 0$, $v = 20$, so:

$-\frac{1}{20} = -0.1(0) + c$ *[1 mark]* $\Rightarrow c = -\frac{1}{20}$ *[1 mark]*

So, when $v = 10$, $-\frac{1}{10} = -0.1t - \frac{1}{20}$

$\Rightarrow t = 0.5$ seconds *[1 mark]*

Q6 a) Using $F = ma$:

$-kv = 2 \times \frac{dv}{dt}$ *[1 mark]*

So, $\frac{dv}{dt} = \frac{-kv}{2}$ *[1 mark]*

b) Separate the variables and integrate:

$\frac{dv}{dt} = \frac{-kv}{2} \Rightarrow \frac{1}{v}dv = -\frac{k}{2}dt$

So $\int \frac{1}{v} dv = \int -\frac{k}{2} \, dt$

$\Rightarrow \ln v = -\frac{kt}{2} + c$ *[1 mark]*

When $t = 0$, $v = 12$, so:

$\ln 12 = 0 + c \Rightarrow c = \ln 12$ *[1 mark]*

Take exponentials of both sides to get an equation for v:

$v = e^{-\frac{kt}{2} + \ln 12} = e^{-\frac{kt}{2}} \times e^{\ln 12}$ *[1 mark]*

So, $v = 12e^{-\frac{kt}{2}} = 12\sqrt{e^{-kt}}$ *[1 mark]*

Chapter 3: Work, Energy and Power

1. Work Done

Exercise 1.1 — Work done

Q1 Work done = Fs
Work done = $500 \times 300 = 150\ 000$ J
Remember to convert the distance into metres.

Q2 Work done = $F \times s$
$8 = P \times 1.6$
$\Rightarrow P = 8 \div 1.6 = 5$ N

Q3 Work done = Fs
$0.428 = 84 \times d$
$\Rightarrow d = 0.428 \div 84 = 5.10 \times 10^{-3}$ m (3 s.f.)

Q4 **a)** Work done against friction = $50 \times 0.7 = 35$ J

 b) The resultant force is 350 N – 50 N = 300 N in the direction of motion.
 So work done = $300 \times 0.7 = 210$ J

Q5 Resolving horizontally:
$F = 2000\cos18°$
Work done = $Fs = 2000\cos18° \times 1150$
$= 2\ 190\ 000$ J (3 s.f.)

Q6 Resolving horizontally, taking direction of motion as positive, and using $F_{net} = ma$:
$P\cos30° – F = m \times 0$
$\Rightarrow F = P\cos30°$, where F is the frictional force acting between the particle and the plane.
So, using 'Work done = Force × distance':
Work done against friction = $F \times 25$
Substituting in $F = P\cos30°$:
$55 = P\cos30° \times 25$
$\Rightarrow P = 55 \div 25\cos30° = 2.54$ N (3 s.f.)

Q7 **a)**

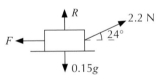

Resolving vertically:
$R + 2.2\sin24° = 0.15g$
$\Rightarrow R = 0.575...$ N
Using $F = \mu R$:
$F = 0.14 \times 0.575... = 0.0805...$ N
Work done against friction = Fs
$= 0.0805... \times 6 = 0.483$ J (3 s.f.)

 b) Resolving horizontally, taking direction of motion as positive, and using formula for work done:
 Work done = $(2.2\cos24° – 0.0805...) \times 6$
 $= 11.6$ J (3 s.f.)

Q8 **a)**

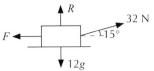

Resolving vertically:
$R + 32\sin15° = 12g$
$\Rightarrow R = 109.317...$ N
Using $F = \mu R$:
$F = 0.18 \times 109.317... = 19.677...$ N
Work done against friction = Fs
$45 = 19.677... \times s$
$\Rightarrow s = 2.286... = 2.29$ m (3 s.f.)

 b) Resolving horizontally, taking direction of motion as positive, and using formula for work done:
 Work done = $(32\cos15° – 19.677...) \times 2.286...$
 $= 25.7$ J (3 s.f.)

Q9 Using 'Work done = Force × distance':
$28 = (60\cos40° – F) \times 3.5$
$8 = 60\cos40° – F$
$\Rightarrow F = 37.962...$ N
Resolving vertically:
$R = 60\sin40° + 28g = 312.967...$ N
Using $F = \mu R$:
$37.962... = \mu \times 312.967...$
$\Rightarrow \mu = 0.12$ (2 d.p.)

Exercise 1.2 — Gravity

Q1 Work done by gravity = mgh
$= 0.0013 \times 9.8 \times 37 = 0.472$ J (3 s.f.)
You need to change the mass from grams to kilograms to get an answer in joules.

Q2 Work done against gravity = mgh
$16\ 367 = 57 \times 9.8 \times h$
$\Rightarrow h = 16\ 367 \div (57 \times 9.8) = 29.3$ m (3 s.f.)

Q3 Work done against gravity = mgh
$22\ 491 = m \times 9.8 \times 2.7$
$\Rightarrow m = 22\ 491 \div (9.8 \times 2.7) = 850$ kg

Q4 Gravity only does work vertically, so you only need to take the vertical motion into account.
Work done = $mgh = 48 \times 9.8 \times 3 = 1410$ J (3 s.f.)

Q5 **a)** **(i)** Resolving vertically and using $F = ma$:
 $T – mg = m \times 0$
 $\Rightarrow T = mg = 3 \times 9.8 = 29.4$ N

 (ii) Work done = $F \times s = T \times h$
 $= 29.4 \times 9.5 = 279.3$ J
 You could also do this using the fact that the work done by the rope is equal to the work done against gravity, so Work done = mgh.

 b) **(i)** Resolving vertically and using $F_{net} = ma$:
 $T – mg = ma$
 $\Rightarrow T = ma + mg = m(a + g)$
 $= 3(1.5 + 9.8) = 33.9$ N

 (ii) Work done = $F_{net} \times h$
 $= (T – mg) \times h = (33.9 – 3g) \times 9.5$
 $= 42.75$ J

Q6 a) Using $s = ut + \frac{1}{2}at^2$, taking down as positive:

$u = 0$, $a = 9.8$, $s = s$, $t = 3$

$s = (0 \times 3) + \frac{1}{2} \times 9.8 \times 3^2 = 44.1$ m

b) Work done by gravity $= mgh = 2 \times 9.8 \times 44.1$
$= 864.36$ J

c) E.g. there is no air resistance or any other external forces, the stone is a particle, g is constant at 9.8 ms^{-2}.

Q7 a) Resolving vertically, taking up as positive, and using $F = ma$:

$44 - mg = m \times 0.16$

$44 = m(0.16 + 9.8)$

$\Rightarrow m = 4.417... = 4.42$ kg (3 s.f.)

b) Resolving vertically, taking up as positive, and using the formula for work done:

Work done $= (44 - (4.417...)g) \times 9$
$= 6.3614... = 6.36$ J (3 s.f.)

Q8 a) $u = 0$, $v = 4.2$, $s = s$, $t = 10$

Using $s = \left(\frac{u + v}{2}\right)t$:

$s = 2.1 \times 10 = 21$ m

Work done against gravity $= mgh$
$= 25 \times 9.8 \times 21 = 5145$ J

b) $u = 0$, $v = 4.2$, $a = a$, $t = 10$

Using $v = u + at$:

$4.2 = 10a$

$\Rightarrow a = 0.42$ ms^{-2}

Resolving vertically, taking up as positive, and using $F = ma$:

$T - 25g = 25 \times 0.42$

$\Rightarrow T = 255.5$ N

c) Work done $=$ Force $\times$ distance
$= 255.5 \times 21 = 5365.5$ J

Exercise 1.3 — Friction and gravity

Q1 Resolving vertically, the body travels a vertical distance of $1.4\sin70°$ m.

Work done $= mgh = 90 \times 9.8 \times 1.4\sin70°$
$= 1160$ J (3 s.f.)

Q2 a) Work done by gravity $= mgh$
$= 0.45 \times 9.8 \times 2\sin25° = 3.73$ J (3 s.f.)

b) Resolving perpendicular to the plane:
$R = 0.45g\cos25° = 3.996...$ N
$F = \mu R = 0.37 \times 3.996... = 1.478...$ N
Work done against friction $= Fs$
$= 1.478... \times 2 = 2.96$ J (3 s.f.)

Q3 a)

Work done against gravity $= mgh$
$= 8 \times 9.8 \times 1.5\sin22° = 44.1$ J (3 s.f.)

b) Resolving perpendicular to the plane:
$R = 8g\cos22° = 72.691...$ N
$F = \mu R = 0.55 \times 72.691... = 39.980...$ N
Work done against friction $= Fs$
$= 39.980... \times 1.5 = 60.0$ J (3 s.f.)

Q4 Resolving perpendicular to the plane:
$R = 11g\cos5° = 107.389...$ N
$F = \mu R = 0.08 \times 107.389... = 8.591...$ N
Resolving parallel to the plane, taking up the plane as positive, and using $F_{net} = ma$:
$P - 8.591... - 11g\sin5° = 11 \times 0$
$\Rightarrow P = 8.591... + 11g\sin5° = 17.986...$ N
So, using 'Work done $=$ Force $\times$ distance':
Work done by $P = 17.986... \times 16 = 287.785...$
$= 288$ J (3 s.f.)

Q5 $u = 0$, $v = 5$, $a = a$, $s = 4.5$

$v^2 = u^2 + 2as$

$25 = 9a$

$\Rightarrow a = 2.777...$ ms^{-2}

Resolving parallel to the plane, taking up the plane as positive, and using $F_{net} = ma$:

$F_{net} = 1.2 \times 2.777... = 3.333...$ N

Work done $=$ Force $\times$ distance
$= 3.333... \times 4.5 = 15$ J

Q6 a) Resolving perpendicular to the plane:
$R = 23g\cos18° = 214.368...$ N
$F = \mu R = 0.36 \times 214.368... = 77.172...$ N
Resolving parallel to the plane, taking up the plane as positive, and using $F_{net} = ma$:
$T - 23g\sin18° - 77.172... = 23 \times 0.95$
$\Rightarrow T = 21.85 + 146.824... = 168.674...$ N
$= 169$ N (3 s.f.)

b) Work done $=$ Force $\times$ distance $= mas$
$= 23 \times 0.95 \times 0.75 = 16.3875$ J

2. Kinetic and Gravitational Potential Energy

Exercise 2.1 — Kinetic energy

Q1 K.E. $= \frac{1}{2}mv^2 = \frac{1}{2} \times 0.045 \times 20^2 = 9$ J

Don't forget to convert grams to kilograms.

Q2 K.E. $= \frac{1}{2}mv^2$

$94\,080 = \frac{1}{2} \times 60 \times v^2$

$v^2 = 3136$

$\Rightarrow v = 56$ ms^{-1}

Q3 $1462 \times 1000 \div 3600 = 406.11...$ ms^{-1}

K.E. $= \frac{1}{2}mv^2 = \frac{1}{2} \times 11\,249 \times (406.11...)^2$
$= 9.28 \times 10^8$ J (to 3 s.f.)

Q4 K.E. $= \frac{1}{2}mv^2 = \frac{1}{2} \times (6.64 \times 10^{-27}) \times (1.5 \times 10^6)^2$
$= 7.47 \times 10^{-15}$ J

Q5 $v = \frac{s}{t} = 14 \div 3.5 = 4$ ms^{-1}

K.E. $= \frac{1}{2}m(4)^2 = 22$

$\Rightarrow m = 22 \div 8 = 2.75$ kg

Q6 Let v be the velocity of B. The velocity of A is then $2v$. The ratio of K.E. is:

$\frac{1}{2}m(2v)^2 : \frac{1}{2}mv^2$

$(2v)^2 : v^2$

$4v^2 : v^2$

$4 : 1$

Exercise 2.2 — Kinetic energy and work done

Q1 a)

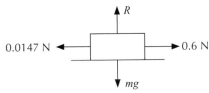

Change in K.E. = Work done on the particle
3.62×10^{-3} = Force × Distance
$3.62 \times 10^{-3} = F_{net} \times s$
Resolving horizontally, taking direction of motion as positive:
$F_{net} = 0.6 - 0.0147 = 0.5853$ N
So:
$3.62 \times 10^{-3} = 0.5853 s$
$\Rightarrow s = 6.18 \times 10^{-3}$ m (3 s.f.) = 6.18 mm (3 s.f.)

b) Work done = $\frac{1}{2}m(v^2 - u^2)$

$3.62 \times 10^{-3} = \frac{1}{2}m(1.222^2 - 0.210^2)$
$\Rightarrow m = 4.995... \times 10^{-3}$ kg
$= 5.00 \times 10^{-3}$ kg (3 s.f.) = 5.00 g (3 s.f.)

Q2 Work done = change in K.E.
So, Work done = $\frac{1}{2}m(v^2 - u^2)$
$= \frac{1}{2} \times 1800(0^2 - 11^2) = -108\,900$ J
So there is a loss in K.E. of 108 900 J.
Therefore, the work done is 108 900 J.
Work done = Force × Distance
$108\,900 = R \times 96$
$\Rightarrow R = 1134.375$ N = 1130 N (3 s.f.)

Q3 a) Change in K.E. = $\frac{1}{2}m(v^2 - u^2)$
$= \frac{1}{2} \times 3(7^2 - 3^2) = 60$ J

b) $R = mg = 3 \times 9.8 = 29.4$ N
$F = \mu R = 0.2 \times 29.4 = 5.88$ N

c) Work done = change in K.E.
$(T - F) \times s = 60$
$(15.88 - 5.88) \times s = 60$
$\Rightarrow s = 6$ m

Q4 a) K.E. = $\frac{1}{2}mv^2 = \frac{1}{2} \times 0.022 \times 8^2 = 0.704$ J

b) Work done = change in K.E.
Final velocity is zero, so change in K.E. is the same as the initial K.E.
So the work done = 0.704 J.

c) Work done = Fs
$0.704 = F \times 0.005$
$\Rightarrow F = 140.8$ N

Q5

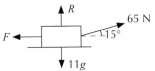

Resolving vertically:
$R + 65\sin 15° = 11 \times 9.8$
$\Rightarrow R = 90.976...$ N
So $F = \mu R = 0.19 \times 90.976... = 17.285...$ N
Change in K.E. = $\frac{1}{2}m(v^2 - u^2)$
$= \frac{1}{2} \times 11 \times (14^2 - 2^2) = 1056$ J
Change in K.E. = Work done
1056 = Force × distance
$1056 = (65\cos 15° - 17.285...) \times s$
$1056 = 45.499... \times s$
$\Rightarrow s = 23.2$ m (3 s.f.)

Exercise 2.3 — Gravitational potential energy

Q1 Gain in G.P.E. = mgh
$= 3.7 \times 9.8 \times (0.73 - 0.41)$
$= 11.6032$ J = 11.6 J (3 s.f.)

Q2 Loss of G.P.E. = mgh
$7.2 \times 10^{-5} = m \times 9.8 \times (1.63 - 1.02)$
$\Rightarrow m = 1.204... \times 10^{-5} = 1.20 \times 10^{-5}$ kg (3 s.f.)

Q3 Gain in G.P.E. = mgh
$5 \times 10^{12} = 3\,039\,000 \times 9.8 \times h$
$\Rightarrow h = 1.678... \times 10^5$ m = 168 km (to nearest km)

Q4 The vertical component of the distance travelled, h, is
$3.7 \sin \theta = 3.7 \sin\left(\sin^{-1}\frac{1}{8}\right) = 3.7 \times \frac{1}{8} = 0.4625$ m.
So G.P.E. = $mgh = 20 \times 9.8 \times 0.4625 = 90.65$ J

Q5 The vertical component of the distance travelled, h, is $240\sin 13°$.
G.P.E. = mgh
$1\,000\,000 = m \times 9.8 \times 240 \times \sin 13°$
$\Rightarrow m = 1890.055... = 1890$ kg (3 s.f.)

Q6

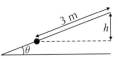

The vertical component of the distance travelled, h, is $3\sin\theta$.
Loss of G.P.E. = mgh
$6.032 = 0.6 \times 9.8 \times 3 \times \sin\theta$
$\sin\theta = 0.341...$
$\Rightarrow \theta = 19.995... = 20.0°$ (3 s.f.)

Q7

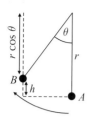

Using trigonometry, the height gained by the pendulum, h, is $(r - r\cos\theta)$. So:
Gain in G.P.E. $= mgh = mg(r - r\cos\theta)$
$= mgr(1 - \cos\theta)$

3. The Work-Energy Principle

Exercise 3.1 — The principle of conservation of mechanical energy

Q1 Total mechanical energy is conserved, so
total M.E. at the top = total M.E. at the bottom
$= $ K.E. + G.P.E.
So G.P.E. at bottom = total M.E. at top − K.E. at bottom
$= 70\,560 - 52\,920 = 17\,640$ J

Q2 a) Total M.E. $= $ K.E. + G.P.E. $= 0 + mgh$
$= 0.057 \times 9.8 \times 1.13 = 0.631218$
$= 0.631$ J (3 s.f.)

b) When it hits the ground, G.P.E. is zero, so, using the fact that total mechanical energy is conserved:
Total M.E. before = Total M.E. after
$0.631218 = \frac{1}{2}mv^2 + mgh$
$0.631218 = (\frac{1}{2} \times 0.057 \times v^2) + 0$
$v^2 = 22.148$
$\Rightarrow v = 4.71$ ms^{-1} (3 s.f.)

Q3 At the instant it is dropped, the object has G.P.E. but no K.E., and at the instant it hits the ground, it has K.E. but no G.P.E.
Total mechanical energy is conserved, so:
G.P.E. lost = K.E. gained
$mgh = \frac{1}{2}mv^2$
$gh = \frac{1}{2}v^2$
$h = (\frac{1}{2} \times 11^2) \div 9.8 = 6.17$ m (3 s.f.)

Q4 Loss in K.E. = gain in G.P.E.
$1.47 \times 10^{-3} = mgh$
Using trigonometry, the bead moves a distance of $(0.06\sin30°)$ m vertically upwards.
$1.47 \times 10^{-3} = m \times 9.8 \times 0.06\sin30°$
$\Rightarrow m = 0.005$ kg $= 5$ g

Q5 a) Total mechanical energy $= $ K.E. + G.P.E.
$= \frac{1}{2}mv^2 + mgh$
$= (\frac{1}{2} \times 0.05 \times 10.1^2) + (0.05 \times 9.8 \times 52)$
$= 28.03025$ J $= 28.0$ J (3 s.f.)

b) When it reaches its maximum height, it will momentarily be at rest, so it will have no K.E.
As total mechanical energy is conserved:
G.P.E. at highest point $= 28.03025$
$mgh = 28.03025$
$\Rightarrow h = 28.03025 \div (0.05 \times 9.8)$
$= 57.2$ m (3 s.f.)

c) It is projected from ground level, so it will have no G.P.E. at the instant it is projected.
As total mechanical energy is conserved:
K.E. at projection $= 28.03025$
$\frac{1}{2}mv^2 = 28.03025$
$\frac{1}{2} \times 0.05 \times v^2 = 28.03025$
$v^2 = 1121.21$
$\Rightarrow v = 33.5$ ms^{-1} (3 s.f.)

Q6 a) Change in G.P.E. $= 4 \times 9.8 \times 7 \times \sin40°$
$= 176.380... = 176$ J (3 s.f.)

b) Mechanical energy is conserved, so:
gain in K.E. = loss in G.P.E.
$\frac{1}{2}m(v^2 - u^2) = 176.380...$ J
$\frac{1}{2} \times 4 \times (v^2 - 3^2) = 176.380...$
$v^2 = 97.190...$
$\Rightarrow v = 9.86$ ms^{-1} (3 s.f.)

Q7 Mechanical energy is conserved, so:
gain in K.E. = loss in G.P.E.
$\frac{1}{2}m(v^2 - u^2) = mgh$
$\frac{1}{2}(v^2 - u^2) = gh$
$\frac{1}{2}(4.5^2 - 0^2) = 9.8h$
$\Rightarrow h = 1.033...$ m
This is the vertical distance travelled by the body.
Using trigonometry:
$x\sin19° = 1.033...$ (where x is the length of the sloped surface of the ramp)
So $x = 1.033... \div \sin19° = 3.17$ m (3 s.f.)

Q8 a) Take the bottom of the plane as the base level (i.e. the point where the particle's height is measured from).
At the bottom of the plane, when it is fired, it has K.E. but no G.P.E.
At the point it comes to rest, it has G.P.E. but no K.E.
Change in K.E. $= \frac{1}{2}m(v^2 - u^2)$
$= \frac{1}{2} \times 13 \times (0^2 - 16^2) = -1664$ J
So 1664 J of K.E. has been lost.
Change in G.P.E. $= mgh$
$= 13 \times 9.8 \times h = 127.4h$ J
K.E. lost = G.P.E. gained
$1664 = 127.4h$
$\Rightarrow h = 13.061...$ m
This is the vertical distance travelled.
Using trigonometry, the distance travelled up the plane, x, satisfies:
$x\sin25° = 13.061...$
$\Rightarrow x = 30.9$ m (3 s.f.)

b) Change in K.E. $= \frac{1}{2}m(v^2 - u^2)$

$= \frac{1}{2} \times 13 \times (10^2 - 16^2) = -1014$ J

As in part a), change in G.P.E. is 127.4h J
K.E. lost = G.P.E. gained
$1014 = 127.4h$
$\Rightarrow h = 7.959...$ m
This is the vertical distance travelled.
Using trigonometry, the distance travelled up the plane, x, satisfies:
$x\sin25° = 7.959...$
$\Rightarrow x = 18.8$ m (3 s.f.)

Exercise 3.2 — The work-energy principle

Q1 Take the block's position when it has moved 12 m down the ramp as the 'base level' — the point where the block's height is measured from, and where it has no gravitational potential energy.
First, you need to find the block's initial mechanical energy — i.e. its mechanical energy at the top of the ramp:
Initial Mechanical Energy = Initial K.E. + Initial G.P.E.

$= \frac{1}{2}mu^2 + mgh_{initial}$

$= (\frac{1}{2} \times 5 \times 0^2) + (5 \times 9.8 \times 12\sin10°) = 102.105...$ J

Next, find the block's final mechanical energy — i.e. its mechanical energy when it has moved 12 m down the ramp:
Final Mechanical Energy = Final K.E. + Final G.P.E.

$= \frac{1}{2}mv^2 + mgh_{final}$

$= (\frac{1}{2} \times 5 \times 3.5^2) + (5 \times 9.8 \times 0) = 30.625$ J

Now, using the work-energy principle:
Initial Mechanical Energy – Final Mechanical Energy
= Work done against friction
$102.105... - 30.625 = 71.480... = 71.5$ J (3 s.f.)

Q2 **a)** Take the body's initial position as the 'base level'.
Initial M.E. = Initial K.E. + Initial G.P.E.

$= \frac{1}{2}mu^2 + mgh_{initial}$

$= (\frac{1}{2} \times 50 \times 8^2) + (50 \times 9.8 \times 0) = 1600$ J

Final M.E. = Final K.E. + Final G.P.E.

$= \frac{1}{2}mv^2 + mgh_{final}$

$= (\frac{1}{2} \times 50 \times 1.5^2) + (50 \times 9.8 \times 3.4\sin30°)$
$= 889.25$ J

Now, using the work-energy principle:
Initial Mechanical Energy – Final Mechanical Energy = Work done against friction
$1600 - 889.25 = 710.75$ J

b) Work done $= Fs$
$710.75 = F \times 3.4$
$\Rightarrow F = 209.044... = 209$ N (3 s.f.)

Q3 **a)** Take the body's final position (i.e. 5 m down the slide) as the 'base level'.
Initial M.E. = Initial K.E. + Initial G.P.E.

$= \frac{1}{2}mu^2 + mgh_{initial}$

$= (\frac{1}{2} \times 7.9 \times 0^2) + (7.9 \times 9.8 \times 5\sin45°) =$
$273.721...$ J
Final M.E. = Final K.E. + Final G.P.E.

$= \frac{1}{2}mv^2 + mgh_{final}$

$= (\frac{1}{2} \times 7.9 \times 6^2) + (7.9 \times 9.8 \times 0) = 142.2$ J

Now, using the work-energy principle:
Initial Mechanical Energy – Final Mechanical Energy = Work done against friction
$273.721... - 142.2 = 131.521... = 132$ J (3 s.f.)

b) Work done $= Fs$
$131.521... = F \times 5$
$\Rightarrow F = 26.304...$ N
Resolving perpendicular to the slope:
$R = 7.9g\cos45° = 54.744...$ N
$F = \mu R$
$\Rightarrow \mu = F \div R = 26.304... \div 54.744...$
$= 0.48$ (2 d.p.)

Q4 Initial M.E. = Initial K.E. + Initial G.P.E.

$= \frac{1}{2}mu^2 + mgh_{initial}$

$= (\frac{1}{2} \times 0.025 \times 0^2) + (0.025 \times 9.8 \times 0.3) = 0.0735$ J
Final M.E. = Final K.E. + Final G.P.E.

$= \frac{1}{2}mv^2 + mgh_{final}$

$= (\frac{1}{2} \times 0.025 \times 0.7^2) + (0.025 \times 9.8 \times 0.1)$
$= 0.030625$ J
Now, using the work-energy principle:
Initial Mechanical Energy – Final Mechanical Energy
= Work done against friction
$0.0735 - 0.030625 = 0.042875$ J
You could answer this question by redefining the base level as being 0.1 m above the ground — it would make the calculation a bit simpler.

Q5 **a)** Initial M.E. = Initial K.E. + Initial G.P.E.

$= \frac{1}{2}mu^2 + mgh_{initial}$

$= (\frac{1}{2} \times 9 \times 14^2) + (9 \times 9.8 \times 0) = 882$ J
Final M.E. = Final K.E. + Final G.P.E.

$= \frac{1}{2}mv^2 + mgh_{final}$

$= (\frac{1}{2} \times 9 \times 0^2) + (9 \times 9.8 \times 9) = 793.8$ J
Now, using the work-energy principle:
Initial Mechanical Energy – Final Mechanical Energy = Work done against resistive force
$882 - 793.8 = 88.2$ J

b) The work done by the resistive force as the particle travels upwards and back down again will be $2 \times 88.2 = 176.4$ J.
Using the work-energy principle:
Initial Mechanical Energy – Final Mechanical Energy = Work done against resistive force
$882 - \text{Final M.E.} = 176.4$
$\Rightarrow$ Final M.E. $= 705.6$ J
When the particle lands, it will have K.E., but no G.P.E., so:
$705.6 = \frac{1}{2}mv^2$
$705.6 = \frac{1}{2} \times 9 \times v^2$
$v^2 = 156.8$
$\Rightarrow v = 12.5$ ms^{-1} (3 s.f.)

Q6 a)

Let x be the distance travelled before the object comes to rest.
Initial M.E. = Initial K.E. + Initial G.P.E.
$= \frac{1}{2}mu^2 + mgh_{\text{initial}}$
$= (\frac{1}{2} \times 5.5 \times 6.25^2) + (5.5 \times 9.8 \times 0)$
$= 107.421...$ J
Final M.E. = Final K.E. + Final G.P.E.
$= \frac{1}{2}mv^2 + mgh_{\text{final}}$
$= (\frac{1}{2} \times 5.5 \times 0^2) + (5.5 \times 9.8 \times x\sin17°)$
$= (15.758...)x$ J
Work done by friction $= Fx = \mu Rx$
$= 0.22 \times 5.5g\cos17° \times x = (11.339...)x$ J
Now, using the work-energy principle:
Initial Mechanical Energy – Final Mechanical Energy = Work done against friction
$107.421... - (15.758...)x = (11.339...)x$
$107.421... = (27.098...)x$
$\Rightarrow x = 3.964... = 3.96$ m (3 s.f.)

b) The object's initial M.E. (i.e. when it is first projected) $= 107.421...$ J
The object's final M.E. (i.e. when it returns to its point of projection) is given by:
Final M.E. $= \frac{1}{2}mv^2 + mgh_{\text{final}}$
$= (\frac{1}{2} \times 5.5 \times v^2) + (5.5 \times 9.8 \times 0)$
$= 2.75v^2$ J
The work done by friction as the particle moves up the slope and back down again is given by:
Work done = Force × distance
$= F \times 2x = \mu R \times 2x$
$= 0.22 \times 5.5g\cos17° \times 2(3.964...) = 89.904...$ J
Now, using the work-energy principle:
Initial Mechanical Energy – Final Mechanical Energy = Work done against friction
$107.421... - 2.75v^2 = 89.904...$
$v^2 = 6.369...$
$\Rightarrow v = 2.52$ ms^{-1}

Q7 Let B be the 'base level'.
Initial M.E. = Initial K.E. + Initial G.P.E.
$= \frac{1}{2}mu^2 + mgh_{\text{initial}}$
$= (\frac{1}{2} \times 980 \times U^2) + (980 \times 9.8 \times 65\sin10°)$
$= (490U^2 + 108\,401.6...)$ J
Final M.E. = Final K.E. + Final G.P.E.
$= \frac{1}{2}mv^2 + mgh_{\text{final}}$
$= (\frac{1}{2} \times 980 \times 10^2) + (980 \times 9.8 \times 0) = 49\,000$ J
Work done = Force × distance
$= F \times 65 = \mu R \times 65$
$= 0.32 \times 980g\cos10° \times 65 = 196\,728.3...$ J
Now, using the work-energy principle:
Initial Mechanical Energy – Final Mechanical Energy = Work done against friction
$490U^2 + 108\,401.6... - 49\,000 = 196\,728.3...$
$U^2 = 280.258...$
$U = 16.7$ ms^{-1} (3 s.f.)

4. Elastic Potential Energy

Exercise 4.1 — Hooke's law

Q1 a) $T = \frac{\lambda}{l}e = \frac{6}{2} \times 0.5 = 1.5$ N

b) $T = \frac{\lambda}{l}e = \frac{10}{4} \times (5 - 4) = 2.5$ N

c) $T = \frac{\lambda}{l}e = \frac{25}{l} \times (2l - l) = 25$ N

Q2 $T = \frac{\lambda}{l}e = \frac{30}{5} \times (5 - 3) = 12$ N

Q3 $\lambda = \frac{T}{e}l = \frac{12}{1 - 0.8} \times 0.8 = 48$ N

Q4 $T = \frac{\lambda}{l}e = \frac{40}{l} \times (l - 0.5l) = 20$ N

Q5 a)

Resolving vertically:
$T = 3g = 3 \times 9.8 = 29.4$ N

b) $T = \frac{\lambda}{l}e \Rightarrow e = \frac{T}{\lambda}l = \frac{29.4}{49} \times 2 = 1.2$ m

Q6 Resolving vertically:
$T = 3.2g = 3.2 \times 9.8 = 31.36$ N
$T = \frac{\lambda}{l}e \Rightarrow 31.36 = \frac{38}{l}(6 - l)$
$\Rightarrow 31.36l = 228 - 38l$
$69.36l = 228$
$\Rightarrow l = 228 \div 69.36 = 3.29$ m (3 s.f.)

Q7 Resolving vertically:
$T = mg$
$T = \frac{\lambda}{l}e \Rightarrow mg = \frac{35}{1.2}(1.2 - 0.9)$
$\Rightarrow m = 8.75 \div 9.8 = 0.893$ kg (3 s.f.)

Exercise 4.2 — Elastic potential energy

Q1 **a)** E.P.E. $= \frac{\lambda}{2l}e^2 = \frac{10}{2 \times 5} \times 1^2 = 1$ J

b) E.P.E. $= \frac{\lambda}{2l}e^2 = \frac{24}{2 \times 6} \times (8 - 6)^2 = 8$ J

c) E.P.E. $= \frac{\lambda}{2l}e^2 = \frac{30}{2 \times 1.5} \times 0.3^2 = 0.9$ J

Q2 The initial length of extension is 0.6 m, which is then increased to 1.5 m, so:

E.P.E. gained $= \frac{\lambda}{2l}e^2 = \frac{20}{2 \times 3} \times (1.5^2 - 0.6^2) = 6.3$ J

Q3 **a)** Resolving vertically when the particle is in equilibrium:

$T = mg = 1 \times 9.8 = 9.8$ N

$T = \frac{\lambda}{l}e \Rightarrow 9.8 = \frac{\lambda}{l} \times 0.01 \Rightarrow \lambda = 980l$

Now consider the system once the particle has been pulled down a further 2 cm.

The particle is released from rest, so initially it has no kinetic energy. So, using conservation of mechanical energy:

E.P.E. lost = K.E. gained + G.P.E. gained

E.P.E. lost $= \frac{\lambda}{2l}e^2 = \frac{980l}{2l} \times 0.03^2 = 0.441$ J

The particle stretches the string by 1 cm, then it is pulled down a further 2 cm, so e = 3 cm = 0.03 m.

K.E. gained $= \frac{1}{2}mv^2 = \frac{1}{2} \times 1 \times v^2 = 0.5v^2$ J

G.P.E. gained $= mgh = 1 \times 9.8 \times 0.03 = 0.294$ J

h is just the extension length of the string, as it has returned to its natural length when it is slack.

So: $0.441 = 0.5v^2 + 0.294$

$\Rightarrow v^2 = 0.294$

$\Rightarrow v = 0.542$ ms^{-1} (3 s.f.)

b) Take the position of the particle at the point that the string goes slack as the base level. At this point, it has K.E., but no G.P.E. or E.P.E. At its highest point, the particle will momentarily be at rest, so it will have G.P.E., but no K.E. or E.P.E. So, using conservation of mechanical energy:

K.E. lost = G.P.E. gained

$\frac{1}{2}mv^2 = mgh$

$\frac{1}{2} \times 0.294 = 9.8 \times h$

$\Rightarrow h = 0.147 \div 9.8 = 0.015$ m ($= 1.5$ cm)

Q4 **a)** Resolving vertically:

$T = mg = 2 \times 9.8 = 19.6$ N

$T = \frac{\lambda}{l}e \Rightarrow 19.6 = \frac{98}{1.5}e$

$\Rightarrow e = 29.4 \div 98 = 0.3$ m

b) Take the point from which the block is released as the base level. At this point, it has only E.P.E. At its highest point, the block will have only G.P.E.

Using conservation of mechanical energy:

E.P.E. lost = G.P.E. gained

$\frac{\lambda}{2l}e^2 = mgh$

$\frac{98}{2 \times 1.5} \times (0.3 + 0.5)^2 = 2 \times 9.8 \times h$

$\Rightarrow h = 20.906... \div 19.6 = 1.07$ m (3 s.f.)

c) If the block was attached to a spring, the block would have E.P.E. as well as G.P.E. at its maximum height (because the spring would be compressed).

So, using conservation of mechanical energy:

E.P.E. lost = G.P.E. gained

$\frac{\lambda}{2l}e^2 - \frac{\lambda}{2l}c^2 = mgh$

Here, c is the length of compression of the spring when the block is at its highest point.

The maximum height that the block reaches above its point of release is equal to the original length of extension of the string e ($= 0.3 + 0.5 = 0.8$ m) plus the length of compression of the string when the block is at it's highest point:

$h = 0.8 + c \Rightarrow c = h - 0.8$

$\Rightarrow \frac{\lambda}{2l}e^2 - \frac{\lambda}{2l}(h - 0.8)^2 = mgh$

$\frac{98}{3}(0.8)^2 - \frac{98}{3}(h - 0.8)^2 = 2 \times 9.8 \times h$

$\frac{98}{3}(0.64) - \frac{98}{3}(h^2 - 1.6h + 0.64) = 19.6h$

$\frac{98}{3}(0.64 - h^2 + 1.6h - 0.64) = 19.6h$

$-h^2 + 1.6h = 0.6h$

$h^2 - h = 0$

$h(h - 1) = 0$

$\Rightarrow h = 0$ or $h = 1$

$h = 0$ is when the block is at its lowest point, before it is released. So the maximum height reached by the block is 1 m.

Q5 $T = \frac{\lambda}{l}e \Rightarrow 40 = \frac{\lambda}{1.8} \times (3.4 - 1.8)$

$\Rightarrow 40 = \lambda \times 0.888...$

$\Rightarrow \lambda = 45$ N

When the string is stretched, the system has only E.P.E. When the block hits the wall, the system has only K.E.

Using the work-energy principle:

Initial M.E. – Final M.E. = Work done against friction

So: Initial E.P.E. – Final K.E. = Work done

$\frac{\lambda}{2l}e^2 - \frac{1}{2}mv^2 = Fd$

Resolving vertically for the block, $R = mg$.

So, using $F = \mu R \Rightarrow F = \mu mg$:

$\frac{45}{2 \times 1.8}(3.4 - 1.8)^2 - (\frac{1}{2} \times m \times 2.5^2)$

$= 0.12 \times m \times 9.8 \times 3.4$

$32 - 3.125m = 3.9984m$

$32 = 7.1234m$

$\Rightarrow m = 32 \div 7.1234 = 4.49$ kg (3 s.f.)

Q6 **a)** Using conservation of mechanical energy:

G.P.E. lost = E.P.E. gained + K.E. gained

$mgh = \frac{\lambda}{2l}e^2 + \frac{1}{2}mv^2$

$20 \times 9.8 \times y = \frac{60}{2 \times 15}(y - 15)^2 + (\frac{1}{2} \times 20 \times v^2)$

$196y = 2(y^2 - 30y + 225) + 10v^2$

$196y = 2y^2 - 60y + 450 + 10v^2$

$10v^2 = 256y - 2y^2 - 450$

$v^2 = -0.2y^2 + 25.6y - 45$, as required.

b) Substitute $y = 30$ into your equation from a):

$v^2 = -0.2(30)^2 + 25.6(30) - 45 = 543$

$\Rightarrow v = 23.3$ ms^{-1} (3 s.f.)

c) Substitute $v = 4$ into your equation from a):
$4^2 = -0.2y^2 + 25.6y - 45$
$16 = -0.2y^2 + 25.6y - 45$
$0.2y^2 - 25.6y + 61 = 0$
$y^2 - 128y + 305 = 0$
$(y - 64)^2 - 3791 = 0$
$y = 64 \pm \sqrt{3791}$
$\Rightarrow y = 2.428...$ or $y = 125.571...$
y must be greater than 15, so you can ignore the solution $y = 2.428...$
Therefore, the extension of the rope is
$125.571... - 15 = 111$ m (3 s.f.)

Q7 When the spring is initially stretched, the system has only E.P.E. When the particle passes through point A, the system has K.E. and E.P.E. (because the spring is compressed).
Using the work-energy principle:
Initial M.E. − Final M.E. = Work done against friction
So:
Initial E.P.E. − (Final K.E. + Final E.P.E.) = Work done
$\frac{\lambda}{2l}e^2 - (\frac{1}{2}mv^2 + \frac{\lambda}{2l}c^2) = Fd$
Where c is the compression length of the spring.
A is 0.6 m from the wall, and the spring's natural length is 1.25 m, so $c = 1.25 - 0.6 = 0.65$ m.
So:
$\frac{32}{2 \times 1.25}(2 - 1.25)^2 - (\frac{1}{2} \times 0.2 \times v^2) - \frac{32}{2 \times 1.25}(0.65)^2$
$= Fd$
Resolving vertically, $R = mg$, so, using $F = \mu R$:
$Fd = \mu mgd$
$\Rightarrow 7.2 - 0.1v^2 - 5.408 = 0.3 \times 0.2 \times 9.8 \times (2 - 0.6)$
$0.9688 = 0.1v^2$
$v^2 = 9.688$
$\Rightarrow v = 3.11$ ms^{-1} (3 s.f.)

Q8 a) Using conservation of mechanical energy:
E.P.E. lost = K.E. gained + G.P.E. gained
$\frac{\lambda}{2l}e^2 = \frac{1}{2}mv^2 + mgh$
The vertical height through which the block moves is $h = (8 - 1)\sin\theta = 7 \times \frac{3}{5} = 4.2$ m
$\frac{44}{2 \times 8}(8 - 1)^2 = (\frac{1}{2} \times 1.6 \times v^2) + (1.6 \times 9.8 \times 4.2)$
$134.75 = 0.8v^2 + 65.856$
$68.894 = 0.8v^2$
$v^2 = 86.1175$
$\Rightarrow v = 9.28$ ms^{-1} (3 s.f.)

b) Using the work-energy principle:
Initial M.E. − Final M.E. = Work done
E.P.E. − (K.E. + G.P.E.) = Fd
Using $F = \mu R$ and resolving perpendicular to the plane:
$F = \mu \times mg\cos\theta$
$\sin\theta = \frac{3}{5} \Rightarrow \cos\theta = \frac{4}{5}$
$\Rightarrow F = 0.55 \times 1.6 \times 9.8 \times \frac{4}{5} = 6.8992$ N
So: $\frac{\lambda}{2l}e^2 - \frac{1}{2}mv^2 - mgh = 6.8992d$
$134.75 - 0.8v^2 - 65.856 = 6.8992 \times (8 - 1)$
$20.5996 = 0.8v^2$
$v^2 = 25.7495$
$\Rightarrow v = 5.07$ ms^{-1} (3 s.f.)

5. Power

Exercise 5.1 — Power

Q1 At maximum speed, the acceleration is zero, and so the resultant force is zero. Therefore:
Driving force = resistance to motion = 85 N.
$P = Fv = 85 \times 1.8 = 153$ W

Q2 $P = Fv$
$23\ 100 = F \times 11$
$\Rightarrow F = 2100$ N
Resolving horizontally in the direction of motion:
$F - 1140 = ma$
$2100 - 1140 = 900 \times a$
$a = 1.066.... = 1.07$ ms^{-2} (3 s.f.)

Q3 At maximum speed, the acceleration is zero.
Resolving horizontally, taking the direction of motion as positive:
$F - R = 0$
$F - (1360 + 1070) = 0$
$\Rightarrow F = 2430$ N
$P = Fv$
$95\ 000 = 2430v$
$\Rightarrow v = 95\ 000 \div 2430 = 39.1$ ms^{-1} (3 s.f.)
Add together the individual resistive forces to find the overall total resistance to motion.

Q4 a) Find the driving force F using $P = Fv$:
$96\ 000 = F \times 32$
$\Rightarrow F = 3000$ N
Resolving horizontally in the direction of motion, where there is no acceleration:
$F - R = ma = 0$
$\Rightarrow R = F = 3000$ N

b) Going up the hill you need to include a component of the weight opposing the motion, so resolving parallel to the slope, with no acceleration, gives:
$F - R - mg\sin\theta = ma$
$F - 3000 - (250 \times 9.8\sin\theta) = 0$
$F = 3000 + 2450\sin\theta$
$P = Fv$
$96\ 000 = F \times 28$
$\Rightarrow F = 3428.5...$ N
So $3000 + 2450\sin\theta = 3428.5...$
$\sin\theta = 0.174...$
$\Rightarrow \theta = 10.1°$ (3 s.f.)

Q5 Resolving vertically, taking up as positive, and using $F_{net} = ma$:
$T - 52 - 4.2 = m \times 0$
$\Rightarrow T = 56.2$ N
(where T is the tension in the rope).
So, work done in lifting the object = Force × distance
$= 56.2 \times 2.4 = 134.88$ J
Rate of working $= \frac{\text{Work Done}}{\text{Time}} = \frac{134.88}{11}$
$= 12.261... = 12.3$ W (3 s.f.)
You could answer this question by finding the object's velocity, and then using Power = Force × Velocity.

Q6 a)

140 N, N, F, 17°, 660g

When travelling at max speed, acceleration is zero, so resolving parallel to the ramp, taking up the ramp as positive, and using $F_{net} = ma$:
$F - 140 - 660g\sin17° = 660 × 0$
$\Rightarrow F = 2031.0...$ N
$P = Fv$
$16\,000 = 2031.0... × v$
$\Rightarrow v = 7.877... = 7.88$ ms^{-1} (3 s.f.)

b)

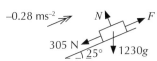

140 N, N, 17°, 660g

Resolving parallel to the ramp, taking up the ramp as positive, and using $F_{net} = ma$:
$-140 - 660g\sin17° = 660a$
$\Rightarrow a = -3.077...$ ms^{-2}
$u = 7.877..., v = 0, a = -3.077..., s = s$
$v^2 = u^2 + 2as$
$0 = (7.877...)^2 + 2(-3.077...)s$
$\Rightarrow s = 62.057... ÷ 6.154... = 10.1$ m (3 s.f.)
You could've done this using the work-energy principle.

Q7

-0.28 ms^{-2}, N, F, 305 N, 25°, 1230g

Resolving parallel to the ramp, taking up the ramp as positive, and using $F_{net} = ma$:
$F - 305 - 1230g\sin25° = 1230 × -0.28$
$\Rightarrow F = 5054.8...$ N
$P = Fv$
$P = 5054.8... × 8 = 40\,438.7... = 40.4$ kW (3 s.f.)

Q8 Resolving parallel to the slope, taking down the slope as positive, and using $F_{net} = ma$:
$F + 720\sin5° - 25 = (720 ÷ 9.8) × 0.733$
$\Rightarrow F = 16.100...$ N
$P = Fv = 16.100... × 6.5$
$= 104.656... = 105$ W (3 s.f.)

Exercise 5.2 — Variable resistive forces

Q1 When the car is travelling at its maximum speed, $a = 0$. Resolving horizontally, taking the direction of motion as positive:
$F_{net} = ma$
$F - 22v = 800 × 0$
$\Rightarrow F = 22v$
$P = Fv \Rightarrow 62\,000 = 22v^2$
$2818.18... = v^2$
$\Rightarrow v = 53.1$ ms^{-1} (3 s.f.)

Q2 When the vehicle is travelling at its maximum speed, $a = 0$. Resolving horizontally, taking the direction of motion as positive:
$F_{net} = ma$
$F - 0.9v^2 = m × 0$
$\Rightarrow F = 0.9v^2$
$P = Fv = 0.9v^3$
Substituting $v = 52$:
$P = 0.9 × 52^3 = 126\,547.2$ W (= 127 kW (3 s.f.))

Q3 Resolving horizontally, taking the direction of motion as positive:
$F_{net} = ma$
$F - 89v = ma$
When $v = 17$, $a = 1.05$, so:
$F - (89 × 17) = 1.05m$
$P = Fv \Rightarrow F = \dfrac{P}{v} = \dfrac{200\,000}{17} = 11764.7...$ N
$\Rightarrow 11\,764.7... - (89 × 17) = 1.05m$
$\Rightarrow m = 10\,251.70... ÷ 1.05 = 9763.52...$
$= 9760$ kg (3 s.f.)

Q4 a) Resolving horizontally, taking the direction of motion as positive:
$F_{net} = ma$
$F - 25v = 600 × 2$
$F - 25v = 1200$
$P = Fv \Rightarrow F = \dfrac{P}{v} = \dfrac{40\,000}{v}$
$\Rightarrow \dfrac{40\,000}{v} - 25v = 1200$
$\Rightarrow 40\,000 - 25v^2 = 1200v$
$\Rightarrow 25v^2 + 1200v - 40\,000 = 0$
$\Rightarrow v^2 + 48v - 1600 = 0$, as required.

b) Solve the equation from part a):
$v^2 + 48v - 1600 = 0$
$(v + 24)^2 - 2176 = 0$
$v + 24 = ±\sqrt{2176}$
$\Rightarrow v = 22.647...$ or $v = -70.647...$
The direction of motion was taken as positive, so you can ignore the negative solution.
So the car's velocity is 22.6 ms^{-1} (3 s.f.)

Q5 a) When the body is travelling at its maximum speed, $a = 0$. Resolving horizontally, taking the direction of motion as positive:
$F_{net} = ma$
$F - 1.3v^2 = 1200 × 0$
$\Rightarrow F = 1.3v^2$
$P = Fv = 1.3v^3$
Convert the body's speed to ms^{-1}:
$(216 × 1000) ÷ 60^2 = 60$ ms^{-1}
Substituting $v = 60$:
$P = 1.3 × 60^3 = 280\,800$ W (= 280.8 kW)

b) Call the new driving force of the body T.
Convert the body's speed to ms⁻¹:

$(70 \times 1000) \div 60^2 = 19.444...$ ms⁻¹

Using $P = Tv$:

$T = \dfrac{P}{v} = \dfrac{280\,800}{19.444...} = 14\,441.1...$ N

Resolving horizontally, taking the direction of motion as positive:

$F_{net} = ma$

$14\,441.1... - (1.3 \times 19.444...^2) = 1200a$

$13\,949.6... = 1200a$

$\Rightarrow a = 13\,949.6... \div 1200 = 11.6$ ms⁻² (3 s.f.)

Q6 a)

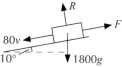

Resolving parallel to the slope, taking up the slope as positive:

$F_{net} = ma$

$F - 80v - 1800g\sin10° = 1800 \times 0.8$

$\Rightarrow F - 80v - 4503.153... = 0$

Using $P = Fv$:

$F = \dfrac{P}{v} = \dfrac{30\,000}{v}$

So: $\dfrac{30\,000}{v} - 80v - 4503.153... = 0$

$\Rightarrow 30\,000 - 80v^2 - (4503.153...)v = 0$

Rearranging and substituting $v = u$:

$80u^2 + (4503.153...)u - 30\,000 = 0$

$u^2 + (56.289...)u - 375 = 0$

$u^2 + 56.3u - 375 = 0$, to 3 s.f., as required.

b) Solve $u^2 + 56.3u - 375 = 0$:

$u = \dfrac{-56.3 \pm \sqrt{56.3^2 - (4 \times 1 \times -375)}}{2 \times 1}$

$\Rightarrow u = 6.017...$ or $u = -62.317...$

The vehicle is moving up the slope, which is the positive direction, so you can ignore the negative solution. Therefore, $u = 6.02$ (3 s.f.)

The question says 'Hence find...', so you can use the rounded coefficient 56.3 rather than 56.289... to find the value of u. Don't worry if you used the unrounded value though — the final answer's the same to 3 significant figures.

Review Exercise — Chapter 3

Q1 Work done $= Fs = 250 \times 3 = 750$ J

Q2 Work done $= Fs$

$1.3 = T\cos60° \times 0.4$

$\Rightarrow T = 6.5$ N

Q3 Work done against gravity $= mgh$

$34\,000 = m \times 9.8 \times 12$

$\Rightarrow m = 289$ kg (3 s.f.)

Q4 Work done against gravity $= mgh$

$2.92 = 3 \times g_{moon} \times 0.6$

$\Rightarrow g_{moon} = 1.62$ ms⁻² (3 s.f.)

Q5

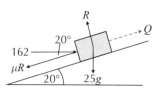

Resolving forces parallel to the plane to find the resultant force Q gives:

$Q = 162\cos 20° - \mu R - 25g\sin 20°$

Resolving perpendicular to the plane to find R gives:

$R = 25g\cos 20° + 162\sin 20° = 285.6319...$ N

So:

$Q = 162\cos 20° - (0.19 \times 285.6319...) - 25g\sin 20°$

$\quad = 14.16519...$ N

Work done by $Q = Qs$

$\quad = 14.16519... \times 10 = 142$ J (3 s.f.)

Q6 Kinetic Energy $= \frac{1}{2}mv^2 = \frac{1}{2} \times 450 \times 13^2$

$\quad = 38\,025$ J $= 38.0$ kJ (3 s.f.)

Q7 Work done = Change in Kinetic Energy

$800 = \frac{1}{2}m(v^2 - u^2)$

$u = 0$ and $m = 65$, so:

$v^2 = \dfrac{1600}{65}$

$\Rightarrow v = 4.96$ ms⁻¹ (3 s.f.)

You might not always need to use all the information given in the question — here, you don't need to use the fact that the skater has travelled 40 m.

Q8 a) To find the work done you need to know the stopping distance. You can find this using constant acceleration equations, as long as you know the acceleration. Acceleration can be found by resolving forces horizontally, in the opposite direction to motion:

$F_{net} = ma$

$590 + 8500 = 1000a$

$\Rightarrow a = 9.09$ ms⁻² (= −9.09 in direction of motion)

Now using $v^2 = u^2 + 2as$:

$0^2 = 100^2 + (2 \times -9.09 \times s)$

$\Rightarrow s = 550.055...$ m

So work done by braking force $= Fs$

$\quad = 8500 \times 550.055... = 4\,675\,467.5...$

$\quad = 4.68$ MJ (3 s.f.)

b) Work done by resistance $= Fs$

$\quad = 590 \times 550.055... = 324\,532.4...$

$\quad = 325$ kJ (3 s.f.)

c) Work done by resultant force $= Fs$
$= (8500 + 590) \times 550.055... = 5\,000\,000$ J $= 5$ MJ
Change in K.E. $= \frac{1}{2}m(u^2 - v^2)$
$= \frac{1}{2} \times 1000 \times (100^2 - 0) = 5\,000\,000$ J $= 5$ MJ
So the work done by the resultant force = change in K.E.

Q9 Increase in P.E. $= mg \times$ increase in height
$= 0.5 \times 9.8 \times 150 = 735$ J

Q10 When the hat reaches its maximum height, its velocity will be zero. Using conservation of energy:
Change in P.E. = Change in K.E.
$mgh = \frac{1}{2}m(u^2 - v^2)$
Cancel m from both sides, and substitute $u = 5$, $v = 0$ and $g = 9.8$:
$9.8h = \frac{1}{2} \times 25$
$\Rightarrow h = 1.28$ m (3 s.f.)

Q11 Using the principle of conservation of mechanical energy, Initial M.E. = Final M.E., so:
Initial K.E. + Initial P.E. = Final K.E. + Final P.E.
Final K.E. = Initial K.E. + Initial P.E. – Final P.E.
$= 39.2 + 0 - mgh$
(assuming the ball is kicked from the ground so initial P.E. = 0).
Final K.E. $= 39.2 - (0.4 \times 9.8 \times 1.94) = 31.6$ J (3 s.f.)

Q12

Take the bottom of the ramp as the 'base level'.
Initial M.E. = Initial K.E. + Initial P.E.
$= \frac{1}{2}mu^2 + mgh_{\text{initial}}$
$= (\frac{1}{2} \times 15 \times 0^2) + (15 \times 9.8 \times 9\sin11°) = 252.440...$ J
Final M.E. = Final K.E. + Final P.E.
$= \frac{1}{2}mv^2 + mgh_{\text{final}}$
$= (\frac{1}{2} \times 15 \times 4.2^2) + (15 \times 9.8 \times 0) = 132.3$ J
Now, using the work-energy principle:
Initial Mechanical Energy – Final Mechanical Energy = Work done against friction
$252.440... - 132.3 = 120.140... = 120$ J (3 s.f.)

Q13 a) Take the body's initial position as the 'base level'.
Initial M.E. = Initial K.E. + Initial P.E.
$= \frac{1}{2}mu^2 + mgh_{\text{initial}}$
$= (\frac{1}{2} \times 14 \times 5.5^2) + (14 \times 9.8 \times 0) = 211.75$ J
Final M.E. = Final K.E. + Final P.E.
$= \frac{1}{2}mv^2 + mgh_{\text{final}}$
$= (\frac{1}{2} \times 14 \times 0.4^2) + (14 \times 9.8 \times 2.5\sin30°)$
$= 172.62$ J
Now, using the work-energy principle:
Initial Mechanical Energy – Final Mechanical Energy = Work done against friction
$211.75 - 172.62 = 39.13$ J

b) Work done $= Fs$
$39.13 = F \times 2.5$
$\Rightarrow F = 15.652$ N
Resolving perpendicular to the slope:
$R = 14g\cos30° = 118.818...$ N
$F = \mu R$
$\Rightarrow \mu = F \div R = 15.652 \div 118.818...$
$= 0.131... = 0.13$ (2 d.p.)

Q14 a) $T = \frac{\lambda}{l}e = \frac{25}{3} \times (3 - 1.5) = 12.5$ N

b) E.P.E. $= \frac{\lambda}{2l}e^2 = \frac{25}{2 \times 3} \times (3 - 1.5)^2 = 9.375$ J

Q15 a) Let e_1 be the string's extension when the particle is 8.4 m from the wall and e_2 be the string's extension when the particle is 4.2 m from the wall. The natural length of the string is 2 m, so when the particle is 4.2 m from the wall, the string will still have E.P.E. stored in it.
Using conservation of mechanical energy:
E.P.E. lost = K.E. gained
$\frac{\lambda}{2l}e_1^2 - \frac{\lambda}{2l}e_2^2 = \frac{1}{2}mv^2$
$\frac{10}{2 \times 2}[(8.4 - 2)^2 - (4.2 - 2)^2] = \frac{1}{2} \times 3 \times v^2$
$90.3 = 1.5v^2$
$v^2 = 60.2$
$\Rightarrow v = 7.76$ ms^{-1} (3 s.f.)

b) When the particle hits the wall, the string will be slack, so there will be no E.P.E. stored in the string.
Using conservation of mechanical energy:
E.P.E. lost = K.E. gained
$\frac{\lambda}{2l}e^2 = \frac{1}{2}mv^2$
$\frac{10}{2 \times 2}(8.4 - 2)^2 = \frac{1}{2} \times 3 \times v^2$
$102.4 = 1.5v^2$
$v^2 = 68.266...$
$\Rightarrow v = 8.26$ ms^{-1} (3 s.f.)
This is the particle's speed when the string first goes slack — but as there is no resultant force acting on the particle from the point that the string goes slack to the point that the particle hits the wall, the particle's speed is constant between these two points.

Q16 Power of engine = driving force × velocity
$350\,000 = F \times 44$
$\Rightarrow F = 7950$ N (3 s.f.)

Q17

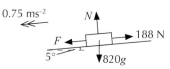

Resolving parallel to the slope, taking down the slope as positive, and using $F_{\text{net}} = ma$:
$F + 820g\sin5° - 188 = 820 \times 0.75$
$\Rightarrow F = 102.616...$ N
$P = Fv$
$P = 102.616... \times 10 = 1026.1...$
$= 1.03$ kW (3 s.f.)

Q18

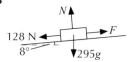

When moving with max speed, acceleration is zero. Resolving parallel to the slope, taking up the slope as positive, and using $F_{net} = ma$:
$F - 128 - 295g\sin 8° = 295 \times 0$
$\Rightarrow F = 530.34... \text{ N}$
$P = Fv$
$22\,000 = 530.34... \times v$
$\Rightarrow v = 41.5 \text{ ms}^{-1}$ (3 s.f.)

Q19 When the bicycle is moving at its maximum speed, $a = 0$. So, resolving horizontally, taking the direction of motion as positive:
$F - kv = m \times 0$
$\Rightarrow F = kv \text{ N}$
$P = Fv \Rightarrow F = \dfrac{P}{v} = \dfrac{240}{16} = 15 \text{ N}$
So $15 = kv$
$15 = 16k$
$\Rightarrow k = 0.9375$

Exam-Style Questions — Chapter 3

Q1 a) Take B as the 'base level'.
Initial M.E. = Initial K.E. + Initial P.E.
$= \dfrac{1}{2}mu^2 + mgh_{initial}$
$= (\dfrac{1}{2} \times 90 \times 8^2) + (90 \times 9.8 \times 100\sin 20°)$
[1 mark]
$= 33\,046.1... \text{ J}$
Final M.E. = Final K.E. + Final P.E.
$= \dfrac{1}{2}mv^2 + mgh_{final}$
$= (\dfrac{1}{2} \times 90 \times 7^2) + (90 \times 9.8 \times 0)$ *[1 mark]*
$= 2205 \text{ J}$
Initial M.E. – Final M.E. = $33\,046.1... - 2205$
$= 30\,841.1... \text{ J}$
$= 30\,800 \text{ J}$ (3 s.f.) *[1 mark]*

b) Using the work-energy principle:
change in mechanical energy = work done against friction
So, using 'Work done = Force × distance':
$30\,841.1... = F \times 100$ *[1 mark]*
$\Rightarrow F = 308.411... \text{ N}$ *[1 mark]*
Resolving perpendicular to the plane:
$R = 90g\cos 20° = 828.808... \text{ N}$ *[1 mark]*
(where R is the normal reaction force of the plane on the man)
So, using $F = \mu R$:
$308.411... = \mu \times 828.808...$ *[1 mark]*
$\Rightarrow \mu = 0.37$ (2 d.p.) *[1 mark]*

Q2 a) Find T, the driving force of the car, using $P = Tv$:
$T = P \div v = 20\,000 \div 10 = 2000 \text{ N}$. *[1 mark]*
Resolve forces parallel to the slope:
$T - mg\sin\theta - kv = 0$ *[1 mark]*.
$\Rightarrow 2000 - (1000 \times 9.8 \times 0.1) - 10k = 0$
$\Rightarrow 10k = 1020$
$\Rightarrow k = 102$ *[1 mark]*

b) (i) Call the new driving force F.
Using Power = Fv:
$F = \dfrac{50\,000}{u}$ *[1 mark]*
Resolve forces parallel to the slope:
$\dfrac{50\,000}{u} - mg\sin\theta - 102u = 0$. *[1 mark]*
Rearranging and substituting known values gives:
$50\,000 - (1000 \times 9.8 \times 0.1)u - 102u^2 = 0$
[1 mark]. This rearranges to:
$102u^2 + 980u - 50\,000 = 0$ — as required
[1 mark].

(ii) Solve for u using the quadratic formula:
$u = \dfrac{-980 + \sqrt{980^2 - (4 \times 102 \times -50\,000)}}{2 \times 102}$
$u = 17.9 \text{ ms}^{-1}$ (3 s.f.)

[2 marks available in total]:
- *1 mark for correctly using quadratic formula*
- *1 mark for correct value for u*

You don't need to worry about the negative part of ± in the formula, as you're after a speed — which is always positive.

c) Using $F = ma$ gives $T - 102v = ma$. *[1 mark]*
This time, $T = P \div v = 21000 \div 12$, and so:
$(21000 \div 12) - (102 \times 12) = 1000a$ *[1 mark]*
$\Rightarrow a = 0.526 \text{ ms}^{-2}$. *[1 mark]*

Q3 a) Work done = Force × distance moved
$= 3500\cos 40° \times 820 = 2.20 \text{ MJ}$ (3 s.f.)
[3 marks available in total]:
- *1 mark for using the horizontal component of the force*
- *1 mark for correct use of formula for work done*
- *1 mark for correct final answer.*

b)

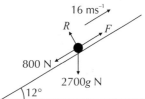

Resolving vertically:
$R + 3500\sin40° = 1100g$
$R = 1100 \times 9.8 - 3500\sin40° = 8530.2... N$
[1 mark]
$F = \mu R = (8530.2...)\mu$
The log is moving only horizontally, so:
Work done on log = change in kinetic energy
[1 mark]
Force $\times$ distance $= \frac{1}{2}m(v^2 - u^2)$

Modelling the rope as a light, inextensible string, the speed of the log will be the same as the speed of the truck, so resolving horizontally:
$(3500\cos40° - (8530.2...)\mu) \times 820$
$= \frac{1}{2} \times 1100 \times (6^2 - 5^2)$ *[1 mark]*
$\Rightarrow 2673.7... = (8530.2...)\mu$
$\Rightarrow \mu = 0.31$ (2 d.p.) *[1 mark]*

Q4 a) Use $P = Fv$ to find the 'driving' force, F, of the cyclist:
$250 = F \times 4$ *[1 mark]*
$\Rightarrow F = 62.5 N$ *[1 mark]*
Resolving parallel to the slope, taking up the slope as positive, and using $F_{net} = ma$:
$62.5 - 35 - 88g\sin\alpha = m \times 0$ *[1 mark]*
$\alpha = \sin^{-1}\frac{27.5}{88g} = 1.83°$ (3 s.f.) *[1 mark]*

b) Use $P = Fv$ to find the new 'driving' force, F':
$370 = F' \times 4$ *[1 mark]*
$F' = 92.5 N$ *[1 mark]*
Resolving parallel to the slope, taking up the slope as positive, and using $F_{net} = ma$:
$92.5 - 35 - 88g\sin\alpha = 88a$ *[1 mark]*
$a = 0.341$ ms^{-2} (3 s.f.) *[1 mark]*

Q5 a) The system is in equilibrium, so resolving forces vertically gives $T = mg$, where T is the tension in the string. *[1 mark]*
So, using Hooke's law:
$T = \frac{\lambda}{l}e = mg$ *[1 mark]*
$\Rightarrow \lambda = \frac{mgl}{e} = \frac{3 \times 9.8 \times 2}{(5 - 2)} = 19.6 N$ *[1 mark]*

b) E.P.E. $= \frac{\lambda}{2l}e^2$ *[1 mark]*
So $\frac{19.6}{2 \times 2} \times 3^2 = 44.1 J$ *[1 mark]*

c) By the Principle of Conservation of Mechanical Energy:
E.P.E. lost = G.P.E. gained + K.E. gained *[1 mark]*
Assuming that the block starts with no K.E. or G.P.E.:
$\frac{\lambda}{2l}(8 - 2)^2 - \frac{\lambda}{2l}(3 - 2)^2 = mg(8 - 5) + \frac{1}{2}mv^2$
[1 mark]
$\frac{19.6}{4}(36) - \frac{19.6}{4}(1) = (3 \times 9.8 \times 5) + (\frac{1}{2} \times 3 \times v^2)$
[1 mark]
$v^2 = \frac{2}{3}(171.5 - 147) = 16.333...$
$v = 4.04$ ms^{-1} (3 s.f.) *[1 mark]*

Q6 a)

Let F be the driving force of the van's engine.
Resolving parallel to the slope, taking up the slope as positive, and using $F_{net} = ma$ with $a = 0$:
$F - 800 - 2700g\sin12° = 0$ *[1 mark]*
$\Rightarrow F = 6301.343...$ *[1 mark]*
Rate of work of engine $= Fv$ *[1 mark]*
$= 6301.343... \times 16 = 101$ kW (3 s.f.) *[1 mark]*

b) Work done against resistive force $= 800x$ *[1 mark]*
Take A as the 'base level'.
First find initial mechanical energy
(i.e. mechanical energy at A):
Initial M.E. = Initial K.E. + Initial P.E.
$= \frac{1}{2}mu^2 + mgh_{initial}$
$= (\frac{1}{2} \times 2700 \times 16^2) + (2700 \times 9.8 \times 0)$ *[1 mark]*
$= 345\,600 J$
Now find final mechanical energy:
Final M.E. = Final K.E. + Final P.E.
$= \frac{1}{2}mv^2 + mgh_{final}$
$= (\frac{1}{2} \times 2700 \times 0^2) + (2700 \times 9.8 \times x\sin12°)$
[1 mark]
$= (5501.343...)x J$
Now using the work-energy principle:
Initial mechanical energy – Final mechanical energy = Work done against resistive force
$345\,600 - (5501.343...)x = 800x$ *[1 mark]*
$345\,600 = (6301.343...)x$
$\Rightarrow x = 54.8$ m (3 s.f.) *[1 mark]*

c) Resolve parallel to the slope using $F = ma$ to find a:

$-800 - 2700g\sin12° = 2700a$ *[1 mark]*

$a = -2.333...$ ms^{-2} *[1 mark]*

Use $v = u + at$ to find the time taken to come to rest:

$0 = 16 - (2.333...)t$ *[1 mark]*

$t = 16 \div 2.333... = 6.86$ s (3 s.f.) *[1 mark]*

Rather than finding a, you could've answered this question using $s = \left(\frac{u + v}{2}\right)t$, where s is the value of x you found in b).

Q7 a) K.E. $= \frac{1}{2}mv^2 = \frac{1}{2} \times 0.3 \times 20^2$ *[1 mark]*

$= 60$ J *[1 mark]*

b) The only force acting on the stone is its weight, so use conservation of mechanical energy.
Take the surface of the water as the 'base level'. Immediately before it is dropped, the stone has P.E. but no K.E. When it hits the surface of the water, it has K.E. but no P.E. Therefore:

Gain in K.E. = Loss in P.E. *[1 mark]*

$60 = 0.3 \times 9.8 \times h$ *[1 mark]*

$\Rightarrow h = 20.4$ m (3 s.f.) *[1 mark]*

c) Let the depth the stone sinks be y.
Work done by resistive forces = Force × Distance

$= 23y$ J *[1 mark]*

Now find the change in mechanical energy.
Take the depth of the stone when its speed has been reduced to 1 ms^{-1} as the 'base level'.
First find the initial mechanical energy (i.e. the mechanical energy when it hits the surface of the water):

Initial M.E. = Initial K.E. + Initial P.E.

$= \frac{1}{2}mu^2 + mgh_{initial}$

$= (\frac{1}{2} \times 0.3 \times 20^2) + (0.3 \times 9.8 \times y)$ *[1 mark]*

$= (60 + 2.94y)$ J

Now find final mechanical energy (i.e. mechanical energy when speed has been reduced to 1 ms^{-1}).

Final M.E. = Final K.E. + Final P.E.

$= \frac{1}{2}mv^2 + mgh_{final}$

$= (\frac{1}{2} \times 0.3 \times 1^2) + (0.3 \times 9.8 \times 0)$ *[1 mark]*

$= 0.15$ J

Now using the work-energy principle:
Initial Mechanical Energy – Final Mechanical Energy = Work done against resistive force

$60 + 2.94y - 0.15 = 23y$ *[1 mark]*

$59.85 = 20.06y$

$\Rightarrow y = 2.98$ m (3 s.f.) *[1 mark]*

Q8 a) E.P.E. $= \frac{\lambda}{2l}e^2$ *[1 mark]*

$= \frac{50}{2 \times 5} \times (d - 5)^2 = 5(d - 5)^2$ *[1 mark]*

b)

There is no motion vertically, so $R = 10$ N *[1 mark]*

Particle is moving, so friction is limiting $\Rightarrow$ frictional force, $F = \mu R = 0.5 \times 10 = 5$ N *[1 mark]*

Work done against $F = F \times$ distance moved $= 5d$ *[1 mark]*.

There is no change in K.E. or G.P.E. between the start and end of motion, so the only change in mechanical energy is the loss of E.P.E. *[1 mark]*

When the particle reaches the wall, the string will be slack, so E.P.E. at this point will be zero.
So, by the work-energy principle:

Initial M.E. – Final M.E. = Work done against F

Initial E.P.E. – Final E.P.E. = Work done against F

$\Rightarrow 5(d - 5)^2 - 0 = 5d$ *[1 mark]*

Rearranging: $d = d^2 - 10d + 25$

$\Rightarrow d^2 - 11d + 25 = 0$.

Solve using the quadratic formula: *[1 mark]*

$d = 7.79$ or $d = 3.21$ (each to 3 s.f.)

The question says that $d > 5$, so take $d = 7.79$ m. *[1 mark]*

Chapter 4: Uniform Circular Motion

1. Horizontal Circular Motion

Exercise 1.1 — Circular motion

Q1 a) The particle moves through an angle of $100 \times 2\pi = 200\pi$ rad.
It moves through this angle in 60 seconds, so:
$\omega = \frac{\theta}{t} = \frac{200\pi}{60} = \frac{10\pi}{3}$ rad s^{-1}

b) The particle moves through an angle of 2π rad in 3 seconds, so:
$\omega = \frac{\theta}{t} = \frac{2\pi}{3}$ rad s^{-1}

c) The particle moves through an angle of $\theta = 10 \times 2\pi = 20\pi$ rad.
It moves through this angle in 240 seconds, so:
$\omega = \frac{\theta}{t} = \frac{20\pi}{240} = \frac{\pi}{12}$ rad s^{-1}

Q2 a) $v = r\omega = 2 \times 5 = 10$ ms^{-1}

b) $\theta = 7 \times 2\pi = 14\pi$ rad
$\omega = \frac{\theta}{t} = \frac{14\pi}{20} = \frac{7\pi}{10}$ rad s^{-1}
$v = r\omega = 0.5 \times \frac{7\pi}{10} = \frac{7\pi}{20} = 1.10$ ms^{-1} (3 s.f.)

c) $\theta = 300 \times 2\pi = 600\pi$ rad
$\omega = \frac{\theta}{t} = \frac{600\pi}{60} = 10\pi$ rad s^{-1}
$v = r\omega = 2 \times 10\pi = 20\pi = 62.8$ ms^{-1} (3 s.f.)

Q3 a) $a = \frac{v^2}{r} = \frac{10^2}{0.5} = 200$ ms^{-2}

b) $F = ma = 2 \times 200 = 400$ N

Q4 $\theta = 10 \times 2\pi = 20\pi$ rad
$\omega = \frac{\theta}{t} = 20\pi$ rad s^{-1}
$v = r\omega$
$\Rightarrow r = \frac{v}{\omega} = \frac{20}{20\pi} = \frac{1}{\pi} = 0.318$ m (3 s.f.)

Q5 $v = r\omega$
$\Rightarrow \omega = \frac{v}{r} = \frac{8}{5} = 1.6$ rad s^{-1}
$\omega = \frac{\theta}{t}$
$\Rightarrow t = \frac{\theta}{\omega} = \frac{2\pi}{1.6} = 3.93$ s (3 s.f.)

Q6 a) $a = \frac{v^2}{r} = \frac{5^2}{4} = 6.25$ ms^{-2}

b) $F = ma = 40 \times 6.25 = 250$ N

c) $\omega = \frac{5}{4} = 1.25$ rad s^{-1}
$v = r\omega = (4 - 2.5) \times 1.25 = 1.875$ ms^{-1}

Q7 $a = r\omega^2 \Rightarrow F = mr\omega^2$
$400 = 250 \times 8 \times \omega^2$
$\omega^2 = 0.2$
$\omega = 0.447...$ rad s^{-1}
$\omega = \frac{\theta}{t}$
$\Rightarrow t = \frac{\theta}{\omega} = \frac{2\pi}{0.447...} = 14.0$ s (3 s.f.)

Q8 $F = \mu R = 0.45 \times 0.35 \times 9.8 = 1.5435$ N
$F = mr\omega^2 \Rightarrow 1.5435 = 0.35 \times 0.95 \times \omega^2$
$\Rightarrow \omega^2 = 1.5435 \div 0.3325 = 4.642...$
$\Rightarrow \omega = 2.15$ rad s^{-1}

Q9 $F = mr\omega^2 = 800 \times 40 \times 0.2^2 = 1280$ N
Resolving vertically, $R = mg = 800 \times 9.8 = 7840$ N
$F \le \mu R$
$1280 \le \mu \times 7840$
$\Rightarrow \mu \ge 1280 \div 7840$
$\Rightarrow \mu \ge 0.1632...$
So the least value of μ is 0.16 (2 d.p.)

Exercise 1.2 — Conical pendulums

Q1 a)

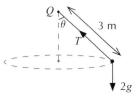

$r = 3\sin\theta$
Resolving horizontally for the particle, taking inwards as positive, and using $F = mr\omega^2$:
$\Rightarrow T\sin\theta = 2 \times 3\sin\theta \times \pi^2$
$\Rightarrow T = 6\pi^2 = 59.217... = 59.2$ N (3 s.f.)

b) Resolving vertically for the particle:
$T\cos\theta = mg$
$\cos\theta = 19.6 \div 59.217... = 0.330...$
$\Rightarrow \theta = 70.7°$ (3 s.f.)

Q2 a)

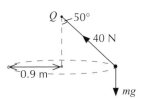

b) $\sin 50° = \frac{0.9}{l}$
$\Rightarrow l = \frac{0.9}{\sin 50°} = 1.174... = 1.17$ m (3 s.f.)

c) Resolving vertically for the particle:
$40\cos 50° = mg$
$\Rightarrow m = 40\cos 50° \div 9.8 = 2.623...$
$= 2.62$ kg (3 s.f.)

d) Resolving horizontally for the particle, taking inwards as positive:
$F_{net} = ma$
$40\sin 50° = mr\omega^2$
$40\sin 50° = 2.623... \times 0.9 \times \omega^2$
$\omega^2 = 12.976...$
$\omega = 3.602...$ rad s^{-1}
So the particle moves through 3.602... radians each second, and therefore $3.602... \times 60 = 216.140...$ radians each minute.
This is equivalent to $216.140... \div 2\pi = 34.399...$ revolutions each minute.
Therefore, the particle makes 34 full revolutions in one minute.

Q3 a)

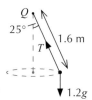

Resolving vertically for the body:
$T\cos25° = 1.2g$
$\Rightarrow T = 12.975...$ N
Resolving horizontally for the body, taking inwards as positive:
$F_{net} = ma$
$(12.975...)\sin25 = 1.2a$
$\Rightarrow a = 4.569... = 4.57$ ms^{-2} (3 s.f.)

b) $a = r\omega^2$
$\Rightarrow \omega^2 = 4.569... \div (1.6\sin25°) = 6.758...$
$\Rightarrow \omega = 2.60$ rad s^{-1} (3 s.f.)

c) $a = \dfrac{v^2}{r}$
$\Rightarrow v^2 = 4.569... \times (1.6\sin25°) = 3.090...$
$\Rightarrow v = 1.76$ ms^{-1} (3 s.f.)
You could also answer this part using v = rω.

Q4 a)

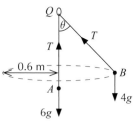

Resolving vertically for A:
$T = 6g = 58.8$ N

b) Resolving vertically for B:
$58.8\cos\theta = 4g$
$\cos\theta = 0.666...$
$\Rightarrow \theta = 48.189...°$
Resolving horizontally for B, taking inwards as positive:
$F_{net} = mr\omega^2$
$58.8\sin(48.189...°) = 4 \times 0.6 \times \omega^2$
$\omega^2 = 18.261...$
$\Rightarrow \omega = 4.273... = 4.27$ rad s^{-1} (3 s.f.)

c) B moves through 4.273... radians each second, and therefore $4.273... \times 60 = 256.398...$ radians each minute.
This is equivalent to $256.398... \div 2\pi = 40.807...$ revolutions each minute.
Therefore, B makes 40 full revolutions in one minute.

Q5 a)

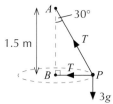

Resolving vertically for P:
$T\cos30° = 3g$
$\Rightarrow T = \dfrac{3g}{\cos30°} = \dfrac{3g}{\sqrt{3}/2} = \dfrac{6g}{\sqrt{3}} = \dfrac{6\sqrt{3}g}{3}$
$= 2\sqrt{3}g$ N — as required.

b) Resolving horizontally for P, taking inwards as positive:
$F_{net} = \dfrac{mv^2}{r}$
$2\sqrt{3}g + 2\sqrt{3}g\sin30° = \dfrac{mv^2}{r}$
$2\sqrt{3}g + (2\sqrt{3}g \times \dfrac{1}{2}) = \dfrac{mv^2}{r}$
$3\sqrt{3}g = \dfrac{mv^2}{r}$
Using trigonometry, $\tan30° = \dfrac{r}{1.5}$
$\Rightarrow r = 1.5\tan30° = \dfrac{1.5}{\sqrt{3}}$
So:
$3\sqrt{3}g = \dfrac{3v^2}{1.5/\sqrt{3}}$
$3\sqrt{3}g = \dfrac{3\sqrt{3}v^2}{1.5}$
$1.5g = v^2$
$\Rightarrow v = \sqrt{1.5g}$ ms^{-1} — as required.

Q6 a)

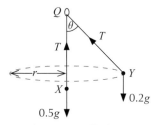

Resolving vertically for X:
$T = 0.5g$
Resolving vertically for Y:
$0.5g\cos\theta = 0.2g$
$\cos\theta = 0.4$
$\Rightarrow \theta = 66.421...°$
Resolving horizontally for Y, taking inwards as positive, and using $F_{net} = ma$:
$0.5g\sin(66.421...°) = 0.2a$
$\Rightarrow a = 22.454... = 22.5$ ms^{-2} (3 s.f.)

b) Y moves through an angle of $40 \times 2\pi = 80\pi$ rad in 60 seconds, so:
$\omega = \dfrac{80\pi}{60} = \dfrac{4\pi}{3}$ rad s^{-1}
$a = r\omega^2$
$22.454... = r \times \left(\dfrac{4\pi}{3}\right)^2$
$\Rightarrow r = 1.28$ m (3 s.f.)

Q7

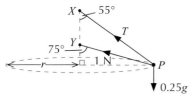

Resolving vertically for P:
$0.25g = 1\cos75° + T\cos55°$
$\Rightarrow T = 2.191... \div 0.573... = 3.820...$ N
Resolving horizontally for P, taking inwards as positive, and using $F_{net} = \frac{mv^2}{r}$:
$(3.820...)\sin55° + 1\sin75° = \frac{0.25 \times 2.25^2}{r}$
$\Rightarrow r = \frac{1.265...}{4.095...} = 0.309$ m (3 s.f.)

Q8

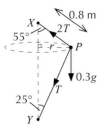

Resolving vertically for P:
$0.3g + T\cos25° = 2T\cos55°$
$T(2\cos55° - \cos25°) = 0.3g$
$\Rightarrow T = 2.94 \div 0.240... = 12.207...$ N
Using trigonometry, $r = 0.8\sin55°$, so, resolving horizontally for P, taking inwards as positive:
$F_{net} = mr\omega^2$
$(2 \times 12.207...)\sin55° + (12.207...)\sin25° = 0.3 \times 0.8\sin55° \times \omega^2$
$\omega^2 = 25.157... \div 0.196... = 127.966...$
$\Rightarrow \omega = 11.3$ rad s^{-1} (3 s.f.)

2. Vertical Circular Motion

Exercise 2.1 — Vertical circular motion

Q1 Take the level of the body's position when it has moved through 70° from the highest point as the base level. At this point, it has moved downwards through a vertical height of $0.95 - 0.95\cos70° = 0.625...$ m. Using conservation of mechanical energy:
$(\frac{1}{2} \times m \times 7.5^2) + (m \times 9.8 \times 0.625...) = \frac{1}{2}mv^2$
$68.501... = v^2$
$\Rightarrow v = 8.28$ ms^{-1} (3 s.f.)

Q2 a) Take the lowest point on the circle as the base level. When the particle is vertically level with O, it will have moved upwards through a vertical height of 0.6 m. Using conservation of mechanical energy:
$(\frac{1}{2} \times m \times 5^2) = \frac{1}{2}mv^2 + (m \times 9.8 \times 0.6)$
$v^2 = 13.24$
$\Rightarrow v = 3.64$ ms^{-1} (3 s.f.)
It doesn't matter whether the particle is on its way up or down. The motion is symmetrical, so the speed is the same either side of the centre of the circle.

b) When the particle is vertically above O, it will have moved upwards through a vertical height of 1.2 m. Using conservation of mechanical energy:
$(\frac{1}{2} \times m \times 5^2) = \frac{1}{2}mv^2 + (m \times 9.8 \times 1.2)$
$v^2 = 1.48$
$\Rightarrow v = 1.22$ ms^{-1} (3 s.f.)

c)

When the string makes an angle of 20° with the upward vertical, it will have moved upwards though a vertical height of $0.6 + 0.6\cos20° = 1.163...$ m. Using conservation of mechanical energy:
$(\frac{1}{2} \times m \times 5^2) = \frac{1}{2}mv^2 + (m \times 9.8 \times 1.163...)$
$v^2 = 2.189...$
$\Rightarrow v = 1.48$ ms^{-1} (3 s.f.)
Again, it doesn't matter if you draw the particle 20° 'before' the top of the circle (i.e. on the way up), or 20° 'past' the top of the circle (i.e. on the way back down).

Q3 **a)**

b) Take the level of point A as the base level.
When the object is at A, it has moved downwards through a vertical distance of 0.8sin40° m.
Using conservation of mechanical energy:
$(\frac{1}{2} \times 3 \times 0^2) + (3 \times 9.8 \times 0.8\sin40°) = \frac{1}{2} \times 3 \times v^2$
$10.078... = v^2$
$\Rightarrow v = 3.174... = 3.17$ ms⁻¹ (3 s.f.)

c)

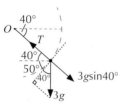

Resolving radially, taking inwards as positive:
$F_{net} = ma$
$T - 3g\sin40° = \frac{mv^2}{r}$
$T = \frac{3 \times 10.078...}{0.8} + 3g\sin40° = 56.693...$
$= 56.7$ N (3 s.f.)
Resolving forces to find their radial components can be quite tricky, but drawing right-angled triangles usually helps. Depending on how you drew your triangle, and which angle you used to resolve, you could've used cos50° rather than sin40° in this question — it's the same thing.

Q4 **a)** Take the bottom of the circle as the base level.
When the string has moved through an angle θ, the object has moved through a vertical height of
$h = 0.4 - 0.4\cos\theta = 0.4(1 - \cos\theta)$
Using conservation of mechanical energy:
K.E. lost = G.P.E. gained
$\frac{1}{2}mv^2 = mgh$
$\frac{1}{2} \times 0.75 \times 2.5^2 = 0.75 \times 9.8 \times 0.4(1 - \cos\theta)$
$2.34375 = 2.94(1 - \cos\theta)$
$0.797... = 1 - \cos\theta$
$\cos\theta = 0.202...$
$\Rightarrow \theta = 78.298...° = 78.3°$ (3 s.f.)

b)

Resolving radially, taking inwards as positive, using $F_{net} = \frac{mv^2}{r}$ with $v = 0$:
$T - 0.75g\cos(78.298...°) = 0$
$\Rightarrow T = 0.75g\cos(78.298...°) = 1.49$ N (3 s.f.)
At this point, the object is stationary, so it has no angular speed, and hence no radial acceleration. This means that the radial component of the resultant force is zero, and so the tension in the string must be balanced by the radial component of the object's weight acting in the opposite direction.

Q5 **a)** Take the bottom of the circle as the base level.
The vertical height the particle moves through in going from the top to the bottom of the circle is $2 \times 1.2 = 2.4$ m.
Using conservation of mechanical energy:
$(\frac{1}{2} \times m \times 2^2) + (m \times 9.8 \times 2.4) = \frac{1}{2}mv^2$
$51.04 = v^2$
$\Rightarrow v = 7.14$ ms⁻¹ (3 s.f.)

b) Take the level of the particle's position when its speed is 3 ms⁻¹ as the base level. At this point, it has moved downwards through a vertical height of $1.2 - 1.2\cos\theta = 1.2(1 - \cos\theta)$ m.
Using conservation of mechanical energy:
$(\frac{1}{2} \times m \times 2^2) + (m \times 9.8 \times 1.2(1 - \cos\theta))$
$= \frac{1}{2} \times m \times 3^2$
$11.76(1 - \cos\theta) = 2.5$
$1 - \cos\theta = 0.212...$
$\cos\theta = 0.787...$
$\Rightarrow \theta = 38.1°$ (3 s.f.)

c) Take the level of the particle's position when its speed is 6 ms⁻¹ as the base level. At this point, it has moved downwards through a vertical height of $1.2 + 1.2\cos\varphi = 1.2(1 + \cos\varphi)$ m.
Using conservation of mechanical energy:
$(\frac{1}{2} \times m \times 2^2) + (m \times 9.8 \times 1.2(1 + \cos\varphi))$
$= \frac{1}{2} \times m \times 6^2$
$11.76(1 + \cos\varphi) = 16$
$1 + \cos\varphi = 1.360...$
$\cos\varphi = 0.360...$
$\Rightarrow \varphi = 68.9°$ (3 s.f.)

Q6 a)

Take the bottom of the circle as the base level.
Using conservation of mechanical energy:
$$\tfrac{1}{2}m(2v)^2 = \tfrac{1}{2}mv^2 + (m \times 9.8 \times 4)$$
$$1.5v^2 = 39.2$$
$$v^2 = 26.133...$$
$$\Rightarrow v = 5.112... = 5.11 \text{ ms}^{-1} \text{ (3 s.f.)}$$

b) $2v = 2 \times 5.112... = 10.224... = 10.2 \text{ ms}^{-1}$ (3 s.f.)

c)

Let u be the body's speed when the string is horizontal.
Take the bottom of the circle as the base level.
Using conservation of mechanical energy:
$$\tfrac{1}{2}m(2v)^2 = \tfrac{1}{2}mu^2 + (m \times 9.8 \times 2)$$
$$\tfrac{1}{2}(10.224...)^2 = \tfrac{1}{2}u^2 + 19.6$$
$$u^2 = 65.333...$$
$$\Rightarrow u = 8.082... = 8.08 \text{ ms}^{-1} \text{ (3 s.f.)}$$

d)

Resolving vertically at the top of the circle, taking down as positive, and using $F_{net} = \frac{mv^2}{r}$:
$$mg + T_1 = \frac{(26.133...)m}{2}$$
$$\Rightarrow T_1 = m(13.066... - 9.8) = (3.266...)m$$
$$= 3.27m \text{ N (3 s.f.)}$$

e)

Resolving horizontally when the string is horizontal, taking towards O as positive, and using $F_{net} = \frac{mv^2}{r}$:
$$T_2 = \frac{m \times u^2}{2} = \frac{m \times 65.333...}{2}$$
$$T_2 = 32.7m \text{ N (3 s.f.)}$$

Q7 a) (i) Let the level of the particle's position when it has moved through an angle of 60° from the top of the circle be the base level.
At this point, it has moved downwards through a vertical height of $l - l\cos60° = \tfrac{1}{2}l$.
Using conservation of mechanical energy:
$$\tfrac{1}{2}mu^2 + mg(\tfrac{1}{2}l) = \tfrac{1}{2}mv^2$$
$$u^2 + gl = v^2$$
$$\Rightarrow v = \sqrt{u^2 + gl}$$

(ii)

Let the level of the particle's position when it has moved through an angle of 150° from the top of the circle be the base level. At this point, it has moved downwards through a vertical height of $l + l\sin60° = \left(1 + \frac{\sqrt{3}}{2}\right)l$.
Using conservation of mechanical energy:
$$\tfrac{1}{2}mu^2 + mg\left(1 + \frac{\sqrt{3}}{2}\right)l = \tfrac{1}{2}mv^2$$
$$u^2 + gl(2 + \sqrt{3}) = v^2$$
$$\Rightarrow v = \sqrt{u^2 + gl(2 + \sqrt{3})}$$

(iii) When the particle has moved through 180°, it is at the bottom of the circle. At this point, it has moved downwards through a vertical height of $2l$. Taking the bottom of the circle as the base level, and using conservation of mechanical energy:
$$\tfrac{1}{2}mu^2 + mg(2l) = \tfrac{1}{2}mv^2$$
$$u^2 + 4gl = v^2$$
$$\Rightarrow v = \sqrt{u^2 + 4gl}$$

b) (i)

Resolving radially, taking inwards as positive:
$$T + mg\cos60° = \frac{mv^2}{r}$$
$$T = \frac{m(u^2 + gl)}{l} - \frac{mg}{2} = \frac{2m(u^2 + gl) - mgl}{2l}$$
$$= \frac{2mu^2 + mgl}{2l} = m\left(\frac{u^2}{l} + \frac{g}{2}\right)$$

(ii)

Resolving radially, taking inwards as positive:

$T - mg\sin 60° = \dfrac{mv^2}{r}$

$T = \dfrac{m(u^2 + gl(2 + \sqrt{3}))}{l} + \dfrac{mg\sqrt{3}}{2}$

$= \dfrac{2m(u^2 + gl(2 + \sqrt{3})) + mgl\sqrt{3}}{2l}$

$= \dfrac{2mu^2 + mgl(4 + 3\sqrt{3})}{2l}$

$= m\left(\dfrac{u^2}{l} + \dfrac{g(4 + 3\sqrt{3})}{2}\right)$

(iii)

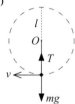

Resolving radially, taking inwards as positive:

$T - mg = \dfrac{mv^2}{r}$

$T = \dfrac{m(u^2 + 4gl)}{l} + mg = m\left(\dfrac{u^2}{l} + 5g\right)$

Exercise 2.2 — Circular wires and surfaces

Q1 a) (i)

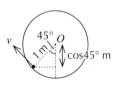

Take the bottom of the circle as the base level. When $\theta = 45°$, the particle has moved upwards through a vertical height of

$1 - 1\cos 45° = (1 - \dfrac{1}{\sqrt{2}})$ m

Using conservation of mechanical energy:

$(\dfrac{1}{2} \times 3 \times 10^2) =$

$(\dfrac{1}{2} \times 3 \times v^2) + (3 \times 9.8 \times (1 - \dfrac{1}{\sqrt{2}}))$

$v^2 = 94.259...$

$\Rightarrow v = 9.71$ ms^{-1} (3 s.f.)

(ii) Using the same reasoning as in part (i):

$(\dfrac{1}{2} \times 3 \times 10^2) =$

$(\dfrac{1}{2} \times 3 \times v^2) + (3 \times 9.8 \times (1 - \cos 75°))$

$v^2 = 85.472...$

$\Rightarrow v = 9.25$ ms^{-1} (3 s.f.)

(iii)

When $\theta = 135°$, the particle has moved upwards through a vertical height of

$1 + 1\cos 45° = (1 + \dfrac{1}{\sqrt{2}})$ m

Using conservation of mechanical energy:

$(\dfrac{1}{2} \times 3 \times 10^2) =$

$(\dfrac{1}{2} \times 3 \times v^2) + (3 \times 9.8 \times (1 + \dfrac{1}{\sqrt{2}}))$

$v^2 = 66.540...$

$\Rightarrow v = 8.16$ ms^{-1} (3 s.f.)

b) (i)

Resolving radially, taking inwards as positive:

$F_{net} = \dfrac{mv^2}{r}$

$R - 3g\cos 45° = \dfrac{3 \times 94.259...}{1}$

$\Rightarrow R = 282.777... + 20.788... = 304$ N (3 s.f.)

(ii)

Resolving radially, taking inwards as positive:

$F_{net} = \dfrac{mv^2}{r}$

$R - 3g\cos 75° = \dfrac{3 \times 85.472...}{1}$

$\Rightarrow R = 256.418... + 7.609... = 264$ N (3 s.f.)

(iii)

Resolving radially, taking inwards as positive:

$F_{net} = \dfrac{mv^2}{r}$

$R + 3g\cos 45° = \dfrac{3 \times 66.540...}{1}$

$\Rightarrow R = 199.622... - 20.788... = 179$ N (3 s.f.)

Q2 a)

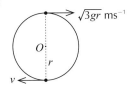

Take the bottom of the ring as the base level.
Using conservation of mechanical energy:
$(\frac{1}{2} \times m \times (\sqrt{3gr})^2) + (m \times g \times 2r) = (\frac{1}{2} \times m \times v^2)$
$\Rightarrow 3gr + 4gr = v^2$
$\Rightarrow v = \sqrt{7gr}$ ms^{-1}

b)

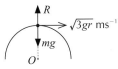

Resolving vertically, taking down as positive:
$F_{net} = \frac{mv^2}{r}$
$mg - R = \frac{m(\sqrt{3gr})^2}{r}$
$\Rightarrow R = mg - 3mg = -2mg = -19.6m$ N
So the normal reaction has magnitude 19.6m N, and acts downwards, towards the centre of the circle.

c)

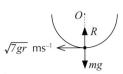

Resolving vertically, taking up as positive:
$F_{net} = \frac{mv^2}{r}$
$R - mg = \frac{m(\sqrt{7gr})^2}{r}$
$\Rightarrow R = 7mg + mg = 8mg = 78.4m$ N

Q3 a) Take the body's position when it has moved through the angle θ as the base level.
The vertical height between this point and the top of the circle is:
$h = 2 - 2\cos\theta = 2(1 - \cos\theta)$ m.
Using conservation of mechanical energy:
$(\frac{1}{2} \times m \times 4^2) + (m \times g \times 2(1 - \cos\theta)) =$
$(\frac{1}{2} \times m \times v^2)$
$\Rightarrow 16 + 4g(1 - \cos\theta) = v^2$ — as required.

b)

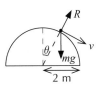

Resolving radially, taking inwards as positive:
$F_{net} = \frac{mv^2}{r}$
$mg\cos\theta - R = \frac{m(16 + 4g(1 - \cos\theta))}{2}$
$\Rightarrow R = \frac{2mg\cos\theta - m(16 + 4g(1 - \cos\theta))}{2}$
$= (3mg\cos\theta - 8m - 2mg)$ N

c) At A, $\theta = 0$, so:
$R_A = 3mg\cos 0 - 8m - 2mg = mg - 8m = 1.8m$ N
So when the normal reaction is half that at A:
$0.9m = 3mg\cos\theta - 8m - 2mg$
$0.9 = 3g\cos\theta - 2g - 8$
$\cos\theta = (0.9 + 2g + 8) \div 3g = 0.969...$
$\Rightarrow \theta = 14.2°$ (3 s.f.)

Q4 First find the bead's speed at B. Take A as the base level. The vertical distance between A and B is:
$h = a\cos 30° + a\cos\theta = a\left(\frac{\sqrt{3}}{2} + \cos\theta\right)$

Using conservation of mechanical energy:
$\frac{1}{2}mv^2 + mga\left(\frac{\sqrt{3}}{2} + \cos\theta\right) = \frac{1}{2}mu^2$
$\Rightarrow v^2 = u^2 - ga(\sqrt{3} + 2\cos\theta)$

Resolving radially at B, taking inwards as positive:
$F_{net} = \frac{mv^2}{r}$
$mg\cos\theta - R = \frac{m(u^2 - ga(\sqrt{3} + 2\cos\theta))}{a}$
$R = \frac{amg\cos\theta - m(u^2 - ga(\sqrt{3} + 2\cos\theta))}{a}$
$= \frac{amg\cos\theta - mu^2 + mga\sqrt{3} + 2mga\cos\theta}{a}$
$= \frac{3amg\cos\theta - mu^2 + mga\sqrt{3}}{a}$
$= mg(3\cos\theta + \sqrt{3}) - \frac{mu^2}{a}$
So the magnitude of the reaction force is:
$|mg(3\cos\theta + \sqrt{3}) - \frac{mu^2}{a}|$ — as required.
The reaction force could act inwards or outwards — that's why you're asked for its magnitude. The method shown here assumes that it acts outwards. If you'd assumed that it acts inwards, then you'd have got $R = \frac{mu^2}{a} - mg(3\cos\theta + \sqrt{3})$ — but the magnitude would still be the same.

Exercise 2.3 — Completing the circle

Q1 a)

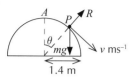

Let P's position when OP makes an angle θ with OA be the base level. The vertical distance between P and A at this point is:
$h = 1.4(1 - \cos\theta)$ m
Using conservation of mechanical energy:
$(\frac{1}{2} \times m \times 2^2) + (m \times g \times 1.4(1 - \cos\theta)) = \frac{1}{2}mv^2$
$\Rightarrow v^2 = 4 + 2.8g(1 - \cos\theta)$
Resolving radially for P, taking inwards as positive:
$F_{net} = \frac{mv^2}{r}$
$mg\cos\theta - R = \dfrac{m(4 + 2.8g(1 - \cos\theta))}{1.4}$
$\Rightarrow R = mg\cos\theta - \dfrac{m(4 + 2.8g(1 - \cos\theta))}{1.4}$
$= mg\cos\theta - \dfrac{20m}{7} - 2mg(1 - \cos\theta)$
$= \left(mg(3\cos\theta - 2) - \dfrac{20m}{7}\right)$ N

b) P leaves the surface when $R = 0$:
$mg(3\cos\theta - 2) - \dfrac{20m}{7} = 0$
$3\cos\theta - 2 = \dfrac{20}{7g}$
$\cos\theta = 0.763...$
$\Rightarrow \theta = 40.195... = 40.2°$ (3 s.f.)

c) From part a):
$v^2 = 4 + 2.8g(1 - \cos(40.195...°)) = 10.48$
$\Rightarrow v = 3.24$ ms^{-1} (3 s.f.)

Q2 a) Take the bottom of the circle as the base level. When the body has moved through an angle θ from the bottom of the circle, it has moved through a vertical height of:
$h = 0.8(1 - \cos\theta)$ m
Using conservation of mechanical energy:
$\frac{1}{2}mv^2 + (m \times g \times 0.8(1 - \cos\theta)) = \frac{1}{2} \times m \times 5^2$
$v^2 = 25 - 1.6g(1 - \cos\theta)$
$= 9.32 + 15.68\cos\theta$
$\Rightarrow v = \sqrt{9.32 + 15.68\cos\theta}$ ms^{-1}

b)

Resolving horizontally, taking towards the centre of the circle as positive:
$F_{net} = \dfrac{mv^2}{r}$
$T = \dfrac{m(9.32 + 15.68\cos 90°)}{0.8} = 11.65m$ N
The tension in the string is positive, so the string is still taut.

c) Assuming that the body does have enough energy to reach the top of the circle, substitute $\theta = 180°$ into your expression from a):
$v = \sqrt{9.32 + 15.68\cos 180°} = \sqrt{-6.36}$
The value inside the square root is negative, so the initial assumption was wrong, and the body doesn't have enough energy to reach the top of the circle.

d)

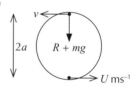

Resolving radially, taking inwards as positive:
$F_{net} = \dfrac{mv^2}{r}$
$T + mg\cos(180° - \theta) = \dfrac{m(9.32 + 15.68\cos\theta)}{0.8}$
Using the identity $\cos(180° - \theta) = -\cos\theta$, this becomes:
$T - mg\cos\theta = \dfrac{m(9.32 + 15.68\cos\theta)}{0.8}$
The body leaves the circle when $T = 0$, i.e. when:
$-mg\cos\theta = \dfrac{m(9.32 + 15.68\cos\theta)}{0.8}$
$-g\cos\theta = 11.65 + 19.6\cos\theta$
$\cos\theta = -0.396...$
$\Rightarrow \theta = 113.344... = 113°$ (3 s.f.)

e) Substitute $\theta = 113.344...°$ into your expression from a):
$v = \sqrt{9.32 + 15.68\cos 113.344...°}$
$= 1.76$ ms^{-1} (3 s.f.)

Q3 a)

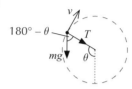

Take the bottom of the circle as the base level. Let v be the particle's speed when it reaches the top of the circle.
Using conservation of mechanical energy:
$\frac{1}{2}mv^2 + (m \times g \times 2a) = \frac{1}{2}mU^2$
$v^2 + 4ga = U^2$
$\Rightarrow v^2 = U^2 - 4ga$
Resolving vertically at the top of the circle, taking down as positive:
$F_{net} = \dfrac{mv^2}{r}$
$R + mg = \dfrac{m(U^2 - 4ga)}{a}$
$R = \dfrac{mU^2}{a} - 5mg$
If the particle just completes the circle, then the reaction at the top of the circle will be zero:
$0 = \dfrac{mU^2}{a} - 5mg$
$U^2 = 5ag$
$\Rightarrow U = \sqrt{5ag}$

b) Take the bottom of the circle as the base level. Let v be the particle's speed when it reaches X. Using conservation of mechanical energy:

$\frac{1}{2}mv^2 + mga = \frac{1}{2}mU^2$

If the particle just reaches X, then its speed at X will be zero (i.e. $v = 0$):

$mga = \frac{1}{2}mU^2$

$2ga = U^2$

$\Rightarrow U = \sqrt{2ag}$

c)

Resolving horizontally at X, taking towards the centre of the circle as positive:

$F_{net} = \frac{mv^2}{r}$

$R = \frac{mv^2}{r}$

$\Rightarrow R = 0$ N, because $v = 0$ at this point.

Q4 a) The bead can't leave the circle, so you only need to check that it has enough energy to reach the top. Take the bottom of the circle as the base level. When the bead reaches the top of the circle, it will have moved through a vertical distance of $h = 2r$ m.

Assuming that the bead does make it to the top, and using conservation of mechanical energy:

$\frac{1}{2}mv^2 + (m \times g \times 2r) = \frac{1}{2} \times m \times (\sqrt{kgr})^2$

$v^2 + 4gr = kgr$

$v^2 = gr(k - 4)$

$\Rightarrow v = \sqrt{gr(k - 4)}$

For the bead to reach the top, the value under the square root must be greater than or equal to zero:

$gr(k - 4) \geq 0$

g and r are both positive constants, so:

$k - 4 \geq 0$

$\Rightarrow k \geq 4$ — as required.

b) When the bead reaches its maximum vertical height above the lowest point on the circle, it will momentarily come to rest (i.e. $v = 0$).

So, using conservation of mechanical energy:

$mgh = \frac{1}{2} \times m \times (\sqrt{3gr})^2$

$2gh = 3gr$

$\Rightarrow h = 1.5r$ m

c)

The bead has moved through a vertical distance of $h = r(1 - \cos\theta)$.

Using conservation of mechanical energy:

$\frac{1}{2}mv^2 + mgr(1 - \cos\theta) = \frac{1}{2} \times m \times (\sqrt{gr})^2$

$v^2 + 2gr(1 - \cos\theta) = gr$

$\Rightarrow v^2 = gr(2\cos\theta - 1)$

Resolving radially, taking inwards as positive:

$F_{net} = \frac{mv^2}{r}$

$R - mg\cos\theta = \frac{mgr(2\cos\theta - 1)}{r}$

$\Rightarrow R = 3mg\cos\theta - mg = mg(3\cos\theta - 1)$

So when $R = 0$:

$mg(3\cos\theta - 1) = 0$

$3\cos\theta - 1 = 0$

$\Rightarrow \cos\theta = \frac{1}{3}$ — as required.

Review Exercise — Chapter 4

Q1 a) $\omega = \frac{\theta}{t} = \frac{2\pi}{1.5} = \frac{4\pi}{3}$ rad s^{-1}

$a = r\omega^2 = 3\left(\frac{4\pi}{3}\right)^2 = \frac{16\pi^2}{3}$ ms^{-2}

b) $\omega = \frac{\theta}{t} = \frac{15 \times 2\pi}{60} = \frac{\pi}{2}$ rad s^{-1}

$a = r\omega^2 = 3\left(\frac{\pi}{2}\right)^2 = \frac{3\pi^2}{4}$ ms^{-2}

c) $\omega = \frac{\theta}{t} = \frac{160/360 \times 2\pi}{1} = \frac{8\pi}{9}$ rad s^{-1}

$a = r\omega^2 = 3\left(\frac{8\pi}{9}\right)^2 = \frac{64\pi^2}{27}$ ms^{-2}

d) $\omega = \frac{v}{r} = \frac{10}{3}$ rad s^{-1}

$a = \frac{v^2}{r} = \frac{10^2}{3} = \frac{100}{3}$ ms^{-2}

Q2 a) $F = mr\omega^2 = 2 \times 0.4 \times (10\pi)^2 = 80\pi^2$ N

b) $F = \frac{mv^2}{r} = \frac{2 \times 4^2}{0.4} = 80$ N

Q3 a) Resolving vertically, taking up as positive:

$T\cos 45° - 4g = 0$

$\Rightarrow T = 55.437... = 55.4$ N (3 s.f.)

b) Resolving horizontally:

$T\sin 45° = \frac{mv^2}{r}$

$\Rightarrow r = \frac{4v^2}{(55.437...)\sin 45°} = 0.102v^2$ m (3 s.f.)

Q4 a)

b) Using conservation of mechanical energy, taking the level of B as the base level:

$(\frac{1}{2} \times m \times 2.2^2) + mg(0.2 - 0.2\cos45°) = \frac{1}{2}mv_B^2$

$v_B^2 = 5.988...$

$\Rightarrow v_B = 2.447... = 2.45$ ms^{-1} (3 s.f.)

c) Resolving radially, taking inwards as positive:

$$F_{net} = \frac{mv^2}{r}$$

$$R + mg\cos45° = \frac{m \times (2.447...)^2}{0.2}$$

$$\Rightarrow R = (29.940...)m - mg\cos45°$$

$$= 23.0m \text{ N (3 s.f.)}$$

Q5 a) Assume that it will complete the circle. First find its speed, v, at the highest point. Using conservation of mechanical energy, taking the bottom of the circle as the base level:

$$\frac{1}{2}mv^2 + 4mg = \frac{1}{2} \times m \times 9^2$$

$$v^2 + 8g = 81$$

$$v^2 = 2.6$$

$$\Rightarrow v = 1.61 \text{ ms}^{-1} \text{ (3 s.f.)}$$

The velocity at the top of the circle is positive (i.e. the body is moving at the top of the circle), so the body has enough energy to complete the circle. This means that if it is a bead on a smooth wire, then it will complete the circle.

To check if a particle on a string will complete the circle, you need to find the tension in the string at the highest point:

1.61 ms⁻¹

$mg + T$

Resolving vertically, taking down as positive:

$$F_{net} = \frac{mv^2}{r}$$

$$T + mg = \frac{2.6m}{2}$$

$$\Rightarrow T = 1.3m - 9.8m = -8.5m \text{ N}$$

The tension is negative, so a particle on a string will not complete a full circle.

That's the difference between things that can leave the circle and things that can't. If something's stuck on the circle (like a bead on a wire), it only needs enough energy to get to the top. If something can leave the circle (like a particle on a string), it also needs a positive (or zero) tension or reaction at the top.

b)

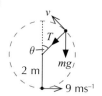

Let θ be the angle the string makes with the upward vertical when the particle leaves the circular path. First find v, the particle's speed when it leaves the circular path, using conservation of mechanical energy. Taking the bottom of the circle as the base level:

$$\frac{1}{2}mv^2 + mg(2 + 2\cos\theta) = \frac{1}{2} \times m \times 9^2$$

$$v^2 + 4g(1 + \cos\theta) = 81$$

$$\Rightarrow v^2 = 81 - 4g(1 + \cos\theta)$$

Resolving radially, taking inwards as positive:

$$F_{net} = \frac{mv^2}{r}$$

$$T + mg\cos\theta = \frac{m(81 - 4g(1 + \cos\theta))}{2}$$

When the particle leaves the circle, $T = 0$, so:

$$mg\cos\theta = \frac{m(81 - 4g(1 + \cos\theta))}{2}$$

$$2g\cos\theta = 81 - 4g(1 + \cos\theta)$$

$$2g\cos\theta = 81 - 4g - 4g\cos\theta$$

$$6g\cos\theta = 41.8$$

$$\cos\theta = 0.710...$$

$$\Rightarrow \theta = 44.7° \text{ (3 s.f.)}$$

Exam-Style Questions — Chapter 4

Q1 **a)** Take the level of B as the base level.
Using conservation of mechanical energy:
$(\frac{1}{2} \times 2 \times 0^2) + 2g(0.5\sin30°) = (\frac{1}{2} \times 2 \times v^2)$
[1 mark]
$\frac{g}{2} = v^2$ **[1 mark]**
$\Rightarrow v = \sqrt{\frac{g}{2}}$ ms⁻¹ **[1 mark]**

b)

Resolving radially, taking inwards as positive:
$F_{net} = \frac{mv^2}{r}$
$T - 2g\sin30° = \frac{2(\frac{g}{2})}{0.5}$
$T = 2g + g$
$\Rightarrow T = 3g$ N

[3 marks available in total]:
- *1 mark for resolving radially*
- *1 mark for correct working*
- *1 mark for correct answer*

c) Using v from part a):
$\omega = \frac{v}{r} = \frac{\sqrt{\frac{g}{2}}}{0.5}$ **[1 mark]**
$= \frac{2\sqrt{g}}{\sqrt{2}} = \sqrt{2g}$ rads⁻¹ **[1 mark]**

Q2 **a)**

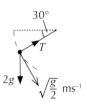

Resolving vertically for P, taking up as positive:
$55\sin40° - mg = 0$ **[1 mark]**
$\Rightarrow m = 55\sin40° \div 9.8 = 3.607...$
$= 3.61$ kg (3 s.f.) **[1 mark]**

b) Resolving horizontally for P,
taking inwards as positive:
$F_{net} = \frac{mv^2}{r}$
$55\cos40° + 80 = \frac{3.607... \times 3^2}{r}$
$\Rightarrow r = \frac{3.607... \times 3^2}{55\cos40° + 80} = 0.2658...$
$= 0.266$ m (3 s.f.)
The radius is the length of the horizontal string.

[3 marks available in total]:
- *1 mark for resolving horizontally*
- *1 mark for correct working*
- *1 mark for correct answer*

c) $\omega = \frac{v}{r} = \frac{3}{0.2658...} = 11.285...$ rads⁻¹ **[1 mark]**

$\frac{11.285...}{2\pi} = 1.796...$ revolutions per second
[1 mark]
$1.796... \times 60 = 107.76...$ revolutions per minute
So the particle makes 107 complete revolutions
in one minute. **[1 mark]**
*You could have answered this by using the linear speed
to work out that P travels 180 m in one minute, then
dividing this by the circumference of the circle.*

Q3 **a)** Using conservation of mechanical energy, taking
the level of A as the base level:
$\frac{1}{2}mv^2 + (m \times g \times 1) = \frac{1}{2} \times m \times \sqrt{20}^2$ **[1 mark]**
$v^2 + 2g = 20$ **[1 mark]**
$v^2 = 20 - 19.6 = 0.4$
$\Rightarrow v = \sqrt{0.4}$ ms⁻¹ **[1 mark]**

b)

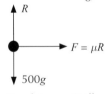

Resolving vertically, taking down as positive:
$F_{net} = \frac{mv^2}{r}$ **[1 mark]**
$mg - R = \frac{0.4m}{1}$ **[1 mark]**
$\Rightarrow R = m(9.8 - 0.4) = 9.4m$ N **[1 mark]**

c) Take the level of A as the base level.
Using conservation of mechanical energy:
$\frac{1}{2}mv_B^2 + (m \times g \times 1) = \frac{1}{2}mu^2$ **[1 mark]**
The bead will complete the circle if $v_B \geq 0$.
Setting $v_B = 0$:
$mg = \frac{1}{2}mu^2$ **[1 mark]**
$u^2 = 2g$
$\Rightarrow u = \sqrt{2g} = 4.43$ ms⁻¹ (3 s.f.) **[1 mark]**
So the minimum value of u for the circle to be
completed is 4.43 ms⁻¹ (3 s.f.)

Q4 If the quad bike is on the point of slipping,
friction is limiting, so $F = \mu R$.

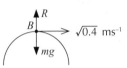

Resolving vertically:
$R = 500g$ **[1 mark]**
Resolving horizontally:
$F = \frac{mv^2}{r}$
$\mu R = \frac{mv^2}{r}$ **[1 mark]**
$\Rightarrow 0.5 \times 500g = \frac{500v^2}{30}$ **[1 mark]**
$\Rightarrow v^2 = 15g$ **[1 mark]**
$\Rightarrow v = 12.1$ ms⁻¹ (3 s.f.) **[1 mark]**

Q5 a) Take the level of J as the base level.
The vertical distance between J and K is:
$h = 5 + 5\cos\theta = 5(1 + \cos\theta)$ m   *[1 mark]*
Using conservation of mechanical energy:
$\frac{1}{2}mv^2 + mg(5(1 + \cos\theta)) = \frac{1}{2} \times m \times 15^2$ *[1 mark]*
$225 = v^2 + 10g(1 + \cos\theta)$ *[1 mark]*
$\Rightarrow v^2 = 225 - 10g(1 + \cos\theta)$ — as required.
[1 mark]

b) Assume that the particle does complete the circle.
Using the formula from part a) with $\theta = 0$:
$v^2 = 225 - 10g(1 + \cos0°) = 29$ *[1 mark]*
$\Rightarrow v = \sqrt{29}$ ms^{-1}
So, it has enough energy to get to the top,
so now find the tension, T, in the string at the top:

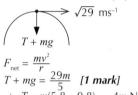
$\sqrt{29}$ ms^{-1}

$F_{net} = \frac{mv^2}{r}$
$T + mg = \frac{29m}{5}$ *[1 mark]*
$\Rightarrow T = m(5.8 - 9.8) = -4m$ N *[1 mark]*
The tension in the string is negative, so the string
is no longer taut and the circle isn't completed
[1 mark].
*You have to find the speed first here — you need it to
work out the tension.*

c)

mg

Resolving radially, taking inwards as positive
(using the expression for v^2 from part a)):
$F_{net} = \frac{mv^2}{r}$
$T + mg\cos\theta = \frac{m(225 - 10g(1 + \cos\theta))}{5}$ *[1 mark]*
When the string first becomes slack, $T = 0$, so:
$mg\cos\theta = \frac{m(225 - 10g(1 + \cos\theta))}{5}$ *[1 mark]*
$5g\cos\theta = 225 - 10g - 10g\cos\theta$
$15g\cos\theta = 225 - 10g$
$\cos\theta = 127 \div 147 = 0.863...$ *[1 mark]*
$\Rightarrow \theta = 30.2°$ (3 s.f.)   *[1 mark]*

Glossary

A

Acceleration
The rate of change of an object's **velocity** with respect to time.

Angular speed
A measure of the **speed** of a body moving on a circular path. Defined by how quickly the radius of the circle is turning, or the rate of change of the angle through which the radius has moved with respect to time.

B

Bead
A **particle** which has a hole in it through which a **string** or **wire** can pass.

Beam
A long, **thin**, straight, **rigid** body.

C

Centre of mass
The point at which a body's **weight** can be considered to act.

Centripetal force
The force which causes the **radial acceleration** of a body moving on a circular path. It is always directed to the centre of the circle.

Component
The effect of a **vector** in a given direction.

Composite shape
A shape that can be broken up into standard parts, such as squares, rectangles and circles.

Conical pendulum
A body attached to the end of a **string**, the other end of which is fixed in place. The body moves on a circular path centred directly below the fixed end of the string.

D

Deceleration
An **acceleration** where the object's **speed** is decreasing.

Displacement
A **vector** measurement of an object's distance from a particular point.

E

Elastic potential energy
The potential energy stored due to the stretching of an elastic **string** (or the stretching/compressing of a spring).

Equilibrium
A state where there is no **resultant force** or **moment** acting on a body, hence the body is at **rest** (or moving with constant **velocity**).

External force
Any force acting on a body other than the **weight** of the body itself or tension in an elastic **string** or spring.

F

Framework
A structure made from **rods** joined together, or a **wire** bent to form a shape.

Friction
A frictional force is a resistive force due to **roughness** between a body and surface. It always acts against motion, or likely motion.

G

g
Acceleration due to gravity.
g is usually assumed to be 9.8 ms^{-2}.

Gravitational potential energy
The potential energy a body has due to its height above a particular base level.

H

Hooke's law
A formula linking the **tension**, **natural length**, length of extension and **modulus of elasticity** for a stretched elastic **string** or spring.

I

i
The horizontal **unit vector**.

Inextensible
Describes a body which can't be stretched. (Usually a **string** or **wire**.)

J

j
A **unit vector** perpendicular to both **i** and **k**.

K

k
A **unit vector** perpendicular to both **i** and **j**.

Kinematics
The study of the motion of objects.

Kinetic energy
The energy a body has due to its **speed**.

L

Lamina
A flat two-dimensional body whose thickness can be ignored.

Light
Describes a body which is modelled as having no mass.

Limiting equilibrium
Describes a body which is at **rest** in **equilibrium**, but is on the point of moving.

Linear speed
The straight-line **speed** of a body moving on a circular path. It is measured in the direction of the tangent to the circle at the point where the body happens to be.

Magnitude
The size of a quantity.

Mechanical energy
The sum of the **gravitational potential**, **elastic potential** and **kinetic energies** of a body.

Modulus of elasticity
A measure of how easily something can be stretched in a way that it will return to its original shape afterwards.

Moment
The turning effect a force has about a pivot point.

Natural length
The length of an elastic **string** or spring when it is not being stretched (or compressed).

Non-uniform
Describes a body whose mass is unevenly distributed throughout the body.

Normal reaction
The reaction force from a surface acting on an object. It acts at 90° to the surface.

Particle
A body whose dimensions are negligible and can be ignored.

Peg
A fixed support which a body can hang from or rest on.

Plane
A flat surface.

Position vector
The position of a point relative to a fixed origin, *O*, given in **vector** form.

Power
The rate at which a force does **work** on a body.

Radial acceleration
The **acceleration** of a body moving on a circular path, due to the constantly changing direction of the body's motion. It is always directed towards the centre of the circle.

Radian
A unit of angular measurement. A full circle has angle 2π radians at its centre.

Resolving
Splitting a **vector** up into **components**.

Rest
Describes a body which is not moving. Often used to describe the initial state of a body.

Resultant (force or vector)
The single force/**vector** which has the same effect as two or more forces/vectors added together.

Rigid
Describes a body which does not bend.

Rod
A long, **thin**, straight, **rigid** body.

Rough
Describes a surface for which a **frictional** force will oppose the motion of a body in contact with the surface.

Scalar
A quantity which has a **magnitude** but not a direction.

Slack
Describes a **string** which is not experiencing a **tension** force.

Smooth
Describes a surface for which there is no **friction** between the surface and a body in contact with it.

Speed
The **magnitude** of an object's **velocity**.

String
A **thin** body, usually modelled as being **light**.

Taut
Describes a **string** or **wire** which is experiencing a **tension** force.

Tension
The force in a **taut wire** or **string**.

Thin
Describes a body which is modelled as having no thickness.

Uniform
Describes a body whose mass is evenly spread throughout the body.

Unit vector
A **vector** of **magnitude** one unit.

Vector
A quantity which has both a **magnitude** and a direction.

Velocity
The rate of change of an object's **displacement** with respect to time.

Weight
The force due to a body's mass and the effect of gravity: $W = mg$.

Wire
A **thin** body often modelled as being **light**. It can be bent to form a shape.

Work
A measure of the energy transferred to or by a moving object due to forces causing or opposing its motion.

Index

MAM2T61